FUTURES AND FICTIONS

FUTURES AND FICTIONS

Edited by
HENRIETTE GUNKEL,
AYESHA HAMEED
AND SIMON O'SULLIVAN

Published by Repeater Books
An imprint of Watkins Media Ltd

19-21 Cecil Court
London
WC2N 4EZ
UK
www.repeaterbooks.com
A Repeater Books paperback original 2017
2

Distributed in the United States by Random House, Inc., New York.

Cover design: Johnny Bull
Typography and typesetting: Stuart Davies
Typefaces: Palatino Linotype

ISBN: 9781910924631
Ebook ISBN: 9781910924648

Printed in the United Kingdom

To Mark Fisher

CONTENTS

FUTURES AND FICTIONS

A Conversation between Henriette Gunkel, Ayesha Hameed and Simon O'Sullivan

Simon O'Sullivan: Perhaps we should begin our conversation by discussing what the particular conjunction of our book's title — futures and fictions — signifies for us? On the one hand our book contains essays on fiction and the future, but it's really the combination of these two terms that, I think, we originally found compelling. Obviously, this relates directly to the genre of science fiction that more often than not involves a depiction of a possible (utopian or dystopian) future, but I'm certainly interested in how these future fictions have a more general traction on the real, not least insofar as they can offer concrete models for other ways of life in the present (or, indeed, might themselves be materially embodied); could we even call this a kind of science fictioning of the real? I think this was one of the things we were especially concerned with during our initial discussions that led to the Visual Cultures Public Programme at Goldsmiths which was the basis for this book: how fiction might be an important category beyond the literary or filmic — especially in terms of the possibility of a different "political imaginary" beyond the impasses of neoliberalism.

Henriette Gunkel: Yes, we were interested in future fictions beyond the ones available in this current political moment, beyond what neoliberalism holds for us — so beyond fiction's impact on the real as already operating in the current systems of financialisation and geopolitical relations as recently highlighted, for example, in Adam Curtis' not unproblematic new film *HyperNormalisation* (2016). The fictioning aspect of the financial system has been foregrounded prior to the film, of course — for example by Mark Fisher in his concept of "SF capital", which emphasises the crossover from science fiction and the apparent future-orientated and speculative nature of capital itself.

While keeping these conceptualisations of future fictions in mind, we were interested in collectively assembled projects that work against neoliberalism's push for competitive individualism and right-wing politics that we can currently see on the rise in Europe as well as in the US. We were also interested in a political imaginary which needs to be read relational to historically situated struggles that give us insights into alternative times and spaces. This is where our shared interest in Afrofuturism as deeply rooted in black radical thought comes in, I would say, which was one of the aspects of future fictions that we foregrounded and which points to an engagement with the future that ceases to devalue the present and the past. As such, Afrofuturism operates differently than a number of Futurisms in the past and brings to the fore how the future is already implicated in the different dimensions of time.

Art and visual culture have the capacity to draw

our attention to these non-linear conceptions of time and inspire our theorisation of futurity as alternative space-times by collapsing the supposedly distinct categories of past/present/future. I am particularly drawn to art strategies that propose different forms of being in the world by cutting familiar lines of association and reassembling new worlds, as visible, for example, in practices of sampling, collage, montage, or the cut-up. We can find this world-making potential of art at the conjuncture between futures and fictions also in Daniel Kojo Schrade's conscious layering of paint in his abstract paintings which produces not only a palimpsest of time but also creates spaces in-between for new subjectivities to emerge. Annett Busch's writing about or with John Akomfrah's films similarly functions as a form of montage — an assemblage of quotes, voice overs and philosophical ideas — which is organised around a key argument Akomfrah made in a recent talk: that the future begins by making an image.

Ayesha Hameed: One of our interests in the conjunction between futures and fictions lies in trying to think through how temporality is spatially embedded, manifest in sedimentations, intensities and condensations. Such condensations have the potential to form a kind of object that operates as what Gilles Deleuze would call a radioactive fossil, and what Walter Benjamin would conceive of as a dialectical image: objects that through their own charge and materiality make transversal cuts through time and destabilise the chronotopes to which they belong. Such objects can act as portals to collapse two temporal moments together.

This book explores how we collect such objects, act as their soothsayers and produce forms of creative misunderstandings. In his conversation with Harold Offeh, Julian Henriques refers to a diagram of sound systems, which highlights the visual and spatial quality of the production of sound — a compilation that also exceeds its components in its affective charge. This kind of prescience runs through John Akomfrah's film *Last Angel of History* on several registers, including sound and its use of props and colour, as Louis Moreno, Kodwo Eshun and I discuss in our conversation. Stefan Helmreich's exploration of the anthropology of the ocean calls attention to a speculative turn intrinsic to scientific studies — a phenomenon he refers to in his contribution to this volume. Something exceeds empirical study and is coded as alien and speculative, and possibly from outer space.

Another theme we consider is how fictioning operates from both above (from the state) and below (at a grassroots level). Benjamin's "Theses on the Philosophy of History" (1969) makes references to this in its articulation of tigers'-leaps into the past and future and warnings about the co-optations of history. In other words, that hallucinations and forms of fictions are being constantly produced from above. The danger today seems to lie in how there's no jolt out of the dream state of state-produced fictions. A constant state of befuddlement is now familiar and the dream state continues. And yet from below we'd like to think there is still the possibility for fictioning to undo the "dreamwork of imperialism", as W.J.T. Mitchell puts it. So fictioning as a tool and a weapon that infiltrates and

4

actively pursues alternatives by posing some "what ifs". From this perspective, futures *plural* can become a tactic that in each instance takes on the guise that the situation requires — not utopic or dystopic; nor as a means to deconstruct the present; nor a repurposing of the past. Rather it is all of these things simultaneously and none of them either.

SOS: Yes, I think for all of us there is an interest — and investment — in the politics of fiction, whether that be how fiction is deployed by the state (what William Burroughs once called "control") or how it might be used as a more resistant practice, not least in articulating and imaging other — *different* — futures (as you suggest, Ayesha, the plural seems crucial). There's something here about how fiction can impact on the real, in fact change it, at least to some extent. This is also at stake — to pull in another important pre-cursor — in the Cybernetic culture research unit's concept of "hyperstition", which names elements of fiction that make themselves real via temporal feedback loops. Hyperstition involves a different, more cybernetic, account of time — almost as if it has been flattened — with different temporal circuits and recursive nestings at work. I think this has some connections with Sun Ra's myth-science that also involves connections between the future and past, but also, as you suggest Henri, with "SF Capital" and the strange temporality of financial instruments such as derivatives in which an idea of the future becomes operative in the present. We increasingly seem to exist in a kind of "patchwork temporality" in this sense.

In relation to this — and some of your remarks
Henri — it's also worth foregrounding that as well as
the future it's also the past (and, again, different pasts)
that interest us, and how these might have a "residual"
potential in the present. I'm sure that we'll come onto
our own contemporary political scene in a moment,
but it's worth saying here that for me it's crucial to
disentangle this interest in the past and future from
what has become known as "neoreaction" and its own
account of a patchwork temporality. I'd also say, as a
bit of a tangent, that it's in fiction per se that we tend
to see experiments with the knotting together of different past-presents-futures. One of my favourite novels
is emblematic in this sense: Russell Hoban's *Riddley
Walker*, which involves a nesting of fictions but also all
sorts of complex temporal loops to the past and future.

So, art practices can certainly represent these other
future-fictions, but, more radically, as you allude to
Ayesha, it can involve the presentation — or instantiation perhaps — of them in the here and now. I think
you're right to mention the cut-up Henri, as, for me,
Burroughs' writings precisely explore this deployment
of other times *in* the present. Indeed, if typical time is
sequential, linear, then the cut-up disrupts this, and,
in so doing, invents other space-times. I think this has
a bearing on other formal experiments in SF writing,
for example with J.G. Ballard, but also on art practice
more generally that can involve this play with language and syntax, and, indeed, with a certain grammar and semantics of objects and images.

As a bit of an aside, the idea of fictioning has res-
onances, I think, with the practice of magick (the "k"

here marks a difference with magic more typically understood as a form of non-scientific causality) that also involves a certain manipulation of the real, or, at least, the exploration of other realities outside the consensual. Magick also names a more wilful self-determination, the idea of "becoming a cause of oneself". Indeed, when it comes to fictioning I think figures like Austin Osman Spare and his various techniques of self-transformation (for example through sygyll magick) have much to teach us (the artist David Burrows has written well on this, see Burrows 2016). This relates to our interest in past modes of existence, but also to the way our book looks to other, non-Western cultures. As far as all this goes, it's especially more syncretic practices — of creolisation and the like — that would seem to offer the possibility of a really *different* future to that predicted by our futures managers.

HG: I would like to take up your reference to other realities outside the consensual, Simon, and link it to our overall interest in different and multiple futures that we have articulated so far in this conversation — which, in one way or another, seem to be linked to the notion of hope and seem to imply that there is at least some form of future available for all of us (and I am not talking about human beings exclusively here).

In his conversation with Elvira Dyangani Ose, Kemang Wa Lehulere points to other realities that seem to complicate our understanding of the chronopolitical when he talks about the archaeological dig that he performed in a backyard in Gugulethu at the outskirts of Cape Town — an archaeological dig that we find articulated in *The Last Angel of History* and a number of SF narratives and practices that connect the future project to the past. In Kemang's case this dig became more than a symbolic gesture the moment he excavated bones, human remains. This discovery speaks to the afterlives of the apartheid regime but also seems to foreground the fact that for certain groups of people the future was/is already foreclosed — which reflects back on Audre Lorde's prominent line "we were never meant to survive" in her poem "A Litany of Survival" (1995). And here we can all think of numerous other historical and contemporary examples that demonstrate how relevant Lorde's poem is today: Europe's politics towards migrants and refugees — a politics that consciously and repeatedly turns the Mediterranean Sea into a graveyard for black and brown bodies — is one of many current examples. Another is the killings of African-Americans by white police, addressed, for example, in the Black Lives Matter movement which not only points to the fact that at this moment in the US black lives do not matter but also mobilises black people, specifically the youth, and their allies to resist state-sanctioned violence (which will be even more pressing now that Trump is elected president).

For me these are important strategies and experiences to consider in our discussion of future fictions. We can find another conceptualisation of "no future" articulated in the punk/post-punk context/moment but also, more recently, and definitely influenced by it, in Lee Edelman's positioning of queer temporality understood as an anti-relational, anti-social politics of "no future" that breaks with teleological conceptions of hope and reproduction in the context of straight time (2004). Against the backdrop of Kemang's work, however, the implications of "no future", as proposed by Edelman, stand in an uncanny tension to the violence that constitutes and defines blackness — and a number of queer scholars have challenged Edelman by foregrounding the relationship between queer temporality and Afrofuturism and explicitly returning to the concept of hope (as for example the important work of José Esteban Muñoz) which in my opinion remains a crucial *feeling* in the context of the political. But it is these different articulations of the chronopolitical that emerge out of the experiences and realities outside the consensual (a consensual that you can also find in left academic writing, at least in the Anglo-American context) that allow us to ask more specifically how certain approaches to time function as pressure points to more conventional understandings/theorisations of the concept of future, but also of fictioning.

AH: I think it is crucial Henri that you bring Black Lives Matter and the recurring deaths of migrants on the Mediterranean Sea into this conversation, as of course the political project of the conjoining of futures and fictions stems precisely from long histories and ongoing occurrences of racialised and neo-colonial forms of violence. Sun Ra's project can only make sense in the wake of racialised slavery in America and the genocide during the middle passage. It is not a whimsical flight of fancy but rather a structured protest whose flight is inextricable from the violence that it is responding to.

There is an affective charge in naming these

9

moments as those with "no future" that I think is crucial to this configuration. When something is named in a manner that has the affective charge of hitting a nail on the head, a lateral sense of possibilities is produced in that moment that produces a line of flight. Lorde's "Litany of Survival" is testament to the kind of curtailment and opening up to possibility that occur in the same instant and cannot be extricated from one another.

Ambivalence is key here as it produces a set of lateral tactics. So, when Simon brings up the cut-up I think these ambivalent concerns are what are at stake. There is a failure on the part of linear time and empirical testimony to adequately address the chronic political and social crises from the long twentieth century on. So even though the cut-up might be seen as an aesthetic gesture now, the possibilities that arise from this gesture do so in part from the violence of the act itself towards a text or a film or whatever media that has been wrung dry of meaning and cannot address the inchoate needs of a present moment. Thus the text is cut up like a corpse on an autopsy table with the same kind of sacrilegious intent. Thus the violence of the cut and the not knowing or understanding what that gesture produces it is constantly generative. The incision into the text or film is akin to the hitting-the-nail-on-the-head feeling produced by naming a moment of no future. There is a despair in the gesture that affectively produces something in another realm. And this is what we attempt to present in our book: transversal cuts between several different forms and objects — imagistic, linguistic, architectural, filmic, that act as the soothsayers that I mentioned above.

This crisis has metastasised though, and as Henri rightly points out our current moment is even more pressing with the recent US elections and the spectre of all kinds of futures likely being curtailed — the erection of the US-Mexico border wall, the irreversible destruction of the environment — the impact is beyond the imaginary of the current moment. The kind of nail-on-the-head affective charge of naming something accurately or the kind of political and libidinal release effected by the cut-up is in danger of being blunted and that we are at a political and epistemic threshold that calls for a similar mutation of these tools.

SOS: Yes, the cut-up is a powerful tool for challenging consensual reality and, especially I think, dominant regimes of subjectivity. The cut-up, or, indeed, other forms of experimentation with images and narrative, does not pander to what Jean-François Lyotard once called the "fantasies of realism" (1984: 74) and the desire for a subjectivity already in place to be reassuringly "mirrored back" by typical narrative structure and image sequences (it's interesting in this respect that Lyotard, along with Deleuze, was at the infamous Schizo-Culture conference where Burroughs delivered his lecture on "The Limits of Control"). For myself this connects to the political importance of art practice that can involve interrogations on what we might call this more subjective level.

In relation to this and what you've just said about the libidinal, Ayesha, I also think some of the material in our book problematises what might be called the new Prometheanism apparent in some areas of the critical humanities (as in "accelerationism"). I would say our investment in futures and fictions, although partaking of the conceptual and rational (especially in its experimental form) also pulls in the libidinal and, of course, the fictional. Actually, I think both Luciana Parisi's introduction to Laboria Cuboniks' xenofeminist manifesto, and the manifesto itself, also attend to this area — and, in terms of the imbrication of the fictional and the technological, there is also AUDINT's future fabulation included in our volume. In fact, with the event of new technologies and especially cheaper and more readily available digital imaging and sampling technology, I think we are at the beginning of some very exciting developments in presenting hybrid times and spaces (I address this — at least a little — in my own essay in our book).

We've talked quite a lot about the concept of futures (again, the plural seems important), but just to turn to fictions for a moment, our book also gathers some interesting "uses" of fiction within contemporary art (when this is broadly construed). I'm thinking of Theo Reeves-Evison's contribution, and especially the part in his essay on Goldin+Sennesby and their play with the surfaces and fictions of financialisation; a kind of generative parasitical practice. Bridget Crone also has recourse to different fictions in her account of the "flicker-image" at work in Tony Conrad's films. Then there's also Oreet Ashery and her use of fiction as method in her own expanded art practice — and how this connects also to her interest in performance. Finally, more generally (and more philosophically), there's also Robin Mackay's account of "yarn work" as a form of fiction or plotting that transits between local and global contexts (and that also relates to therapeutic work).

Staying with fiction, another area not explicitly included in our volume is the work of feminist scholars on science/speculative fiction and "worlding" (an exception to this — at least to a certain extent — being the short story by Ursula K. Le Guin which ends our collection; I know we were all very excited to be able to republish this particular fiction as it both speaks to our thematics but also changes the register of our edited collection). I'm thinking especially of writers like Donna Haraway and Isabelle Stengers (both of whom look to Le Guin's SF writing as a kind of conceptual resource) and their accounts of the co-creation of different worlds and, indeed, how different art practices are involved in this (see Haraway 2016; Stengers 2013). This has implications also for a more ecological consciousness — fictions of the universe in which the human is not the centre. For myself it is especially interesting how "world" is used as a verb by Haraway, as in "to world". My sense is that fiction might also be used in this way ("to fiction") and that this might signal the move from literary examples to something more performative. I think this is where I would situate the move from fiction to fictioning.

HG: I appreciate your focus on the notion of co-creation which you emphasise in relation to the call for being worldly, and that also surfaces in your own scholarship on fictioning (2014) — which you conceptualise as the possible production of different space-times in relation to a collectivity that you seem to understand foremost as a scene (rather than an x amount of people implied) through which one can perform one's own alienation. I always think of Octavia Butler's multispecies storytelling when I read Haraway — in particular her book *Fledgling* which presents this beautifully queer multispecies becoming; or her *Xenogenesis* trilogy. Interestingly, *Parable of the Talents* has been given some attention in the post-Trump election as it seems to have written someone very much like Trump into being nearly twenty years ago, a presidential candidate figure that mobilises his constituency with the very slogan "Make America Great Again".

In her multi-form worlding practice, Haraway also reminds us of the need for denormalisation by arguing that "it matters to destabilise worlds of thinking with other worlds of thinking", or "which ideas we think other ideas with". We can find this form of speculative thinking also articulated in the conversation between Mark Fisher and Judy Thorne — even though not necessarily foregrounded as a multispecies one. In their proposed communist hyperstitional practice they bring together two strikingly disparate concepts, communism and luxury. Not as an attempt to revive each concept through the other but as a form of reassemblage — here the cut-up operates through ideas and concepts that are reassembled and as such become unrecognisable and produce this productive ambivalence that you were pointing towards earlier, Ayesha, that possibly leads to a new platform for dreaming as you call it, Simon, in relation to the potentiality of fictioning. The difference to what is already available to us — and as such experienced and felt, in one way or another — is foregrounded by the unlikely alliance between the two terms, but through their combination they create a form of unpredictability that possibly arrives at a collective potentiality.

To me this sense of collectivity implied in the idea of communism then operates not as an assumed uncritical commonality but, rather, emerges from a shared sense of dissatisfaction with the current political moment which is precisely "not the unproblematic being in common but the mysterious being with" which informs much current writing around the commons in recent years (in this case the notion of the brown commons by Muñoz). It provides a refocus on different forms of being in this world together that is expressed in notions of the commons, in communist hyperstitional practices, in practices of worlding and co-created forms of fabulation.

AH: Haraway's interest in the multispecies implications of worlding also leads to her exploration of the cthulucene as a tactical response to the flash of warning signalled by the anthropocene. This is another register where the war cry of "no future" rings out urgently as well, in the literally seismic shifts that are leading the planet unstoppingly to ecological catastrophe and irreversible breaking points in global warming. Her intervention narrows the anthropocene's indictment of all of humanity to focus on the impact of capitalism and the development of plantations. She also scales down her analysis to the erosions and counter erosions effected at the level of organisms fuelled by feminist commitment to what she calls "staying with the trouble". What's interesting in the context of this discussion is that this form of cohabitation creates fictions where the human is not at the centre anymore. How does one consider this cry of "no future" — its planetary and geological time and space scales — in relation to Black Lives Matter and Edelman's anti-re-productive futurism that Henri flagged earlier? How does the non-human set of actors factor into a response to the end of futures?

If the trouble of this time is the erosion of facticity in a post-Trump era that has left reality as a basis behind, then the tools need to be made of another material. Perhaps one route is to consider the agency of the sooth-saying objects and spatialities that I brought up earlier in constructing alternate worlds. To consider their soothsaying as not needing to be revelatory of facts behind the fictions, but rather producing another con-junction of futures and fictions that took into account new tactics of "troubles" and "scaling". This would add to a growing taxonomy of *futures* plural, another method that scales down the unimaginable into a series of frictions and incommensurables and then stays with those troubles. What would a multispecies, planetary, troubled reworking of futures and fictions look like?

Image credit: Sam Nightingale (2016) Spectral Ecologies, black and white photographs.

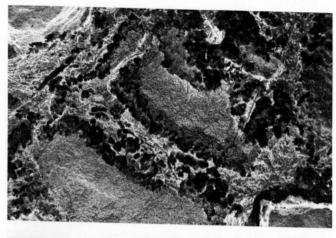

Image credit: Sam Nightingale (2016) Spectral Ecologies, black and white photographs.

Works Cited

Benjamin, Walter (1969), "Theses on the Philosophy of History", in *Illuminations: Essays and Reflections*, ed. Hannah Arendt, trans. Harry Zohn. New York: Schocken Books, 245-55.

Burrows, David (2016), "Self Obliteration through Self Love", in *Black Mirror*. London: Fulgur, 136-57.

Butler, Octavia (1998), *Parable of the Talents*. New York: Seven Stories Press.

— — — (2005), *Fledgling*. New York: Seven Stories Press.

Edelman, Lee (2004), *No Future: Queer Theory and the Death Drive*. Durham: Duke University Press.

Gilroy, Paul (2014), "Hearing our History Now" Lecture. Brilliant Corners, London.

Haraway, Donna J. (2016), *Staying with the Trouble: Making Kin in the Chthulucene*. Durham: Duke University Press.

Lorde, Audre (1995 [1978]), *The Black Unicorn: Poems*. New York: Norton.

Lyotard, Jean-François (1984), *The Postmodern Condition: A Report on Knowledge*, trans. G. Bennington and B. Massumi. Manchester: Manchester University Press.

Mitchell, W.J.T (2002) "Imperial Landscape", in *Landscape and Power*, ed. W.J.T. Mitchell. Chicago: University of Chicago Press, 5-34.

Muñoz, José Esteban (2009), *Cruising Utopia: The Then and There of Queer Futurity*. New York: NYU Press.

O'Sullivan, Simon (2014), "Art Practice as Fictioning (or, myth-science)", in *diakron*, no. 1. http://bit.ly/2ooSMgw; accessed 9 December 2016.

Stengers, Isabelle (2013), "Matters of Cosmopolitics: On the Provocations of Gaïa, Isabelle Stengers in Conversation with Heather Davis and Etienne Turpin", in *Architecture in the Anthropocene: Encounters Among Design, Deep Time, Science and Philosophy*, ed. Etienne Turpin. Michigan: Open Humanities Press.

REVISITING GENESIS >>>

Oreet Ashery

An Intro, a Future, a Fiction

It is awkward to talk about a piece of work that hasn't happened yet. Writing this, I am midway through the process of completing the web series *Revisiting Genesis*. An artist needs time to reflect on their work, and insight is the fruit-child of retrospection > the performance is over, friends say their goodbyes and an hour later you clear up the mess, bent over a brush and dustpan. First you were high, now you are low, adrenalin vacating > I have been on this emotional roller-coaster many times before, but on this occasion the performance hasn't even started and it's already tangential. Telling you about *Revisiting Genesis* now puts me in transitive time, in time of secession. A wishful training in self-belief. I can't really write about the unmade work, so instead I will write around, underneath and beside it. I will introduce influences, references, information, quotes and thoughts, not all connected or resolved, but I assure you > never random. I could have approached it differently, but women shouldn't apologise for something they have not even done yet.

A claimer > when I speak of women, I mean women identified: identified with women, identified as

21

women, sometimes identifying. In *Revisiting Genesis* I am not interested in biochemistry, genitals or forms of essentialism; those are only useful in court cases > the dis/empowerment of being minor is rooted in language. Yesterday I bumped into Onkar Kular who said to me: "Oh I'm going to invent a new language. The future needs a new language. We need a new language, we talk in a new language, of course we do." Kular was referring to *Night School on Anarres*, a space to learn Pravic — based on the *Dispossessed*, a 1974 utopian science-fiction novel by Ursula K. Le Guin. One quote from Le Guin, used in the script for *Revisiting Genesis*, is that women can't successfully pretend to be men, too much hips. This sentiment could be visualised in many ways but a useful difference between Speculative Fiction and Fantasy is that SF has the immediate ability to de-normalise what already exists and as such offers a political satire of the NOW>

A Mood

A mood, an environment, a situation, a heterotopic space. Conceiving of *Revisiting Genesis* is thinking about a mood, trying to communicate THE MOOD > trying to get THE MOOD in the room > feeling something > a kind of a feeling of something distinct yet vaporous. Sometimes a tablecloth of a certain colour is enough to create a mood. It's a struggle telling stories, but I have to tell you this one. Today on my way to the bus stop, time and space screeched to a halt in a hectic central London street when this incredibly old woman > the oldest person you can try to imagine, came to me and said: "I'm dying, everything is dying.

It's all TV and internet. Are you dying?" And I can't stop thinking: Why today, when I'm writing about the death of everything and the internet? What is she trying to teach me? Am I writing my own death? Am I too flippant? The bus stop marked the limitlessness of heterotopia; we were alone, forming a set of conditions for undesirable bodies to come together. This story should have been enough, enough to bring you the mood and the synthesis of *Revisiting Genesis*. If only I could tell the story.

Figure 1. © Oreet Ashery (2016) Revisiting Genesis video still.
Memory stick by Audrey Samson.

The Slideshow, Memory as Identity

Revisiting Genesis follows two nurses, both named Jackie, who assist people actively preparing for death to create biographical slideshows > a *This Is Your Life* type slideshow. The slideshows are used as a tool and a trigger for reflection on cultural and social loss and memory as identity. The script interlaces three narrative modes, the story of Genesis, the story of Bambi and the stories of real people with real life-limiting conditions. Genesis represents a figure of withdrawal and increased dysfunctionality > she is dying > her friends beg the nurse for a slideshow > a memory trigger > a sensory rigger > an emotional pass > a consolidator of events rearranged. The narrative, if you could call it that, centres around the unfolding presentations of the protagonists' slideshows. Genesis' slideshow is made of my archival images and to an extent her partial and fictional biography is mine, although this is not important to know.

When I spoke to doctors and nurses in palliative care and hospices, as well as volunteers who support people who are dying, they told me of the treatment called Reminiscence Therapy. Dr Natasha Arnold explained how photographs, smells, sounds and objects from patients' lives are used to trigger their memory and help consolidate their fragmented sense of self, particularly in cases of dementia. A number of nurses who teach and specialise in palliative care told me that patients' sense of self and identity can disintegrate in the face of terminal illness or old age, and that patients are not the sum of their illness or symptoms, but rather a story to be told. As someone who is interested in the construction and narration of minor identities, fictional and real combined, I was drawn in. I assembled the idea of a *slideshow* made for those who are approaching death as a narrative holder or a continuous spine that runs through *Revisiting Genesis*. The slideshows of Genesis, Bambi and the real people with life-limiting conditions — Julia Warr, Annie Brett, Roger Ely and Joel Sines — bring about questions of friendships, care, afterlife presence, emerging death industries and the death of social structures under neoliberalism. Death and dying has no clear beginning or end — "When I died I continued hearing. One can keep hearing for at least a few days after death. I didn't only hear what the doctor said, I heard him speaking from inside herself." > An account of a patient with a transpersonal near-death experience > When does a piece of *work* start and end? Where does *gender*? Do we ever stop dying?

People with Life-Limiting Conditions in *Revisiting Genesis*

To find people with life-limiting conditions who wanted to participate in the work, we ran audition interviews in August 2015 as part of the exhibition program of Figure 2, at the ICA in London. We spoke about the ways in which life-limiting conditions, chronic and terminal illness create a heterotopic space > a time and space outside that of *the everyday* that is manifest in nuanced states of mind and creative outlets. Like theories of black holes where time and space interchange, stretch and mutate > at one point the nurse asks Genesis' friends if Genesis perhaps fell into such a black hole > "Do you have black holes in your area?" > Genesis' friend replies, "No, luckily we don't have them in our area". In the museum, for example, artworks and artists from different times and geographies are encased in one such heterotopic space during one visitor's journey, sharing many relational existences > one space gives another space a meaning > in *Revisiting Genesis*, the three intersecting narrative modes of Genesis, Bambi and the interviews with real people give one space a new meaning through the cross-referencing of another space.

For minorities > all in different ways > for reasons of precarity, familial circumstances and the lack of established acceptance or belonging > the active processes of dying create unique heterotopic spaces. See for example narrative accounts and case studies in the book *Death and the Migrant*, a sociological account of transnational dying and care in British cities, by Yasmin Gunaratnam.

Audition interview for *Revisiting Genesis* tape 1 — Annie Brett

Friends are very, very important, with a chronic illness such as Crohn's disease, you spend an awful long time in bed, being very, very unwell, being unable to attend events and things like that, and you end up, you end up letting people down. People invite you to things like parties and you say yes of course, I will be there, I wouldn't miss it for the world and then you suddenly become ill and you suddenly have these dark thoughts like you are letting them down and you can't help but think that you are letting them down, and that builds upon itself, but then you see them later and you say I'm really, really sorry that I couldn't be there for you and they're like it doesn't matter, I am your friend, I know you have this illness, I know you flirt with death constantly, going in and out of hospitals, I am always there, and it is those people that get you through the days, it is those people that come to see you if you are in hospital, check up on you, those text messages you get just saying I'm sorry you can't be there, we will do something again soon.

Audition interview *Revisiting Genesis* tape 2 — Julia Warr

I had an art career, I still do, and then I moved to America and I was always worried about getting it again. But I had two more children, naturally, so I was worried and I wasn't worried, but tried to keep stress low. And then moved to America — that's high-stress, with a family of three kids, moving house and all that. So, or not so, I got it again. Same breast. This time the Americans took everything out of me and I went with it. Bilateral mastectomy, chemotherapy, and that took five years for me to stop being angry about agreeing to something that was actually just done as a precaution. But that's a sob story you don't want to hear anymore about that. But two weeks ago I had my ovaries out, just as a precaution, and I am still getting over that. That's a weird one, two ovaries and two tubes, little things (showing with her index fingers and thumbs in both hands, two pea-size hole-shapes).

Audition interview *Revisiting Genesis* tape 3 — Joel Sines

With my condition, the really scary thing for me in it is that I can be talking right now and then fall, fall off, dead. Just boom (clicking his middle finger and thumb), not seeing it even coming. But this is kind of a blessing, because it could be something that I could see coming. I can imagine cancer, something that you see it coming, you see your identity being lost to that condition, right? I feel that that must be much more (clicking his middle finger and thumb), difficult to deal with. But I have no problem talking about death, it is what it is. I was thinking about it the other day, 90% of us are going to die without knowing and we are not going to take care of those details (online accounts, social media, digital content), we are not going to close our accounts. Does Zuckerberg close the accounts of people who die? Do the Microsoft guys get information through our accounts when people have just passed away? Do they think, let's send it to some twisted archive? I was thinking about that. I was in the hospital this week, I had a major pain in my head, but it turned out to be a breakdown, and I posted (wiping his eyes with his hands) I posted "Forever Young" by Alphaville (holding his head in his hands). Watching the sky, I find it beautiful, we don't have the power but we never say never, I like those sentences.

Poo

Heterotopic spaces are places of performance where dirt and purity are one and the same, defining each other in medical and spiritual rituals. The main set for the web series is Genesis' place, or non-place; it has white floors and walls and it is completely empty, indicative of Genesis' condition. The only *object* in the room is the sideshow projection > we will need a 15,000-25,000-lumen projector in order to have a bright white light throughout the shoot and retain a saturated projected image. At some point I plan to have poo on the floor. Who's going to bring the poo? Where from and who's going to clean it? Genesis' friends will be joyous to discover the poo, it means that Genesis is active, functioning, she's still alive, there's still hope. Failing that, someone will trip over a cup of tea left on the floor and a brown liquid stain will linger over the whiteness.

The question of patients' agency became paramount when I spoke to palliative care doctors and nurses. Those preparing for death are often caught up with conflicting family, carers and the health system's agendas, as bit by bit they face the loss of their agency > they told me how important it is to maintain the patient's agency for as long as possible > this presented me with a conflict > Genesis has no agency, she never speaks in the script and we rarely see her. Her there-and-not-there presence is intentional and governed by the wishes of those around her who care for her. There is always something messy in trying to order someone's life, especially someone we care for, especially when they are ill. Mary Douglas states in *Purity and Danger*, "when chasing dirt, decorating, tidying, we are not governed by anxiety to escape disease, but are positively re-ordering our environment, making it conform to an idea".

I went to see Castellucci's *Son of God* > a play about a son who is forced to look after his senile and incontinent father > the surreal and gradual spillage of the excrement over the pristine white stage is like motion painting > every evening before the curtain goes up, various vessels of steaming brown liquid must be churned in order to get the texture, consistency and the smell exactly right > the Barbican Theatre, 2011, stinks of poo as if it's been pumped through the air vent > Castellucci described it as "a play about the spirit of the shit" > the smell of how hard it might be to look after our parents is overwhelming > the stomach is churning, a reminder that we might not be fully up to it > some people feel faint and leave the auditorium.

Women Disappear

Woman's death is not any old death
a woman's death is not normal
Let us make a woman disappear
into a flat black smudge

You seem stitched up in the net
she smiles and cries in the deep deep web
chased, erased, stay in bed
how we live is how we die
Maybe more so

Trolls make goose bumps come alive
Trolls make goose pups come alive
roll and troll and troll and roll and troll
with a laptop on your back

Theses lyrics are from a Kaddish prayer for Genesis, a prayer for those who have died and the last episode of the series > the story of Genesis is the story of the disappearance of women.

In *Men Explain Things to Me*, Rebecca Solnit talks about the many forms of female non-existence.

Wonder to Death is a performing arts project on femicide — telling and retelling the stories of the global pandemic of women who are killed based on their gender, mainly by lovers, partners, former partners, seeking the most extreme forms of erasure.

Some women get erased a little at
a time, some all at once.

Every woman that appears wrestles with the
forces that
would have her disappear.
(Rebecca Solnit)

In her book *Citizen: An American Lyric*, the poet Claudia Rankine describes how Serena Williams' body continuously > over and over again > is being called out to disappear by the media and the umpires. In the racist imagination Williams' body and its gestures do not belong on the tennis court. It is that "again-ness" of those calling-out instances that makes it difficult to distinguish when the umpire's decisions are in fact justifiable or yet again prejudged against Williams.

Rankine describes how the Danish player Caroline Wozniacki performs an impression of Williams by using stuffed towels in her tennis uniform's bra and underpants. Williams responded that she and Wozniacki are friends and said that she does not see Wozniacki as racist, but, she said, "I don't think she'll do it again", and she also said, "So many times I've been mimicked in a racialised way".

I am thinking about the complex ways in which women disappear into women, in this case racially. This is not a case of racism between strangers or competitors only — as Williams explained, they are also friends. Who is disappearing into whom, why and how? Is Williams disappearing into Wozniacki, as some would wish, by the act of racist public humiliation? To quote Rankine, "At last, in this real, and unreal moment, we have Wozniacki's image of smiling blond goddess posing as the best female tennis player of all times". Or is Wozniacki disappearing into Williams, not only by the sheer visual and symbolic allusion to becoming Williams through body towel bumping, but also through the direct exposure of white privilege? Williams' refusal to disappear is the trigger for white fear, anger and shaming.

Women disappearing into women > racially, economically and otherwise > inevitably, those displays of woman-to-woman disappearances are acted out within the patriarchal superstructure. When I look at the various video clips depicting Novak Djokovic "doing" Maria Sharapova to the cheering of the tennis court audience, I cringe.

In a recent *Guardian* interview, the artist Camille Henrot said of her drawing series *My Anaconda Don't*, 2015—"The dance (in Nicki Minaj's "Anaconda" music video) is quite shamanistic and entrancing — she is challenging us to embrace our primal nature". In response, Morgan Quaintance wrote in an e-flux text:

But for all this, *Grosse Fatigue* (a film by Henrot) displayed a troubling and dated tendency. It treated non-white bodies as anthropological curiosities, as examples of the exotic, otherworldly or primitive against which whiteness as rational, modern, cerebral and desirable could be constructed, measured and defined. What's more, it wasn't an isolated instance.

And later on in the same article on Henrot's Minaj:
— "But isn't the objectification of black female bodies,
reduced to the abstract physiological markers of breast
and bum, a centuries-old device of dehumanisation
enacted by what bell hooks called 'white supremacist
patriarchy'?" Is Henrot's *My Anaconda Don't*—the reference, disappearing into Minaj's "Anaconda"—the
referent, through the performances of fetishised racial
appropriation and cultural vulturism?

Another incidence of woman-to-woman racial disappearance that caught my attention was the disturb-
ing images from the *Suffragette* (2015) film premiere >
the stars wearing t-shirts saying: "I'd rather be a rebel
than a slave." Kirsten West Savali writes in *The Root*:

> Pankhurst's full quote may be important, but within
> it lies both the freedom of choice and the choice to be
> free. The message that Streep and company are co-sign-
> ing with their grinning faces and suffragette tees is that
> one cannot be both enslaved and a rebel; and tucked
> between those lines lies the erasure of a dual existence
> that black women have been forced to navigate in one
> form or another throughout history.

How to Make Women Disappear Two
In the art world women retain a state of semi-visibil-
ity through a relative lack of representation in public
collections, solo exhibitions, group exhibitions, gallery representation, magazine covers and reviews,
gender-bias reviewing, gender-bias prices, reviewing,

prices reviewing, monographs, monographs (2.7%), art books, representation, exhibitions, public collections representation.

Representation, as opposed to self-presenting, is part of art-cultural value. For artists > minorities especially > posthumous legacy becomes a re-written cultural and monetary commodity.

A Facebook post by Penny Arcade:

> My biggest nightmare is that after I die some hideous skank will end up writing my obituary or worse some deluded academic or pathetic curator will 'explain' my work to the public. Now I understand why Jack Smith begged me to burn his work on his deathbed. Jack always was right.

Alexis Hunter, Dying on Facebook

I have been following Alexis Hunter's posts on Facebook > obsessively > courageous notes oscillating between descriptions of her deteriorating health and her artistic legacy. Her posts, describing a precarious existence, inscribed themselves onto me. How women artists live > is how women artists die. Often semi-visible > often poor and precarious > and often with an artistic legacy left in a mess. Hunter's posts are a perfect synthesis of the themes in *Revisiting Genesis*, women artists' careers' durability, friendships, care, and posthumous online presence.

16 August 2013
"New show, Wall Street International Magazine,

Alexis Hunter and Jo Spence."

17 August 2013
"I am getting more dependent on mechanical things as I weaken. Think of that character in Doctor Who who has just a brain connected to tubes when they took apart a monster."

21 September 2013
"feminist art in auction, VALIE EXPORT, Jo Spence and me."

23 December 2013
"Today I had a shopping trip in a wheelchair, the rain was glorious on my face and the wind was terrific, buying food I cannot eat for my family, and the Carer having to huff and puff me up Haverstock Hill."

16 January 2014
"I have my carer wash my face, as I don't want to look in a mirror and see the ravages of disease on my face."

30 January 2014
"Feel better today, met with film director who is doing film about my feminist work this morning."

4 February 2014
"I have been looking at interviews I have done over the years and who is this woman I hardly know..."6
February 2014
"Exhibition: *The Weak Sex — How Art Pictures the New Male*."

15 February 2014
"going to hospice on Monday."

16 February 2014
"At the bed bath stage now, put it off as long as possible, but now my personal privacy is not worth the struggle."

18 February 2014
"Morning in hospice. I have two little Japanese nurses taking me to the toilet one on each arm I feel like an empress."

18 February 2014
"Nina Kellgren the cinematographer visited me this morning with ideas for the film we are making about my feminist artwork from my good friend Julia Whitcomb Cahill. At first I could not cope with a conversation but after a shower by one of my hand maidens I could."

23 February 2014
"This is it. My breathing had [sic] got shallow all the time not sometimes. This is how you die with MND, your breathing just gives out, my neighbor in the hospice has turned the colour of the wall! Magnolia."

Hunter died a day later. Her Facebook page has turned into a public memorial space and an online legacy stakeholder; a textual form of expanded mourning and celebration.

25 February 2014
"Alexis Hunter died at 4:30 pm on 24 February. Alexis was brave and strong until the end. We know how much she loved writing posts on Facebook and the reactions she got. It made dealing with the disease easier. RIP Alexis xx"

25 February 2014
"Farewell to my Facebook friend Alexis, an *intrepid* and talented artist that changed the world and shared her hospice experience right up to the last day."

Alexis Hunter's physical archive, currently at the special Collections & Archives at Goldsmiths Library, comprises of six boxes. On one of the boxes, full of slides, there is a post-it note with Hunter's handwriting saying — "What shall I do with these, throw away?"

Hunter's digital archive on Facebook occupies the public space of remembrance and forgetting, the physical archive is a personal artwork of artworks > handwriting as drawings > smell as posture > weight as an assemblage > autonomous.

I continue to read Facebook posts about artists I know who passed away: Ian White, Monica Ross, José Muñoz, Alexis Hunter and very recently a post from Nooshin Farhid about the death of Paul Eatchus who was my tutor, and stayed in her flat for the last three months of his life. They were close friends and neighbours > I admire the care and can only imagine the effects of the absence on Nooshin.

Bambi and the Emerging Death Industries

Bambi's story resides in the scripted and improvised meetings between nurse Jackie and Bambi. Jackie tries to resolve Bambi's digital will and posthumous presence while he still can > Bambi softly resists the intervention. This creates space to contemplate one's attitude to current discussions around digital assets, such as online accounts and subscriptions, websites, blogs and social networks, as well as posthumous presence and emerging technologies of death such as AR (Augmented Reality) gravesites or the developments of supposedly death-defying person-simulated avatars, to quote the robot Bina 48 from a YouTube clip: "Death is optional, we don't have to die! We are futurists!" (Bina 48 (Breakthrough Intelligence via Neural Architecture) is a humanoid robot who is modeled on Martine Rothblatt from more than a hundred hours of her compiled memories, feelings and beliefs. Nurse Jackie shows Bambi the clip in an attempt to persuade him to join a similar avatar program to ensure his posthumous presence.)

In one of their meetings nurse Jackie tells Bambi to consider keeping his online presence alive after his death by making his partner Tom his legacy contact:

> Bambi: Are you kidding? My internet presence is going to help Tom and my mum and everyone to mourn better?

> Nurse: Well, according to our research, digital environments for mourning can prove useful in helping the bereaved cope with their loss.

Bambi: Why should grief be public? It's intimate, isn't it? Poor princess Diana.

Nurse: Digital platforms open the mourning process out to all users, including those outside normative family structures. People can share despair, empathy, advice, even rage. Maybe it could provide some relief.

Bambi: So if someone is feeling worse, then it makes someone else feel better? That kind of sharing?

Nurse: There is nothing wrong with sharing, it's human. There are very few safe public spaces to share grief without being judged. Digital environments help! It's a fact.

Figure 2. © Oreet Ashery (2016) *Revisiting Genesis* video still, Bina 48.

Revisiting Genesis started with my growing awareness of artists around me falling ill or experiencing deep stress and exhaustion, discussing the issue only in private, so as to not expose temporal or chronic professional vulnerabilities. How often have artists "threatened" to stop being artists because it is too precarious, too hard? The fantasy of withdrawal in the face of demands for continuous exposure is evermore appealing. Living artists are under continuous pressure to self-present and promote themselves on established and emerging social networks, for the dying and the dead the same expectations apply.

There are companies that offer afterlife digital-assets management. This includes digital-will services, where one's digital content is dealt with in the same manner as material possessions, this also includes digital storage space and managers, where a person who is dying can assign a trusted digital legacy contact to then have access to all the deceased's digital life. An emotional service includes the delivery of pre-empted video messages from the deceased to friends and family for the span of twenty-five years (see https://www.safebeyond.com). Other companies offer services that will erase all digital content of the deceased from the World Wide Web within a short and limited period — to erase one's digital presence and online accounts from the internet can be a lengthy and a tasking commitment. Questions of access to digital content became more ethically challenging in cases of familial access to social networks, in cases of teenage suicide, for example.

There are new technologies developing around ecological or ethical burial, such as http://www.urban-deathproject.org. Another example of an emergent technology is the possibility of an AR grave environment where relatives and friends can activate digital content on the gravesite through dedicated mobile-phone technologies or retinas (see https://www.

aurasma.com). Ashes are now made into jewellery, tattoos, vinyl records and other products. AI (Artificial Intelligence) experimentations are dedicated to avatars based on real people — one of the most popular and advanced of which is Bina 48. By making avatars like us, we are creating a version of ourselves that never needs to die and only expands.

Capitalism inherently changed the way we live; now it is changing the way we are dying. We are a commodity in life and in death.

Casting for the Future

On the train back from Kingston > where I wrote the script > to Waterloo, I notice a beautiful stranger, who looks like the future. He is young, not fully formed, something between a teenager and an adult, his ethnicity is mixed and for a while I am not sure of his gender. A woman with a baby in her hands boards the train and he immediately lets go of his seat and lets her sit down. He then sits opposite me. After a while I notice that he doesn't hold or check his mobile phone like I do and like everyone else around us incessantly does. I want to ask him to be in my film, but feel embarrassed. It's so cheesy. As we inch towards Waterloo I know that this is my last chance and I ask him if he is an art student, he replies — "no, I study nutrition, what we eat is very important". I ask him if I can contact him on Facebook and he replies that he is not on Facebook, that he doesn't want to waste his life. I ask him if he wants to be The Future in my film and he says yes. His name is George Hard. Casting is how we can affect the future, in Genesis' part of the story there are no white men until episode eleven.

Works Cited

Douglas, Mary (2002), *Purity and Danger: An Analysis of the Concepts of Pollution and Taboo*. London: Routledge.

Emelife, Aindrea (2015), "'She's a wild woman, she's a shaman': Nicki Minaj becomes a feminist art muse", in *The Guardian* 1 September. https://www.the-guardian.com/artanddesign/2015/sep/01/nicki-min aj-anaconda-camille-henrot-feminist-art; accessed 28 August 2016.

Gunaratnam, Yasmin (2013), *Death and the Migrant: Bodies, Borders and Care*. London: Bloomsbury.

Le Guin, Ursula K. (1974), *The Dispossessed.* NY: Harper & Row.

The LifeNaut Project (2014), "Bina 48 Meets Bina Rothblatt - Part One". November 27. https://www.youtube.com/watch?v=KYshJRYCArE; accessed 10 September 2016.

Quaintance, Morgan (2015), "Camille Henrot on Nicki Minaj: exoticising like it's 1989?", in *Flux* 1 September. http://conversations.e-flux.com/t/camille-henrot-on-nicki-minaj-exoticising-like-its-1989/2412; accessed 28 August 2016.

Rankine, Claudia (2014), *Citizen: An American Lyric*. Minneapolis: Graywolf Press.

Solnit, Rebecca (2014), *Men Explain Things to Me.* London: Haymarket Books.

West, Kirsten Savali (2015), "Sister Suffragette: 'Slave' T-Shirts Highlight White Feminism's Race Problem", in *The Root*. 7 October. http://www.theroot.com/articles/culture/2015/10/sister_suffragette_slave_t_shirts_highlight_white_feminism_s_race_problem/; accessed 30 August 2016.

HISTORY WILL BREAK
YOUR HEART

A Conversation between Elvira Dyangani
Ose and Kemang Wa Lehulere

Elvira Dyangani Ose: It seems we have two things in common: first, our personal interest in the African artist collective, and, second, our interest in history. We both thought that this beautiful title that you chose for your mid-career show would be an excellent way to introduce your practice. Maybe we can start with one of your projects to begin the conversation?

Kemang Wa Lehulere: I will begin with a performance piece which was not done for an audience per se, but with the anticipation that an audience might come and witness whatever outcome the performance led to. This is a piece I did in 2008 which was called *Uku-guqula iBatyi* which means "to turn a coat inside out", and it was within the context of an exhibition called *Scratching the Surface* which was curated by a collective called manje-manje projects, meaning "now now" or "in the moment" that operated in South Africa for a short time. We were invited as a collective to take part in this project and activate a space that we had set up in Gugulethu, a township just outside of Cape Town. This was an individual project that I did within a context of working collectively.

I chose to take the concept of the show literarily — especially the idea of "digging". My interest in digging was a symbolic gesture, archeologically, but also something meditative that would take place within a context of other works. So I was digging a hole with an afro-comb in a backyard in Gugulethu. This work becomes interesting and important for me because of the chance discovery of the human bones that I found. The space we worked in was a house that had been turned into a *shebeen*. A *shebeen*, an Irish term for an illicit drinking place, was very important in South Africa for two reasons: one, because the apartheid government had banned the selling of liquor by black South Africans as a way to prevent economic activity amongst blacks. So it was a very repressive law. But, two, within that, *shebeens* became very popular and important, most notably for single women who were running these establishments as a way of generating income. These would be for example single black women whose men had gone off to Johannesburg to work in the mines. *Shebeens* also became very important cultural spaces where intellectuals, musicians and artists met to discuss things — like a form of an open studio really. Our location with the collective, in terms of working space-wise, was in the interest of re-activating these ideas in the historical sense but also to try and re-imagine a way of moving forward with those ideas.

EDO: You are talking about the importance of the transformation of the *shebeen* which I think is crucial for two factors. What the *shebeen* represents during apartheid is a space in which people could gather together, but apart from celebrating and drinking it was also a political space of engagement. You reinvented the format, in a way, to turn it into this plural, more community-oriented cultural space of exchange. Both to empower the local actors, the local agents, but also to bring and to try to dislocate the main focus of cultures in Cape Town and the main cultural activity from the city to the outskirts of the city.

KWL: Yes. To give a bit of context: Gugulethu is a township that was created to house black South Africans who were moved from wherever they lived. So when the Group Areas Act came in, blacks were dispossessed and relocated — if they lived in the city of Cape Town. For example, there is a neighbourhood called District Six which was completely demolished, or another one called Loyolo Village, where all the residents were moved to Gugulethu. My family was moved from an area called Athlone, as this area was then designated for coloured people. There is another one in Johannesburg called Sophiatown, which was very important because it is where a lot of musicians and writers came together specifically and hung out within those *shebeen* spaces. If anyone has further interest to see an example of this, look at a film called *Come Back Africa* (1959) by Lionel Rogosin, which includes a documentary scene where Miriam Makeba as a young woman is singing amongst a group of writers who were called the Drum Writers. So within this kind of geopolitics of Cape Town, and South Africa at large, we were interested in the urban space and urban planning and how these affected the lives of black people for the past half-century, and also how these are still real experiences that affect people in the day-to-day post-1994, which is considered the official end of apartheid. We were interested in re-activating that space and creating a space for dialogue with other artists who created platforms, invited people for film screenings, music gigs and poetry readings, amongst others.

EDO: There is something very interesting about the formation of Gugulective that started in 2007 and includes artists like Zipho Dayile, Unathi Sigenu, who I believe was, together with you, one of the main conceptualisers of the project, alongside Temba Tsoti, Khanyisile Mbongwa and Dathini Mzayiya. The interest in the space, the role of the township in a cultural scene that, perhaps, was dislocated or marginalised was one of your preoccupations, as was the idea of making that composition of the periphery central to the discourse of the artistic community — both in terms of the producer but also the possible audience that was linked to that. One of the aspects of your work that has always been one of my interests is your sense of tradition, your sense of not being pioneers, right? This is one of the things that was extremely important in your conceptualisation of the Gugulective and in the way that you wanted to engage with the socio-historical process that was taking place in South Africa at that point. Ten years after the end of the regime, in a moment in which perhaps the conditions of the community in places like Gugulethu did not change as much as people expected, in a moment in which one can create an account and say: "Well, we can think about what happened and how that was extremely important". And I remember that you occasionally said that you did not have a manifesto but you have a declaration of intention.

KWL: We had a statement of intent, which you could say is a manifesto. But it kept changing because we did not want to theorise ahead too much so that we could leave some room for spontaneity. This is something that reoccurs in my individual work as well. So we kept rewriting the statement of intent as we were discovering things because we would rather do something and then reflect and theorise it, than theorise ahead. It reads as follows:

> We would like to introduce ourselves as the creative intellectualism of a society whose value system is grounded on notions of community or the collective. We do not claim to be pioneers. No! Like every aspect of a society or community we have inherited this, our acute collective eyes spies a grave lack of change in this times of transformation. This lack of change also has a stance in spaces outside of our communities, even in institutions of higher learning. Post-apartheid South Africa is failing to realise transformation. Such an exhibition provided space for interrogation as alternative for this lack of change. At this point in this country's history we need to ask ourselves how do we learn and teach each other that the ideologies that divide us are

not necessarily a basis for ostracism or prejudice.

That is an extract from a bigger text.

EDO: So then almost twelve years down the line, to what extent can you still recognise yourself in that?

KWL: Well, I think my work has always been rooted in the collective experiences I had. And this is why I chose to start with this work. Even though I continued making work as an individual, I was always meditating on the collective experience. For example, a piece I made is called *Remembering the Future of a Hole as a Verb* and it was part meditation on the experience of the digging that I mentioned earlier in the context of the performance piece *Ukuguqula iBatyi*, but also thinking about this hole that presented this skeleton, which speaks to so many things within the context of South Africa — in terms of transformation, in terms of history, in terms of openness. When I did this work a number of things came up — for example, even today there are a lot of missing political activists who were murdered either by the apartheid government or by the ruling party itself, and their grave sites may never be discovered. These missing people still have to be discovered. Families are still searching for their loved ones, many died in South Africa, many died in exile. In a way the collective has always been with me, and the sensibility that I have learned from working collectively is something that I will always carry forth even though I might not be working within a collective at a particular given time.

EDO: There is a sense of the digging, this archaeological research, in the whole of your work. Another aspect that we see in your murals, as we see in many of your works, is this sense of the erasure, what it means to write but also to erase. Perhaps we can take the opportunity to look at that and talk a bit more about what that means in your practice.

KWL: Within the collective, a lot of our work was concerned with the socio-political, but also institutions of power; including the art world itself and how it was structured, its lack of transformation, both racially but also in terms of gender dynamics, queer politics and its lack of representation of the society at large. But we were also concerned with institutions of higher learning. We made works that spoke directly to these issues but we also held workshops with young people. We organised film screenings that were politically oriented, for example, and we would have conversations and dialogues that were very pedagogically driven. And it is interesting that the country is currently on fire where students are standing up because of the lack of transformation in many spheres.

Personally, I took an approach where I was interested in the writing of history. In the case of the discovery of the bones in this residential area, for example, neighbours came and spoke about their experiences and gave testimonies. Because a lot of people did not believe I had discovered the bones, they thought I had planted them. So elderly people came to give evidence to say "no, this was the context of the time", "it was in the early 1970s", and so on. I became interested in both the importance of oral history but also in unwritten narratives. At that time when we were working with the Gugulective, I worked for a television production company and I was given a script by this woman — it is still something that gives me chills when I think about it. It is about someone who had been re-classified in South Africa from "black" to "coloured" in order to be upwardly mobile, both socially and economically. And they had to change their name and relinquish all relations with their family and went to Cape Town to start a new life. Only on his death-bed did he tell his wife and children his real name or his given name. The woman I was working for, the producer happened to be his child, and she gave me it and said, "Would you be interested to develop the script?" They wanted to turn it into a feature film. But that never really happened because I quit working for them for other reasons. However, I was really interested in the erasures of history but also histories that had yet to be told.

EDO: Your practice is multi-faceted, and includes performances, as well as mural drawings that form an extended way of writing; creative writing as a political gesture. And you have mentioned a script and also narratives for movies that you will never make; stories yet to be told that are also part of what you do. I remember talking to you, years ago, about some of the drawings that we presented at the *Arte inVisible* at ARCO in Madrid in 2009, how certain characters keep coming to your practice, and how these consistent narratives are possibly trying to challenge what you have said at other occasions, like the institutional amnesia that is both part of the country and also part of the culture.

KWL: How I came into the art world as I exist in it now was the result of a series of moments. I grew up amongst a theatrical family, spending time at rehearsals, watching the construction of stage plays. So I developed a stronger interest in theatre and film than in the fine arts. I did voiceovers for radio commercials as a teenager that I think really came back in my work. For example, in 2009, before this work was even made, I had a pirate radio station that was about the idea of occupying the public space in an immaterial sense, and I had a newspaper publication which was distributed for free. Both were a direct response to Naomi Klein's *No Logo*. So it was about how to manifest theory. I took the book and I presented it as a project in a literal sense. This was *Recess: Street Credit*, 2009. Then, I had a soccer tournament with various political groups which I was flirting with at the time: the anarchists, the black nationalists and the leftists/socialists. I was flirting with these various kinds of activist groups and

Figure 1. © Kemang Wa Lehulere (2013) *A Homeless Song (Sleep is for the Gifted)*, video still.

became interested in bringing people together. So the soccer tournament became a way to do this, amongst other things. But in terms of the writing, of script writing, it is all based on experiences I had as a child and it was a way of working out how to include these in my practice.

The video entitled *A Homeless Song* (2012), as an example, I co-choreographed with a friend, Khayelihle Gumede, and we worked with four dancers. It was a way of still meditating on the digging piece because it is something that I always go back to, and this time using a stage play that I had seen as a teenager — but a video of it, not the live staging — which was *The Island*. I have always had this image, an opening scene of a play, where you have two characters who are punished and have to move soil from one end to the next in this continuous kind of absurdity. But what was interesting when I went back to the play is that I discovered that the play had no written script for a number of years as the script could be used as evidence for the political nature of the play at a time of gross censorship in South Africa. So when John Kani, Winston Ntshona and Athol Fugard staged the play in South Africa in 1973, later in London and New York, they did not have a script because it could have been used against them. So again, it was in line with my interest in the unwritten and also in a certain kind of erasure, but also in strategies of how people work around these things. *A Homeless Song* is a way of trying to activate that, using the image from this play but also meditating on past works as well.

EDO: The skeleton and the bones: I don't know if you can tell us a little bit about what is happening apart from moving objects from one side to the other. They are moving bones which also connects with the earlier piece.

KWL: Yes, this is a very curious piece because it leads up to the next work I am going to talk about which involves Nat Nakasa, who is a funny character actually. Not funny in the hahaha sense, but very odd. Nat Nakasa left South Africa on an exit permit — he was denied a passport. This was a common thing for the apartheid government to do to punish blacks who wanted to leave South Africa. There is a picture of him taken in Harlem a few months before he died. He fell to his death in 1965 in New York. He was a writer, he was twenty-nine years old when he died, incredibly young, but he was some kind of pioneer and visionary, who started a literary magazine called *The Classic*. *The Classic* was funded by the CIA. I assume that he didn't know — I would like to believe that he didn't know. But the person who was also the front for the CIA, a CIA agent, organised for him to leave South Africa to go and study at Harvard. When he was leaving, the South African government had him on a watch list already because he had been mingling with white people, which was forbidden at the time. He was consequentially marked as a communist. It is curious that the South African government marked him as a communist. In fact, it issued a banning order against him but he left the country before it was signed. This document exists, but unsigned. And interestingly, on the other side, the American government was using him to further their Cold War ideology by promoting capitalism. So he was caught up in this crazy mix.

Interestingly enough, I encountered this work in Paris by Chieko Shiomi, which is called *Spatial Poem No. 3*, because I was due to give a performance lecture at the New Museum with a show I was working on with the Centre for Historical Reenactments with Ryan Inouye. The work is a call for people to submit documentation of things that they make fall intentionally. In the headspace of thinking about this performance, encountering this work led me elsewhere — and sometimes I do things which are not really clear in my head but make sense later on. But because of this work I decided to go read some poetry at Nat Nakasa's grave which I will read now. It is a poem by Syl Cheney-Coker and is entitled "Letter to a Tormented Playwright":

> Amadu I live alone inside four walls of books
> some I have read others will grow cobwebs
> or maybe like some old friends and lovers
> will fade away with their undisclosed logic
> the world that I have seen: New York
> where I suffered the suicidal brother
> and London where I discovered Hinostroza
> Delgado, Ortega, Heraud and other
> Andean poets with a rage very much like ours!
> remember Amadu how terrible I said it was
> that you were in exile and working
> in the Telephone Office in touch with all
> the languages of the world but with no world

to call your own; how sad you looked that winter
drinking your life and reading poetry with me
in the damp chilly English coffee shops
remember I said how furious I was
that Vallejo had starved to death in Paris
that Rabearivelo had killed himself
suffocated by an imaginary France
and I introduced Neruda and Guillen to you
and how in desperation we sought solace in the house
of John La Rose, that courageous Trinidadian poet
Amadu I am writing to you from the dungeon of my heart
the night brings me my grief and I am passive
waiting for someone to come, a woman
a friend, someone to sooth my dying heart!
now the memory of our lives brings a knife to my poems
our deaths which so burdened the beautiful Martiniquan
you said made you happy, she made you so happy, you a
tormented playwright
sadness returns, the apparitions of my brothers
and my mother grows old thinking about them
and also seeing so much sadness in
me her living and dying son
my mother who wishes me happy,
who wants me to relive the son
she lost to poetry like a husband a wife to a trusted friend
but already the walls are closing around me
the rain has stopped and once again I am alone
waiting for them, the politicians of
our country to come for me
to silence my right to shouting poetry loud in the parks
but who can shut up the rage the melodrama of being
Sierra Leone

the farce of seeing their pictures daily in the papers
the knowledge of how though blindfolded and muzzled
something is growing, bloating, voluptuous and not despairing
I say to you for now, I embrace you brother.

This is the poem I read at Nat Nakasa's grave. This was shortly after I had made the video piece called *The Homeless Song*, produced at the time when I was already thinking about Nat Nakasa. Nevertheless, I think that there was a kind of subconscious trait at work. As a result, I decided to write a letter to Chieko Shiomi, which I started writing on my way to the cemetery. So due to *Spatial Poem No. 3* I became interested in time and history, which both feed into my work, especially the drawing works. And I noticed the trait in my writing as well. It was moving between or towards a fictionalising of time in such a way that I was trying to make time elastic. Time did thus not become something that was forward-moving, but rather something that I could change backwards or even intervene in, in real time or in past or historical time as well. I wrote a letter to Chieko Shiomi in 2013, requesting that she include Nat Nakasa's fall to his death, even though my request was forty-eight years late. You actually helped me to get hold of her at the time because I was struggling to find contact details for her. What I also did was to respond directly to the poem at the studio I was in in Amsterdam; I documented a series of things that I made fall intentionally.

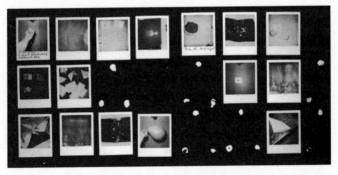

Figure 2. © Kemang Wa Lehulere (2015) *Spatial Poem Reply 1*.

I produced a diptych of Polaroid works and as you can see there are empty spaces there, and those are the photographs which I have taken out and I have sent to Chieko Shiomi in a package. Again, the choice to move into Polaroid as a medium was due to my interest in the kind of ephemerality, that is, something that cannot be really fixed forever like an oil painting but can still live a long life, so to speak.

To come back to this video work, it is all interlinked somehow and it happened over a period of about three years. When I went to read the poetry at the grave, I went back to Amsterdam, recorded this video and I was watching this footage repeatedly in the studio, both when I was sober or if I had gone out for a drink, came back to the studio and watched the footage, so this messy kind of thing. It struck me while doing this, that when I went to the cemetery, I had received a map of the actual grave with information of who owned the title deed of where Nat Nakasa's final resting place was. And it struck me in the studio one night that the person who owned the title deed was the same person who had organised for Nat Nakasa to go the US, the same person who was funding him, who was a CIA agent. And it was the same person who owned the apartment in Manhattan where Nat Nakasa fell to his death. This is something that was really troubling for me. I mean I didn't want to kind of start some conspiracy theory but I was like, "fuck, what a way to exist in the afterlife". And so, in the drunken state I was in the studio, I booked a flight to New York where the intention was to go and cut a piece of grass from the grave. The idea was to take it back to South Africa. So I went back to New York and for me it was my kind of rebellion. So yes, I went there and cut this piece from the grave. I have a text here that I wrote in 2013 which links to this work and also which is part of a film script. It is called *Scene 55*.

Scene 55. A Grave Misunderstanding. Exterior. Somewhere. Day.
I once mistook orthodontia as a fear of death. Upon reading its meaning twice, I realised it was a fear of teeth instead. This is interesting. Because an artist once wrote: 'teeth are the only bones that show'. A few years ago, I was digging in someone's house, I discovered some bones. Where I come from people go to a special school to learn how to 'read' bones. Once read, these bones are said to uncover the past and even unveil the future.

At the end of last year the South African government decided to officially bring Nat Nakasa's remains back to South Africa. It was quite a big state memorial,

which was actually the opposite of what I was trying to do. In fact, we had done a project at the Berlin
Biennial before they announced that they were taking
him back and it was called *Digging Our Own Graves*.
It was a publication project, not about this particular
work but a number of various works. So starting from
the video piece I just wanted to make these links that
it was an extension of a larger body of work which
resulted in the government taking his remains back to
South Africa.

EDO: You follow the traces — spontaneous moments
such as those in which you start with an afro-comb to
dig that grave in Gugulethu that lead to a series of concerns in which your interest in archaeology as a political gesture develops. But it is interesting that you also
in a way leave the project at the very moment in which
that history or that story becomes public. The way you
were engaged with it is over to an extent. You had to
go to other stories that needed to be uncovered. Perhaps we can move to *A Homeless Song 3*, the project that
somehow unveils the work of Gladys Mgudlandlu and
also speaks to some of the collective experiences that
are your interests nowadays.

KWL: How the project came about: when we were
working in the Gugulective, Unathi Sigenu, who
passed away almost two years ago now, was always
obsessed with Gladys Mgudlandlu, who was a black
woman painter, considered the first black woman artist in South Africa. She worked in the 1960s for about
a decade only and she died in 1979. Unathi Sigenu

always wanted us to do something about her but I could never connect to his desire. Partly because he had access to archival material and the owner of the material would only show it to Unathi. He would not show it to any of us because it is stuff that his father collected, like newspaper clippings. He did promise to show it to the rest of us but he never did, so I never saw these things. Last year I was visiting my aunt and a neighbour came who had a book on Gladys Mgudlandlu and gave it to me as a gift. I became interested in Gladys Mgudlandlu then and I started to do research about her. I started working with my aunt because she mentioned that she had seen murals, which for me was the interesting point.

EDO: How important is this return to the Gugulective to you and are you still using archaeology and digging as a way of bringing back history?

KWL: Again, it is not something that I had planned. I had very different plans for this year. But based on the conversations with my aunt I became interested in finding these murals — which she had seen in 1971, when she was a teenager. This interest really was about my own murals, chalk drawings, which, within the context of an exhibition, I would create and that would be destroyed at the end of an exhibition. So I was curious if Gladys Mgudlandlu's murals would still be there. And if so what they would look like — and if they were not there, what that might mean. I was working on a project for the show which is currently travelling and I titled it *History Will Break Your Heart* because I was already anticipating that I might not find the mural. And even if I did find it, I still think it is heartbreaking because this work has not been documented and never been seen. Through the conversation with my aunt they have now kind of come to light. What I did in the meantime was to ask my aunt to recreate the mural from what she remembered and in the course of working on the project, Mgudlandlu's work came up on auction here in London in March 2016. With the help of someone I managed to acquire some of the works. I bought a small portion of the work, not the entirety that was auctioned. What I then did was to exhibit those works and pair them with drawings that my aunt had made, with my intervention. My interventions were mainly erasures and whatever text you would see. In this context the project is something that is still ongoing.

Figure 3. © Kemang Wa Lehulere (2015) *Homeless Song 3: The Bird Lady in 9 Layers of Time*, video still.

When I discovered the mural, in conversation with the art restorer, we only uncovered a little piece as there was a chance that we would destroy the mural through the very exposure. They have been safe all these years, half a century or so. I now need to think about how to move forward with it. This becomes increasingly important to me as I have lost a dear friend, Unathi, who started the Guglective work in terms of the conceptual grounding and who was obsessed with her. Coming back to Gugulethu where I grew up and which was also very formative for my art practice, it feels very important. So in line with that I have a hope to not only establish this house as a museum but also to reactivate some of the programmes that we had started with the Gugulective — be it a film screening programme, poetry, music — to reactivate the kind of work we did because the collective is no longer working at the moment.

I would like to end this conversation with a work entitled *Some Deleted Scenes Too* which also speaks to the notions of future and fiction. I first published this version of the film script in early 2013. It is a text I worked on for many years. I struggled with it until Gladys Mgudlandlu's mural project. Again, with my work I feel like something, a kind of meditation and obsession that materialises itself later on without me necessarily driving it into that direction, but by chance or this offer from the universe, if I were to put it like this. Basically, the script is about 1989 and it was me thinking about the fall of the Berlin Wall. But instead of the wall I used the fall of the stars as a metaphor, also thinking about the fact that 1989 was a very important year not only globally but specifically for South African history. When the wall fell that was when the political parties were unbanned in South Africa and Mandela was released from the prison. I am also interested in a kind of historical narratives and how they are affected by this moment moving forward, but also how we look at the past up to this point. So I was writing this film about a man who was burnt by one of the falling stars. And when the stars fall they wipe out all memories in the world — photographs, any pieces of paper, everything. So there is no kind of archive or history left except for the oral ones which leads to this huge crisis that people feel. Once people discover there is this man who is able to restore these images or memories, there is a pilgrimage to his house to have people restore their memories and images. This speaks to the idea of time-travel — or what I have recently termed as an interest in the intervention in time.

SCENE 47, To the late comers are left the bones
EXT. SOMEWEHERE. DAY.

Since they will never kill us all.
They will never love us all.

Take care not to mention bones
in the presence of the elderly
this makes them nervous.

Walk in an orderly fashion
to where they resuscitate time.

Take note of its grammar
Syntax. Treat it as a verb.
What lyrics would it sing?

I met a woman who said
"There is no song for this,
Even those who have tried gave up long ago",

Ella Jare was incorrect
For this there is a song
Write your own lyrics
Compose your own rhythm but
Never to be sung out aloud.

SCENE 48. The Dark Room Manifesto
INT. SOMEWHERE. DAY.

* (This would be a white text on a black page)* *

The space returns to darkness. The performer
strikes a match, this time setting alight the
pieces of paper on musical note stands 2 and 3.
He watches the paper burn. Hopefully more poetic
than the first. Once these two pieces of paper
have retired the space returns to darkness. Volunteers strike a match. This time the performer
reads the text while periodically inserting siz-
able safety pins in his mouth so that what he is
reading becomes inaudible eventually. He reads:

SCENE 1:
Opening. A black screen. Letters can be seen
behind a mist with a red glow, but it is unclear
what they say. The mist clears, revealing the
words 'Dog Sleep', accompanied by dog barking
sounds in the background. Fade into night, outside. The moon is half sunken in to the screen.
Begin voice over.
V.O. – The year 1989 was a common year that
started on a Sunday. The one thousand nice hundred and eighty ninth of the Common Era, or Anno
Domini; the nine hundred and eighty ninth year
of the second millennium, the eighty ninth year
of the twentieth century, and the tenth and last
year of the nineteen eighties decade. Fade to
black.

SCENE 47
EXT. HOUSE. DAY.

Many people stand in a line that goes around
the neighbourhood. In their hands, under their
arms, or next to them are piles of blank
papers. Next to some people are boxes with the
very same blank pages. Beside the people in the
queue are three women administering and ordering people to maintain straight lines. Thulang
and Familiar Face are also standing in line and
are close to the entrance of the house. Thulang
is facing Familiar Face so that his back is
turned away from the direction of the queue.
Thulang - I can't believe you still won't tell
me what happened to his hand?

Familiar Face - We have been camping out here
for 3 full days and you decide to ask all of
this 5 minutes before we go in?

Thulang turns around to face Familiar Face.

Thulang - Hayibo Mfowe2!

Familiar Face - Well, rumour has it that when
the sky fell along with the stars, one of the
stars fell on this arm burning it. That's why
he's called Black Palm.

Thulang - So why did he hide his hand for so
long? And what does that have to do with the
memories that he produces?

Familiar Face gets irritated.

Familiar Face – Come on dude, don't you listen!?
Shakes his head.

Familiar Face – Because he was scared people
would think that he was the one who slept with
the mermaid. Scared he would be accused of the
fall. I don't know about the pictures he makes,
or memories as you call them. Unlike you, I'm
only here coz my mother sent me. People say when
the star burnt his arm, the star basically
exposed his arm to all its memories. That's why
people come from all over the world to have him
remake images from the past.

Thulang – But why would this star falling on his
arm over-expose and bleach all other photographs? I mean it doesn't make sense….

Familiar Face shoves Thulang forward indicating
it's their term to enter the house.

Familiar Face – (Whispering) We have been camping out here for 3 days and you only decide to
ask these questions 2 minutes before we go in!

Cut to interior of the house.

Familiar Face leads Thulang into the house following the corridor. They both stop when they notice the white squares on the wall. At first these look similar to the white papers that they have brought to be processed by Black Palm, but upon closer observation they realise that these are because of all the absent photographs that once were hanging on the walls.

The space returns to darkness. The performer strikes a match, this time he sets alight the page on musical note stand 4. He watches the paper burn smoothly and without much effort. Once the paper has finished, curling and burning, the space returns to darkness. The performer exits.

Figure 4. © Kemang Wa Lehulere (2013) Some Deleted Scenes Too, film script excerpt.

STAGES, PLOTS AND TRAUMAS[1]

Robin Mackay

Our hero stretches taut the last strand of scarlet twine, pushes the pin home, and steps back to take it all in: the sprawl of facts, the network of inferences, evidence, mug-shots, locations, everything almost tied up, but in waiting for a synoptic overview to coalesce, affording the pivotal insight that will reconfigure this data into a coherent whole, and close the case. The frustration, the pressure, and the dogged working of cognition are palpable.

In this scene, familiar from countless televised police procedurals and thrillers, it's as if the closed chamber of the detective's office serves as a proxy for the internal operations of his mind: a kind of *camera obscura* within which the network of relations between things, people, and places is refracted, projected onto a surface where it promises to finally come into sharp focus.

The operation does not feature in any policing manual or private detective's handbook; there has probably been no instance of any professional dedicating working hours to crafting a pastime of such dubious value. This fictional *in camera* exists only on camera: it is a diagram of a diagram of thought in action. The function of the *yarnwork* is to provide us with a static two-dimensional image of thought, itself embedded within visual narratives which themselves are moving images of the construction of knowledge.

If proof were needed of the popularity and power of the trope, we need only note that the term itself (more Etsy than homicide division) is drawn from a fond parody. In the high-school farce *21 Jump Street* (dir. Phil Lloyd, 2012), presentation of the "yarnwork" sets the scene for a revealing joke. For the failure of communication between two enthusiastic yet incompetent amateur sleuths played by Jonah Hill and Channing Tatum and a disgruntled police captain played by Ice Cube harbours a rather profound truth about the relation between knowledge, art, and the (dis)orientation of the subject in search of truth:

> Schmidt: Okay, so we stayed up all night making this. It's awesome, you're really gonna like it. All yarnwork was done by Jenko.
>
> Captain Dickson: Who put this together? Are you autistic?
>
> Schmidt: It *is* artistic, sir, because the thing is, the yarn actually indicates....

Indeed there is an *art* involved in the construction of the yarnwork, in the sense that there is no self-evident or conventional procedure for stringing together the elements of a case — like the cognitive process it diagrams, the yarnwork is a matter of invention, construction, and perhaps individual talent; usually the result of one individual's more or less competent, distressed, sometimes desperate attempt to gather, connect and map information. In itself the yarnwork asks the methodological question: How to proceed? And in so far as it figures this predicament, there is also something potentially *autistic* about the yarnwork, too: rather than accurately diagramming reality, the yarnworker is always in danger of projecting onto the blank wall his own preoccupations, vendettas, personality flaws and, when things get really murky, sheer delirium. There is always the looming possibility of apophenia, of creating patterns where there are none — a charge with which the detective will inevitably be confronted, when time is short and tempers are high, whether by an impatient superior or by the pen-pushers down at City Hall.

Figure 1. Robin Mackay, Paul Chaney and Sam Forsythe (2015), Installation "Speculum Topographicum". Bergen Kunsthalle.

What does the trope of the yarnwork give us to think as far as the construction of knowledge is concerned? Firstly, in general, plot-driven genre fictions boast this peculiar feature: they are epistemological dramas, dramatisations of the process of obtaining and configuring knowledge. The international thriller, the police procedural and the detective story present fictional inquiries couched within a framework where empirical data are assumed to be causally linked in a way that is subject to rational deduction. As Guy Lardreau observes, "in so far as such narratives present a search for the truth, how can they not envelop a theory of knowledge?" They therefore hold a particular interest for the philosopher in so far as they ask many questions familiar to him or her: "What is a clue, a sign, a proof? What is the status of evidence? What marks allow us to recognise the truth? [...] the questions that govern the detective novel are those that we philosophers have always posed" (Lardreau 1977: 16–17).

Such fictional scenarios present us with a localised object or event (the clue) that stands out from the ground of normality (the everyday crime scene), suggesting forces as yet unaccounted for (unknown accomplices, missing links); at the same time they imply an arsenal of reliable procedures (evidence-gathering, elimination, deduction) and perhaps scientific techniques capable of making objects speak (forensics) — methods capable of uncovering those unknown forces. As mentioned in many studies of detective fiction, it is a form that emerged, and could only emerge, in the modern scientific world, since it reflects the predominance of empirical evidence and rational deductive methods (see Boltanski 2014).

Indeed, the classic predicament of the detective outlined above is similar to that which, according to Jean-Réné Vernes, lies at the origin of the very possibility of scientific knowledge (see Vernes 2000). For Vernes, what is called "Hume's problem" (the fact that reason alone does not allow us to validly posit the existence of laws of nature, or to account for the regularities of empirical experience) constitutes a break in the history of philosophy whose consequences the discipline has yet to fully work through. Since, after Hume's intervention, reason could no longer provide a grounding for the assumption of the existence of independent matter and natural laws, philosophy came loose from its mooring to the scientific spirit, and resigned itself to the examination of perception and the habitual structuring of phenomena within the mind. In response to this disaster, Vernes insists that our perceptions themselves force upon us the hypothesis of a causally determined "external world". In his example, the concept of matter emerges when perceptually identical objects prove to have unaccountably different properties: if we have two coins that look and feel exactly the same, yet turn out to be of different weights, or if an apparently symmetrical die turns up a six on every throw, the probabilistic assumption that "all things are equal" is upset, and one is then compelled to cut open the coin or die in order to ascertain the reason for this departure from equilibrium. According to Vernes, the very meaning of "matter" lies in the enigma of the loaded die, in the disparity between apparent behaviour and an a priori model of the "ideal" die — the probabilistic assumption that "what is equally thinkable [viz. that the die will fall on any one of its faces] is equally possible". This assumption, which becomes evident through its apparent infraction in privileged situations such as that of the loaded die, is identical with the hypothesis of matter, since it posits that any apparent anomaly must stem from our incomplete knowledge of an ulterior, causally consistent reality. This hypothesis "imposes itself upon thought", and it alone can save philosophy from its post-Humean free-fall.

Readers of Quentin Meillassoux's work will easily comprehend how it proceeds from a confrontation with Vernes (see Meillassoux 2008) — indeed, Meillassoux has credited Vernes's earlier work (Vernes 1982) with waking him from his dogmatic slumbers and inspiring his thinking on contingency (see Meillassoux 2008). Meillassoux precisely refuses Vernes's attempt to rees-tablish scientific rationality on the basis of this proba-bilistic assumption, which he also sees tacitly inscribed in Kant's argument on the transcendental necessity of the lawfulness of nature. Instead he chooses to accept the consequences of the reasonlessness of natural phe-nomena: nothing is necessarily as it is, even the laws of nature. Therefore we can have no sure knowledge of phenomena; the only certain knowledge we can possi-bly have is that deduced rationally from this very prin-ciple of "absolute contingency".

It would be an interesting exercise to extend Meil-lassoux's inquiry into the possibility of a coherent "extro-science fiction" (one in which the laws of nature are themselves contingent and subject to change at any moment) (see Meillassoux 2015) to the hypothesis of an "extro-scientific detective fiction". Surely the sleuth's powers of deduction and evidence-gathering would be rendered utterly ineffectual in a universe (whether religious and magical, or "hyperchaotic" like Meillassoux's) where victims could disappear, or be struck down by god, or where "clues" could simply materialise from nowhere, for no reason? For in the background of these fictions is a conception of knowledge founded on a stable causal framework, and their basic narrative device responds more to Vernes's approach: the empirical presence of a salient feature that acts like a sort of mental grit, a cognitive irritant, impelling the protagonist to cut through the surface of things, to dig deeper, to slice open the die and find out why all things are not as equal as they ought to be, why the equation doesn't quite add up. We could therefore say that the narrative motor of these fictions is fuelled by scientific epistemology; and that, philosophically, what they demand of us is to elaborate, not a strictly *rational*, but a *problematic* and *procedural* epistemology, one where knowledge is constructed in the attempt to restore equilibrium by cutting deeper and deeper into a situation in order to discover the unknown elements that continually throw it off-balance.

The figure of the yarnwork is precisely a visual representation of this problematic cognitive state, one where the pieces, when connected systematically, still refuse to "add up", where the die still seems to be loaded. And this brings us to the second intriguing feature of the yarnwork: in its onscreen versions, this form of fiction poses the interesting problem of how to render the cognitive reconfiguration of information *visible,* and visually compelling as image — a problem to which the yarnwork is a reliable and now classic response. Indeed, the yarnwork figures a most crucial moment in the plot: the moment when everything is almost in place, a moment of the highest tension for protagonist and viewer alike. As a kind of provisional summation, a pause in the narrative, the yarnwork moment invites us to join with the protagonist in experiencing this threshold moment, and in readying himself to make the final push toward resolution.

The yarnwork binds together local empirical data in order to make it visible to the concentrated gaze, so that it might reveal what it owes to, and what it might contain of, some wider scheme of things, some more profound, hidden cause. But let us make a further observation about the way in which this information is pursued: rather than cutting into a problematic object such as the loaded die, in this kind of fiction the action of "cutting" moves outward, cleaving from the *local* to the *global*. As the typical situation would have it, arriving on the crime scene, what at first appears as a routine investigation will throw up some anomalous element, inspection of which will provide ingress into a broader intrigue. The ramifications of this anomaly will continue to unfold, with the episodic return of the sentiment that something doesn't add up, and perhaps ultimately leading us to the yarnwork moment — both the cumulation of these episodes and the anticipation of all the missing pieces finally falling into place.

There is also a narrative of the encrypted expression of *power* in play here: the local configurations are only corrupted and partial expressions of some ulterior plot, and the actors of the original crime scene may be mere puppets of a more nefarious crime. In this respect, the nature of these fictions can be clarified by comparing their narrative schema to a model drawn from elsewhere — namely, the quest for *self*-knowledge pursued in the therapeutic process.

In his early model of hysteria, Freud employs a metaphor for trauma that combines geology, cryptography and a theory of psychic defence (Freud 1895): At the core is trauma — the Thing that drives you but which, at the moment of consulting the analyst, you can neither access nor afford to touch. Around the core there are strata, hardened layers that are at once an expression of the trauma — like cooled lava — and an encryption of it, since it cannot be read *clearly* in these secondary residues. Their opaque, perplexing folds both block the way to the truth of the analysand's symptom, and serve as protection against the trauma (like the crust of the earth, upon which the heat of the core can still be felt, and even keeps you warm, but cannot harm you). Yet (as both the geologist and the analyst must assume) these strata contain clues. Symptoms, indeed, are behaviours which, because they are apparently causally unconnected to their immediate context, seem to allude to some unknown factor. During the process of therapy, as the patient attempts to move through these layers to reach the core — i.e. to understand themselves and their trauma — on attaining each subsequent layer they are obliged to assemble a self-narrative using the materials at their disposal, which are always partial and incomplete; and it is the incompleteness of these narratives — something is always missing or not quite right — that continues to drive the meta-narrative of the therapeutic situation. Freud writes of

> the linkage made by a logical thread which reaches as far as the nucleus and tends to take an irregular and twisting path, different in every case. This arrangement has a dynamic character [...] the course of the logical chain would have to be indicated by a broken line which would pass along the most roundabout paths from the surface to the deepest layers and back, and yet would in general advance from the periphery to the central nucleus (Freud 1895: 289).

It is in following this winding thread that one hopes to reach the truth, which will reconfigure both what is known and the knower. This does not happen in a single revelatory moment, but over the course of a tortuous journey during which, episodically, the available data will resolve themselves into new patterns, each time providing a more comprehensive picture of the real source of the power that has a hold over the analysand.

In the process of psychoanalysis (also, let us recall, inspired by the will to forge a "scientific" model of the psyche) as in the political thriller or detective drama, only at the end does one discover the power-source, that Thing that was driving the whole complex, the kingpin, the ultimate villain of the piece. In this sense, the original crime scene, that local, circumscribed and apparently trivial everyday scene which contains some worrying anomaly that doesn't quite fit, is akin to the scene of the symptom, which, whether debilitating or merely peculiar, seems to have no reason, and there-fore, within a "scientific" framework, must testify to the influence of some ulterior power — and thus com-pels continuation of the work.

The question, of course — one to which each fictional detective, and each brand of therapy, provides a differ-ent answer — is how to find the thread from one to the other, or how to target the anomaly correctly and make the correct cuts in order to inspect it, further opening up one's perspective from the local to the global scene. And this is, above all, a question of epistemology, one might almost say *the* question of epistemology, and of the yarnwork too: that of how the subject of knowledge can confidently pass from the gathering of piecemeal bits of information and observation of their asym-metries, to a configuration in which they are rendered coherent from a global point of view.

In this sense, apparent departures within the crime genre are in reality only variations on a theme: *CSI*, for instance, gives us a diagram of contemporary modes of knowledge, but remains concerned with this con-nection between local and global. In *CSI* one proceeds from the crime scene *inward* to discover an ultra-local anomaly that will, in turn, allow one to ascend back to a reconstruction of the crime scene, and thereby to its place within a more global context (the chemi-cal composition of soil particles recovered from the crime scene matches with the land around the cor-porate headquarters where the victim worked until he was fired for insubordination for calling attention to suspicious financial transactions...). In forensic drama the implicit scientific framework of the narrative form is literalised, and it is the microscopic object that provides the symptom, the grit in the otherwise smoothly functioning machine, that will be forensically inspected to reveal the broader scene.

*

The concept of "plot" provides a framework within which we can clarify such an epistemology and its attendant drama; and it is precisely the centrality of *plot* to these kinds of narratives — easy to denounce from a "literary" perspective as its weakness or debility, as in the faintly derogatory term "plot-driven fiction" — that explains their peculiar interest as epistemological dramas, or dramatisations of epistemology. Beyond the conservative gesture of countering the supposed poverty of this "minor" and all too "generic" form by the appeal to majority, perhaps through the hackneyed reference to *Oedipus Rex* as the "first detective story", we can flip this literary denunciation of the supposedly downmarket craft of plotting by taking our lead from an historical account of the notion of plot that concerns not literature but theatre — which then will bring us back to the question of how the construction of knowledge is staged and narrated in visual forms of storytelling.

It is immediately obvious that "plot" is a semantically rich word. Perhaps uppermost for us is plot in the sense of narrative, but not far behind it would come the conspiratorial sense of the word — the manipulation of affairs by some shady agent or agents behind the scenes. Also current, if less prominent, we find the senses of "plot" as territorial (a plot of land), graphic (plotting a graph), and geometrical or projective (plotting one space into another). All of these, as we shall see, are etymologically interlinked in a rather satisfying way, all the more so because this is not a case of returning to a single etymological origin but also (as is in fact common in etymology) one of accidents, convergences and semantic superpositions.

*

In his work on the history of design, Benedict Singleton has identified a set of perennial suspicions relating to the practice and the very notion of "design" and its related terms, all of which have connotations of complicity, connivance, deviousness or intrigue: *craftiness*, having *designs on* something or someone… and *plotting* (see Singleton 2008). Singleton links these misgivings to a well-founded fear concerning the primary act of design: In delimiting a plot — that is to say, in this context, carving out a chunk of material for use to a certain deliberate end — given that the material is never entirely neutral or lacking in its own history and energies, one also invites into one's project forces from the outside; thus design is a constant negotiation with preexisting plots, an attempt to steer and mobilise them in the service of one's own design for the materials at hand.

Design has been seen as suspect, then, according to Singleton, because it deals not with the orderly marshalling of a passive matter — the hylomorphic schema whereby form is impressed upon matter — but with materials whose own proclivities and powers cannot be suppressed, but are to be harnessed and set to work for other purposes. Design is denigrated because the designer does not use her own prowess to tame matter, but colludes with nonhuman forces; which also means that the designer herself is subject to these ulterior plots that pre-existed her intentions and interventions. Design marks an acknowledgement of the designer's own complicity in plots that may exceed her instrumental goals — for using already-existing energies to cunningly achieve your own ends suggests that other agencies may possibly have designs on you, and that, in selecting a plot to work on, you are merely further complicating twisted plots that existed long before you.

The history of the word "plot" itself furnishes some evidence for this nexus of suspicion, intrigue and spatial material practice. In *The English Renaissance Stage*, Henry Turner argues that the modern concept of plot emerged between the end of the sixteenth and beginning of the seventeenth centuries in the context of the dramatic arts, with the advent of a new kind of theatre, and in the attempts of its proponents to define their nascent profession (see Turner 2006).

This involved the physical and cultural construction of a new type of theatre, a spatially enclosed building specifically marked out for dramatic use and with a platform stage (the word *platform* here already hinting at a connection with *plot*). This is the movement from an open-air theatre with journeymen actors and a porosity between players and audience (mystery plays) to an enclosed performance space to which an audience pays for entry, to watch the unfolding of plays whose action often spans more than one setting.

What arose at this moment, as Turner explains, was the need for playwrights to conceptualise for themselves, and to explain to their audiences, the mechanisms of this new theatrical situation and its peculiar powers. The extraordinary nature of the theatre and the platform stage as a space that "can manipulate space, time, and the conventional properties of bodies" (Turner 2006: 32) was a crucial problem for the playwrights of the time not only intellectually but also commercially: to bring in an audience, they needed to justify the artificial construction within which they were to present their narratives. In plays of the period, therefore, we find lengthy defences or apologies which attempt to justify the theatre as spatial device, and to enlist the audience's imaginative powers to make it function.

In constructing these apologies, playwrights turned not to neo-classical literary theory or poetics, but to the conceptual resources provided by what Turner calls the "spatial arts": that is, the practices of an emergent artisan class with whom they had daily contact, and with whom they seem to have identified (*playwright*, after all, refers not to writing but to materials that have been *wrought*, as in *wheelwright*) — and this is where *plot* enters the scene.

Plot and *plat*, and the verb *platting* or later, *emplotment*, are connected with the notion of a *groundplat*: a diagram or working drawing used in practical geometry — for instance in surveying, carpentry and building — involving measurement and reduction to a two-dimensional representation. The *plat, plane* or *flat*, in technical manuals of the time, forms a part of the geometrical triad of a *pricke, platte forme* and a *body* — what we would call today point, area and body. The plot or plat, then, is a schematic geometrical projection, originally a chart or diagram included in a book for the purposes of demonstration. As Turner shows, playwrights conceptualised the capacity of the theatrical situation to achieve startling "imaginative projections" in terms of a power of "translation" or "projection" borrowed from these geometrical diagrams: "an artificial means whereby the viewer may see a series of particular places — remote in time as well as space — that could never be grasped by the naked eye alone" (Turner 2006: 8). A scene of a battle in France, a scene in the royal castle, temporal and spatial ellipses, all contained within the closed space of the theatre... none of this is natural, nor can it be taken for granted that audiences will accept it. So the playwrights forewarn the audience by using the analogy of the "plot" as a rhetorical device to justify the new narrative and spatial form: the action on the stage is "like" the plot of a piece of land or a house, it schematises a more complex reality. In the following examples given by Turner, dating from the end of the sixteenth century, we see the playwrights overtly petitioning the audience to use their power of imagination in order to become complicit in the function of this projective plotting:

And for this small Circumference must stand,
For the imagind Sur-face of much land,
Of many kingdoms, and since many a mile,
Should here be measured out: our *muse intreats,*
Your thoughts to helpe poore Art, and to allow

That I may serve as Chorus to her scenes
She begs your pardon, for sheele send me foorth,
Not when the lawes of Poesy doe call,
But as the storie needes...
The world to the circumference of heaven,
Is as a small point in Geometrie,
Whose greatness is so little, that a lesse
Cannot be made: into that narrow roome,
Your quicke imaginations we must charme,
To turne that world; and (turn'd) again to part it
Into large kingdoms, and within one moment,
To carrie Fortunatus on the wings
Of active thought, many a thousand miles
(Dekker, *Old Fortunatus*)

...But pardon, gentles all,
The *flat unraisèd spirits that hath dared*
On this unworthy scaffold to bring forth
So great an object. Can this cock-pit hold
The vasty fields of France? Or may we cram
Within this wooden O the very casques
That did affright the air at Agincourt?
O pardon: *since a crooked figure may*
Attest in little place a million,
And let us, *ciphers to this great account,*
On your imaginary forces work.
Suppose within the girdle of these walls
Are now confined two mighty monarchies,
Whose high uprearèd and abutting fronts
The perilous narrow ocean parts asunder.
Piece out our imperfections with your thoughts:
Into a thousand parts divide one man,

And make imaginary puissance.
(Shakespeare, *Henry V*)

"Plot" eventually came to mean a diagram of the spatial arrangement of the stage and the various entrances and exits during a play, which was hung on the boundary between off and onstage, and "subdivid[ed] the narrative action of the play into the entrances and exits of the actors, all within carefully ruled columns and boxes" (Turner 2006: 23). And indeed, the pivot of theatrical *emplotment*, as it came to be called, is the boundary between offstage and onstage. This is effectively where the risky business of plotting, the reductive projection of the detailed developments of the story into the limited space and gestures of the theatre, takes place. Emplotment was understood as a kind of projection from the dense complexity of an underlying story into its staged schematisation, in a concept adapted from the popular literature of practical geometry used in the work of the playwrights' fellow artisans, and this trope from the "practical spatial arts" become hybridised with the inherited traditions of poetics. The history of the word "plot" therefore testifies to the emergence of an epistemological model from a body of professional knowhow and its transfer to the spatial device and narrative forms of the theatre — that is, poetics and its reception understood as ways of knowing. As Turner says, what takes place here is an "adapt[ing] [of] a practical knowledge of geometrical form to the realm of aesthetic form, using the methods, habits of thought, and even the economic formations of these technical fields to produce a device — a *thea-*

tron or 'beholding place'" (Turner 2006: 81).

The last piece of this history falls into place with the convergence, in the late sixteenth century, of *plot* with the French word *complot*, originally meaning "dense crowd" — a word that brings with it the connotations of intrigue, strategy, possibly with devious or harmful intent. *Complot* related to a mode of practical intelligence (such as in military strategy) in which deliberation about human action involved the consideration of the spatial disposition of the actors. To the notion of a projection or translation from one space to another, it adds the sense of an ulterior agency controlling the space and players of the *theatron* (here, possibly, a theatre of war) from outside — the one who pulls the strings and directs the action while keeping the full story hidden backstage.

As the designs and devices of a character in a play become assimilated to the projective plottings of the strategist, and to the directing of the play itself, this enriches the concept of emplotment as "the formal decision to represent some events onstage while withholding others from view" (Turner 2006: 213) — as an incomplete, schematic revelation. According to this developed sense of "plot", as Turner argues, at the limit "all modes of ordering perceived experience [...] could be said to constitute a preliminary level of emplotment" (Turner 2006: 24) — plotting, then, as a general epistemological model.

If we make the simple gesture of moving beyond a simple binary model of offstage and onstage, what arises as a speculative surplus from the nexus of the "spatial, geometrical and topographical" and the "strategic, deliberative and pragmatic" senses of *plot* is a very distinctive schema: that of a potentially endless series of points of view, beholding places — *theatrons* — each one an information environment coupled with a perspectival orientation, stabilised by a closure which, however, is compromised by its ultimate contiguity with a (manipulative) outside. Which brings us back to the territorial sense of "plot" as an incomplete circumscription of material, and to Singleton's understanding of design as involving the carving-out of a block of material which may be suspected of carrying with it germs of the outside, ulterior powers that will possibly compromise one's intentions. In short, what *plot* suggests is a circumscription made for the purposes of gaining knowledge of some situation, but one that is always incomplete, and thus brings with it introjections from the outside.[2]

This in turn suggests the schema of the yarnwork, the *in-camera* projection of the investigator's predicament. The detective seeks to move from a particular "beholding place" — the inside of a limited "theatre" in which his perception of events remains constrained by the data immediately available — to a wider field where he would uncover, progressively, the "real story". But the question here is the inverse of the playwright's: how to move *the other way*, from the projected diagram — the plot — to that of which it is a projection. As if thematising their own mechanisms, in yarnwork scenes detective shows visually stage this infospatial drama in which the protagonist is constantly trying to escape the local *theatron*, to discover the way "backstage" so as to reveal the broader global story.

What is really required here — as will be confirmed by any dedicated viewer of such shows — is to maintain a thread between these different mappings of the information-space. Our detective has the local situation, with elements that do not fit, and which solicit her to follow the thread further, or to find the resources to cut *into* some anomalous clue so as to cut herself *out of* her current epistemological constraints. She cannot try to read the outstanding clue in terms of the local site, for this is precisely what it *isn't*: the statement that shows that the dead man was moving millions of dollars into a Swiss bank account obviously is not a part of the local story about a hapless clerk who had split from his girlfriend and may have been suicidal. But the detective also cannot reformat the local plot entirely in terms of the global story she discovers: to see a homicide as "merely" an incidental effect of the movement of global capital also fails to capture the situation, which of course is also a local — human — tragedy! Either of these paths would dissolve the tension that drives the narrative forward.

What is achieved by the most skilled plotters[3] is a kind of stereoscopic — or *multiscopic* — way of looking at things, one that is able to shift between different information-spaces, different *theatrons*, while maintaining their delicate coherence. Knowledge then becomes a form of *navigation*, a shifting of perspectives or a movement across transformations, across contexts or through a staggered series of *theatrons* (and what is navigation, if not *plotting*?).

Plot twists are the turning points in this navigation. Marrying the spatial, topographical or graphical sense of the word *plot* with the temporal sense of a narrative progression, plot twists are the points in the narrative at which one discovers that something which seemed anomalous or counterintuitive at the local level can be explained as the importation or introjection of an element of the wider environment into the local context (what the victim tried to scrawl in blood on the hotel bathroom mirror wasn't her killer's name, but the access code for a restricted-access Department of Defence computer account). Having previously achieved temporary stability with a provisional configuration of the available data, as we shift focus, as we change the mode of projection, this data is entirely reconfigured. As in a kaleidoscope, all of the elements shift in relation to one other, but this gives onto a new stability.

These moments of disorientation and reorientation are what constitute, for the reader or viewer, the pleasure of the plot. In the best fictions, as they take place we feel our sense of ourselves as subject of this knowledge-process shifting along with the protagonist's. Here, Jason Bourne provides the missing link between our fictional and therapeutic models, for the entire conceit of the Bourne series relies on traumatic dissociation. The locality of Bourne's own psyche bears traces of a wider context of which he has no conscious knowledge — so Bourne's brain is both *theatron* and *complot*. Each discovery of an external fact is also a discovery about himself, a reorientation. But in a more general sense, ultimately "trauma" is simply the condition of locality or contingent sitedness as such. Trauma is an epistemological condition, or the condition of epistemology itself: an incomplete cut between a local site and an outside that has already affected it in some way. It is the introjected traces of the outside, clues betraying the emplotment of a deeper story, which at once provide the constitutive disequilibrium that drives the investigation, and promise the possibility of knowledge.

The plot twist, then, comprises both a stability, a new reconciliation of local and global, and a kind of panic that results from the impossibility of achieving this reconciliation in a single image: there is an oscillation between different orientations in which we find it difficult to grasp one without losing the other. This subjective state can of course be "resolved" in a certain sense, and this is the goal of Bourne's quest and the aim of any therapy: to reach a level at which one finds a thread, manages to integrate most of the elements so as to become "functional" again. But in a more essential sense it is never resolved, or at least it could always go further. For the concept of plot makes things more complex and more twisted than reaching a ground, finally discovering the kingpin and closing the case. There is not simply a figure and a ground, but an infinite abyss of "offstages", a constantly shifting relation of *ungrounding*, a potentially endless series of plot twists and complicities which, as in *Bourne*, tend to draw the investigator himself into their kaleidoscopic maelstrom. This is a question of affordance: how many revelations can the subject of knowledge afford before the grounds of his own self-knowledge are eroded, transformed, shifted, twisted so much by the plot that he becomes a patient rather than an agent of the investigation? In some of the best detective fiction this predicament itself is dramatised, as the investigator realises, on the edge of madness, that they themselves are caught up in the plot-threads they are trying to untangle. A peril which is, in fact, insepara-ble from the pursuit of knowledge, as evidenced in the sometimes agonising upheavals of the therapeutic sit-uation.

*

The plot twist is the moment of cognitive reorientation in which the protagonist replots available data accord-ing to a new distribution whose principles were lacking in the situation or *theatron* within which he previously laboured; or rather, *all but lacking*, since precisely what these fictions show us, once again, is that there is never absolute discontinuity. But the yarnwork marks the moment prior to the plot twist, a moment which, within the drama, overtly thematises and figures, in the form of a diagram, the effort of thinking through the plot. If the plot twist is the moment of cognitive disorientation, a moment of the replotting of the avail-able data, then the moment that directly precedes it, figured in visual media by the yarnwork, is a moment of perplexity. The yarnwork scene dramatises the anticipation of reorientation, of an incipient plot twist.

Relating this back to the theatrical origins of the word "plot", we can think of a yarnwork as the *inverse of emplotment*: where the *plat* was the diagrammatic ava-tar of the craft of emplotment — the management of the boundary between onstage and offstage, between story and plot, the projection of a dense unseen out-

Figure 2. Robin Mackay, Paul Chaney and Sam Forsythe (2015),
Installation "Speculum Topographicum". Bergen Kunsthalle.

side (*complot*) into a *theatron*, a beholding place — then
conversely, in the yarnwork, the viewer — thus far
trapped in a limited *theatron* — is given to overtly pon-
der, through the eyes of the protagonist, an incomplete
reconstruction of its connection to another space: a diagram which, if completed, would enable navigation *the
other way*, from a local situation to the dense multitude
of which it is but a partial projection; to the next moment
in the investigation, when the implication of the previous action within a wider plot will become clear. The
yarnwork moment logically precedes the unveiling of
this ulterior space, the passage "backstage".

*

Given all of this, one is tempted to say that the
"extro-scientific detective story" is after all an impos-

sibility. For, from this point of view, Meillassoux's insistence, contra Vernes, that philosophical knowledge demands the jettisoning of all empirical detail in favour of an a priori "intellectual intuition" of the principle of absolute contingency, would leave us with a *global* with no consistent connection to any *locality*, thus denarrativising knowledge, discarding information on every side, dropping every thread, and abandoning all reliable possibility of navigation.

Instead, the universe of the detective story is that of a problematic, not a rational-speculative materialism: one that combines the assumption of universal causal coherence with the drama of incomplete (local) cognitive purchase by way of a *plot* into which anomalous traces of the outside insinuate themselves, drawing the disoriented investigator into ever-widening vistas where his map of the world and of himself will be transformed, twisted, and replotted, across a series of moments whose diachronicity is constitutive of the nature of knowledge itself.

There is always something that stands out from the ground, something that "doesn't add up" and which cannot be accounted for by local principles. What drives investigation is the theatrical introjection or emplotment of data from the global environment, the clue, the index of plotting at work behind the scenes, the element that doesn't fit but will be leveraged in order to drive further plotting. The dice are always loaded; continual navigation and reorientation is inevitable. The essential tools of the detective and the therapist alike are the scalpel and the compass.

1. This essay is part of a long-term research project which began with the seminar "When Site Lost the Plot" at Goldsmiths, University of London, 7–9 May 2013, expanded proceedings of which were published in *When Site Lost the Plot* (Mackay 2015). The project was extended during a residency at Bergen Kunsthall, "The Ultimate Yarnwork", 29 Jan–9 Feb 2015, https://www.urbanomic.com/event/the-ultimate-yarnwork/. Significant contributions to the work presented here came from discussions with Amanda Beech, Paul Chaney, Sam Forsythe, Reza Negarestani and Benedict Singleton.

2. Here we can expand on the analogy with the therapeutic situation by considering how Sandòr Ferenczi's notion of introjection challenges Freud's conception of trauma, in *Beyond the Pleasure Principle*, as extrojective defence against the outside. See my "The Barker Topos", in Mackay 2015: 253–68.

3. See the interview with the "nordic noir" writer Gunnar Staalesen conducted as part of "The Ultimate Yarnwork", https://www.urbanomic.com/podcast/yarncast-gunnar-staalesen-noir-in-ultima-thule/.

Works Cited

Boltanski, Luc (2014), *Mysteries and Conspiracies: Detective Stories, Spy Novels and the Making of Modern Societies*. London: Polity.

Freud, Sigmund (1895), "The Psychotherapy of Hysteria", in Sigmund Freud and Josef Breuer, *Studies on Hysteria*, trans. James Strachey. New York: Basic Books, 253-305.

Lardreau, Guy (1997), *Présentation* criminelle de quelques concepts majeurs de la *philosophie*. Arles: Actes Sud.

Mackay, Robin (ed.) (2015), *When Site Lost the Plot*. Falmouth: Urbanomic.

Meillassoux, Quentin (2008), *After Finitude*, trans. Ray Brassier. London: Continuum.

——— (2015), *Science Fiction and Extro-Science Fiction*, trans. Alyosha Edlebl. Minnesota: Univocal.

Singleton, Benedict (2011), *Subtle Empires: On Craft and Being Crafty*. PhD thesis. University of Northumbria.

Turner, Henry (2006), *The English Renaissance Stage: Geometry, Poetics, and the Practical Spatial Arts, 1580–1630*. Oxford: Oxford University Press.

Vernes, Jean-Réné (1982), *Critique de la raison aléatoire*. Paris: Aubier Montaigne.

——— (2000), *The Existence of the External World: The Pascal-Hume Principle*, trans. Mary Baker. Ottowa: University of Ottawa Press.

AFROFUTURISM, FICTION AND TECHNOLOGY

A Conversation between Julian Henriques and Harold Offeh

Harold Offeh: I wonder if it would be useful for us to start by outlining the presentation that you gave as part of the Visual Cultures "Futures and Fictions" Public Programme. It might help to frame the rest of our conversation.

Julian Henriques: Yeah, certainly. The title of the talk was *Afrofuturism: Technology and Fiction*. We could start by just addressing each of those two last words: *Fiction* and *Technology*. Starting with fiction then, my experience of doing academic research into sound, and sound systems in particular, began as a researcher initially for television and then for my own films. Writing the scripts for these gave me an insight into how to structure stories in a popular medium. And it is really through my ongoing research on a particular project — which is the *Eko* project — that I found my way to Afrofuturism. So it was as a storyteller that I approached the Goldsmiths talk, trying to apply what I have learned about storytelling to describe the development process for *Eko* and also, more generally, to the fiction of Afro-futurism itself. And then in terms of the technology — technology for me has to do with sound, even more particularly to do with reggae sound systems — this is something that I have spent quite a few years research-ing. This has involved fieldwork, listening, hanging out talking to people who own and run sound systems, the engineers and selectors and so on. That was primar-ily in Jamaica with a sound system called "Stone Love Movement", which is one of the longest established — I think it must be celebrating its fortieth anniversary by now. I have also researched in the UK with the "Saxon Studio International" with whom I made the film *We the Ragamuffin*. They are based very near to us at Gold-smiths, in Brockley in fact. I've also done events with Ras Muffet's "Roots Injection" from Bristol, and more recently "Young Warrior", again, from around here.

All the research I have done is very much related to the stories that I have always been telling as well as to the fiction and feature films I have made. In a way, it was through the films that I got to technology, especially needing to understand the technology of the sound systems. And so I have learnt more or less everything I know from the guys, mostly men, actually, and some women — there are quite a few women on the sound-system scene — and in particular the audio engineers. They are the ones who actually design and build these sound systems and who fine-tune them as well. This is engineering in the fullest sense of the word, producing what the sound sounds like for the audience. So you have got these two elements, you have fiction, and you have technology in the sound systems. They came together for me in Afrofuturism. Afrofuturism is a science-fiction story, a story about the future, which very often involves technologies yet to come alongside technologies that are already here. And the "Afro" part of Afrofuturism basically makes the whole enterprise grounded in a particular, I would say, mythical — or fictional — place of Africa. Afrofuturism is a quest both to return home and for a new diasporic future in space.

Figure 1. Channel One Sound System (UK), with five-way frequency split from tweeters to scoops.

HO: Your talk included a first showing of the new fiction work you just mentioned, a kind of graphic novel — *Eko* — can you say something more about that project and how it relates to Afrofuturism?

JH: The development of the *Eko* project — which is still very much work-in-progress — was the motivation for my ongoing exploration of technology and Afro-culture. And in that development process it was very interesting how the fictional character sort of fed into the more academic type of research, published as a book or in journal articles, and how these have also fed back into the fiction. I describe *Captain Eko and her Sonic Warriors: Episode 1 The Clash* (to give it its full title) as a "sonographic" novel, as distinct from a graphic novel. The work includes a soundtrack which, obviously, is not normally the case with graphic novels (though there are apps that do this now). Also the still images are projected, as with a film or slide show, rather than read on a page. This must reflect my background as a filmmaker, I suppose.

Figure 2. Images: Heidi Sincuba, sound: Ben Hauke, concept and story: Julian Henriques. (2014), a frame from *Captain Eko and her Sonic Warriors: Episode 1 The Clash*, 10 min, single screen.

The images are drawings, mostly in charcoal. All the artwork was created by Heidi Sincuba, who is a Goldsmiths MFA alumnus. I gave her the outline of the story, the key events and some reference material from the sound-system scene in which it is set. So the images are by an artist, rather than a graphic artist who would normally do the drawings for a graphic novel or comic strip. They are really powerful, as I thought they would have to be in order to sustain interest and depth when projected on a cinema screen. In fact there is another three-screen version of the piece. The soundtrack that gives an atmosphere or vibe to the piece was specially composed by Ben Hauke. The music reference I gave him was Burial, a dubstep producer from South London. The soundtrack is not in sync with the story as such; the dialogue appears on the screen between the images as inter-titles, as with the silent movies, rather than in speech bubbles.

HO: And how does this relate more specifically to Afrofuturism?

JH: Through sound. I relate everything through sound. With the reggae sound system you are talking about a specific sound-making technology: mechanical, electromechanical, electromagnetic, electronic and digital. All these technologies make up a sound system. And you are also talking about a kind of aspired-to future, which is, if you like, Africa outside Africa. The reggae sound system on which the Eko character plays as the MC is quite steam-punk actually, with vinyl turntables. The future that Captain Eko is exploring is a sonic one, a sonic space-time, a sonic Afrofuture. Like every MC and selector in whatever genre of music they are playing, Eko has to guide the crowd into this better place. But the "consciousness" of reggae lyrics and the idea of Africa or Zion as an idealised destination (like Nirvana in that respect or what Foucault calls a heterotopia [see Foucault 1986]) lends itself the kind of forward projection that Afrofuturism also expresses. To find a better place, escape Babylon. This future is also expressed in the music itself, especially dub, literally the echoic space within the music, with everything but the drum and bass taken out, that gives room for the listener to inhabit with their imagination. For me, dub played on a sound system was an Afrofuture decades before the term was ever coined.

HO: *Eko* is clearly fictional, how does this project connect to your more academic research work?

JH: I was a storyteller before I was an academic, first as a journalist, then as a documentary filmmaker for the BBC and after that I founded my own company — and I did get to write and direct a feature film, entitled *Babymother*. A lot of this work has a music theme, in fact *Babymother* was a reggae musical, so I have spent a lot of time working things out about musical sound, lyrics and story-telling, and how they can come together to take us to new places and engage us at a feeling level. This is a side of myself I like to keep going along with academic research. In fact, as I mentioned earlier, they feed into each other. It was the research for the films, here in the UK and in Jamaica, that I kind of repurposed into academic research, initially as a PhD.

All of this different research — and especially what I have learnt about how sound works on the body and mind from the Jamaican sound engineers (some of which is in my book *Sonic Bodies* [Henriques 2011]) — helps ground Eko's story. Also what I find is that Eko's imaginative world gives her a lot more freedom — to have new crazy ideas — that quite inspires some of my research thinking. The two, fiction and research, work very well together for me. And so that whole way of academic research ideas being kind of informed by creative processes and vice versa was an interesting one, which I continue to pursue. And as her name would suggest, Eko is a sort of fictional interlocutor, someone who answers back. And someone I can tell my thoughts as I am writing them down: "OK Eko, look, how about this?" And she responds and tells me certain stuff and so on.

HO: Are we going to see some more of Eko?

JH: Yes, that was just one episode. It's really important to break a big project down into a process of smaller steps, which have value in themselves, to test it out and get feedback.

HO: You mentioned that you had been thinking more about Afrofuturism since the talk...

JH: Yes, there was some really useful feedback. The "Afro" in Afrofuturism figures very differently in the imagination of those outside the continent than, let's say, of contemporary Nigerians, for example. Now that point was brought home to me when discussing Louis Chude-Sokei's recent work as he was writing about Lucky Dube from South Africa, who in the 1980s was one of the first and maybe biggest African reggae artists (Chude-Sokei 2015). What is interesting is how Rastafarian beliefs that emerged from a New World or disaporic African experience were able to imagine a future Africa. This mythical future was then projected back onto Africa — through reggae rhythms and lyrics — to give Africa itself its future in one sense. This is not unlike the idea of Pan Africanism being born in the metropole with the 1945 Pan African Congress being held in Manchester, for instance. And so this is the kind of mix of cultures and technologies and storytelling that came together for me to motivate my research into Afrofuturism as content for, but also a method of, storytelling.

HO: You mention *The Sound of Culture*, Louis Chude-Sokei's book. Interestingly he is interrogating notions of what the diaspora means, breaking down those constructs into constituent parts. One of the things I really found useful about the book — and where it has some crossover with your talk — is an exploration of the term Afrofuturism, attributed to writer Mark Dery in the 1990s, and how it is often seen as being very much associated with that period. *The Sound of Culture* promotes a much longer history. So, really thinking about going back in time and through history, thinking about industrialisation in relation to modes of technology. There is an interesting and obvious kind of parallel between the Industrial Revolution and slavery, the latter provides labour and capital to support the former. Their interconnectedness is perhaps lost today, but Chude-Sokei fleshes out that link. I think that link to history is very important: it is African labour that fuels the technological and industrial advancement.

JH: Yeah. You have highlighted one of the major points that I think is very useful about the book. I certainly hadn't read it before the talk; it was only very recently published. What he does in effect is to mount a critique of Afrofuturism. Previously I had been thinking the conventional kind of thing about modernism and tradition — African tradition meeting modern technologies, jazz being the primary example. That is fine as far as it goes, but what Chude-Sokei does in quite a lot of detail is to show how modern technologies are imbricated in basically racist, racialised relationships. Technology is not a neutral thing; it cannot be understood outside the social and political circumstances of its development. Similarly, as is now being more broadly recognised, the industrial revolution was basically funded from the slave-wealth generated in the colonies. As you alluded to, this was Eric Williams' basic argument in *Capitalism and Slavery* (Williams 1964).[1] So it is not the case of our understanding of technology having to be supplemented with some sort of detour through Africa, it is that this is entirely necessary to understand the nature of technology itself.

In this vein Chude-Sokei discusses how the so-called stereotyped naturalness of Africa and Africans was used to introduce new technologies to the modern world, with nineteenth-century recording apparatus and so on. So, the threat value of technologies, you know, the Frankenstein kind of thing — that they may turn against us — was mediated or modulated, or sort of ameliorated by the fact that the content very often — literally in terms of recording devices — made use of African speaking voices. A one-time minstrel Bert Williams became a star through this. And so all that is embedded within the idea of modernist technology, basically the master-slave relationship. Chude-Sokei makes use of Ron Eglash's work on this; Eglash has studied when and where the terms "master" and "slave" become part of engineering discourse (Eglash 2007). And so what that is doing is naturalising an artificial medium of the technology, power relations. And, so, the futurism of Afrofuturism takes its name from, basically, from Italian Futurism. Right?

HO: Yes.

JH: Okay. And that was a very uncritical acceptance of the powers of technology; technologies of war, machine. Right?

HO: Yes.

JH: And so, the technology that is embedded as part of Afrofuturism actually has a, well you could say, a racialised, racist and power-oppressive dynamic in it already. Now, I don't think that this has been fully recognised. But it certainly causes us to have a more critical relationship to Afrofuturism. The neutrality of technology, which often Afrofuturism gives us as a de-racialised or a non-racialised world in the future, is actually the means to that end. But this is in fact going to prevent the achieving of this end, because the very idea of technology itself is embedded in a racialised development process, which I don't think most Afrofuturists would be willing to sign up to.

HO: Absolutely. I often think of problematising that link between Italian Futurists, Marinetti et al and their just very obvious links to fascist ideology and how that is now co-opted linguistically and through technology really, even within the Afrofuturist project.

JH: And what is interesting about this is that we are using the African and Africanist or a decentred sensibility to critique the very modernist project itself. And what I find is that Chude-Sokei makes it even more sophisticated and subtle through this understanding of the Caribbean as new world culture, as a creolised, creolising culture, bringing in thinkers such as Sylvia Wynter and the novelist Wilson Harris. So you have a level of sophistication of understanding, a sort of nuanced understanding that is very, very helpful indeed.

HO: One of the other things that I found really useful from the book — in terms of the relationship between kinds of fiction and technology — was the example he cites of the robot, and how as a re-occurring narrative within science fiction, there is a very unsubtle metaphor of the relationship between slave and master that is played out in the role of the robot, with early sci-ence-fiction writers problematising that kind of slav-ery. Some are coming from an abolitionist perspective, but still there is that ongoing, you know, dialogue about the robot's rights, politics, humanity and so on that are often embedded within debates of emancipa-tion.

JH: Yeah. And in the analysis of where the robot as a sort of trope is standing there is a less dangerous way of understanding the master-slave relationship. I just think that's got a lot of substance to it. But let's talk about your work.

HO: I guess there is an intersection with the body of work that I have been making most recently, which is called *Covers*. Essentially it's focused on a series of performances where I re-enact or re-create album cov-ers from a period of the late 1960s to the early 1980s. And, for me, the project has been a way to think about the album cover as a kind of popular archive really. So, as opposed to thinking about or starting with the music, the musical content of the album, I have been very much led by the images and it has been interest-ing to think about the album cover as a kind of func-tional illustrative medium, so something whose sole purpose is to promote, advertise and represent an art-ist's identity, to promote the musical kind of content. So within that kind of function I am interested in how the album cover operates in terms of representing particular artists.

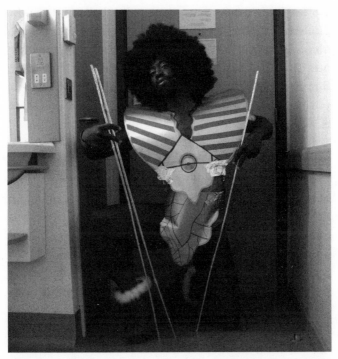

Figure 3. Harold Offeh (2013), *Covers: After Betty Davis. They Say I'm Different*, 1974. Photograph 30cm x 30cm.

I have a particular focus on this period of the 1970s and 1980s in relation to a sense of the African-American artist. So, some of the works I have been looking at are relatively well-known, George Clinton in Funkadelic/ Parliament guise for example, but there are also other less well-known artists, people like Betty Davis and Marlena Shaw. I am always very much led through this idea of an articulation and representation as embodied through the album cover. It is a way of being recon- nected with a particular narrative. Prior to doing this work, I have done a few projects that looked at Sun Ra as a kind of model, particularly of myth. I mean, you mentioned myth (or the mythical) at the beginning of our discussion. I think for me that is really important, that notion of self-mythologising. Within this kind of practice and that particular period, there is this notion of a kind of interrogation of identity through an adoption of myths and narratives, often rather playful, but sometimes more overtly politically positioned than others. The primary strategy for me has been this use of embodiment, this idea of actually interrogating these images, these subordinate images through these kinds of re-enactments.

JH: Do you always just use yourself as model then, I mean, in these different re-enactments?

HO: Yes, but this practice has evolved. Initially I would restage the album covers in my studio, apartment, or other domestic spaces. I would try to recreate things like the Grace Jones' *Island Life* pose as a photograph. I then translated them into durational moments, recorded as videos. Recently, I've presented them as live works where I'm performing the images for an audience. I was thinking about iTunes cover flow and how a performance could be presented like a playlist. I assume the pose for the length of the title track while the album cover art is projected. It's about inviting the audience to look at the image. To look at me and look again at the image.

JH: Yeah. We can broaden or contextualise the discussion; we could say that that in a way, the fact that you have taken a specifically visual approach to a specifically sonic subject, I mean, we could use that as an example of how sound works, that sound is not just what your ears hear or even what your body feels, it's also in the dance. That it is a way of inhabiting other selves. And so this is mythology that we are in. The absolute prime example is of course Sun Ra, from whom everybody draws, but Beyoncé also had Sasha Fierce as her alter ego. So what is being appreciated with music is a whole world, and now in one sense that is very well-known, recognised since the 1980s of MTV and music videos as well. But I think on a more kind of subtle level of talking about myth and imagination, and allowing us to feel and see and know ourselves as different people. This is part of, if you like, the quest of the Afrofuturism project, so in a way the future provides a space for us to reimagine ourselves, right. But also, the sound itself provides a space to reimagine ourselves. In *Noise: The Political Economy of Music*, Jacques Attali talked about music as prophecy; of it being able to go to places and anticipate things that have yet to happen, this is sound in the fullest sense (Attali 1985). Music offers these possibilities for liberation, possibilities for creating a better future.

HO: Absolutely. To return to your Goldsmiths presentation, you had these really interesting diagrams, these graphics that were illustrating sound waves, if I remember correctly? Just on the subject of visualisations of sound…

JH: Yeah, well that is something that the multisensory nature of sound affords. I'm interested in diagrams — in the work of Deleuze and Charles Sanders Peirce in terms of semiotics — as they provide an expression or gesture of relationships, rather than a representation, though they are of course visual. Diagrams as a form of expression are very ancient, as for example in the tradition of alchemy. Some of the finest diagrams are the alchemical ones, the Ripley's Scroll, for example, which is from the sixteenth century and people like the alchemist Robert Fludd and Athanasius Kircher, the seventeenth-century Jesuit priest. Historically, there is a whole tradition of understanding not through text and words and the linearity of language, but in a more holistic and relational way, which of course lends itself — expresses itself — mythically. And so part of Eko's quest, to put it like that, is to find ways to visualise sound. That can be done, starting in a very simple way, by taking an analogy of the light spectrum, the colours of the rainbow, Newton's diagram if you like, and just applying that to sound. So the bass frequencies, the bottom end which takes you from deep reds and purples up through greens, oranges and yellows of the treble, using the colour spectrum to express the pitches of the auditory spectrum.

And then in the dancehall session there is also an actual visual spatalisation of sound with the vertical configuration of each of the speaker stacks with the scoops or bass bins at the bottom and the tweeters on the top of the stack. So you've got a physical vertical dimension, which also expresses frequency. From that it is very easy to visualise how the sound waves come

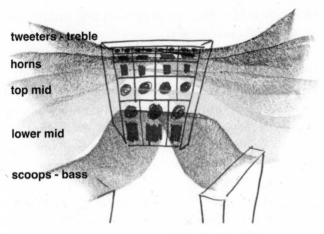

tweeters - treble

horns

top mid

lower mid

scoops - bass

Figure 4. Julian Henriques, Single Speaker Stack Frequency
Rainbow diagram from treble to bass (grayscale version).

out as visual waves, and these in different colours. The
whole business of the spatalisation of sound in the
arena, the space of the dancehall session, is something
I have been researching for a while (see Henriques
2011 and 2014). And the specific thing here is that they
do not use the conventional configuration of speakers
either side of the stage because with the sound system
there is no stage, because there is no artist; it's more
a phonographic medium, in Jamaica. Instead they
set up three speaker stacks, not two. ("Channel One"
sound system over here are also set up in this manner).
So, that gives a triangle, all pointing *inwards* onto the
crowd in the middle. That gives you not a flat plane
of sound, but a three-dimensional *volume* of sound,
an area which is imbued, filled with the sound waves
from the massive speaker stacks pointing inwards.

HO: Like a pyramid of sound. I am just thinking of a kind of triangular set-up...

JH: Yeah, in a way. You could put it like that, a pyramid of sound. Triangulation of sound with the audience in the middle rather than as distinct from the normal stereo where — mimicking the proscenium arch — the performance is located on one side as if it was a live band and the audience positioned on the other side. This idea of the stage, still the default for theatre design, was first formulated by the Jacobean architect Indigo Jones. And so it is us and them — us as the audience and the act on the other side of the divide. By contrast with the sound-system session the sound comes from all around, through us as the audience on the stage, where the stage is everything between the three speaker stacks.

HO: But there is this notion that the audience is inhabiting the architecture of the sound, which is being transformed. It's a kind of teleportation within this defined area of sound that is created by this triangular structure that you are talking about.

JH: Yeah, it's literally taking off...

HO: A sonic transporter?

JH: Yeah, exactly, it is a sonic transporter, at the level of pleasure, right, of just pure bodily delight. The body embodying itself with other people, you are feeling, you know you are feeling with the sound in the music. But also the spiritual level, going back to the alchemy, it's the refinement of the soul, in this case through the sound of music, raising consciousness. This is an ascendance to a more beautiful place, but you need to purify yourself to get to that place — Africa if you like. This is also of course in the bigger picture the next life, which this life is preparing us for, so to say, you know in traditional belief systems, that is often the case. So it is working on all these levels. What is so beautiful about it is the street culture. It's a street technology. So here is all this rich-ness, sophistication, subtlety, understanding, which is happening completely outside any academy, any official anything. It's something that is being developed with the people for the people. And that's a knowledge system, a *way of knowing* how sound works.[2] And that's something to give respect to and to learn from.

HO: Absolutely! It seems to be a seminal narrative that informs a large part of mainstream contemporary media and music. The origins of those experiences we talk about. We could talk about the experience of sur-round sound, for example. Within this kind of street culture and dancehall you talk about, there is a grass-roots culture, a precursor to the commercialisation of similar notions of surround sound that you have in the mainstream. But there is a complete erasure of the link to the grassroots of the sound experience.

JH: Yeah, there are lots of these erasures. Somebody put it to me that Foucault is credited as the man who understands discipline, right. In fact, really that all comes from Black Power in the United States and in terms of what the prison system was doing there. Foucault never makes a single mention of Black Power or the prison-industrial complex that Angela Davis has long been campaigning against. Lee "Scratch" Perry and King Tubby were doing their dub experiments in Jamaica in the 1960s, discovering for themselves the material nature of sound — likewise in the European avant-garde tradition Pierre Schaeffer is widely recognised as pioneering with his *musique concrète*. The history that gets written is invariably only all about the avant-garde pioneers, rather than what was going on in popular culture, where the work was being done out of necessity, in two-track recording studios in Kingston, Jamaica, in the tropics. This is normally not seen or heard as part of the bigger picture. That is what we need to do, we can use the cultural capital of the academy to recognise these narratives. That is to recognise in terms of technology and sound, what popular culture has been doing, where it comes from as black and brown people — and thereby where, if you like, modern civilisation comes from. And that disavowal, that blindness to these origins, is unfortunately as much part of the modernist project, as it is part of the future that Afrofuturism is projecting for us.

HO: It is interesting again you mention that, because I see this also within the work that I am doing — often the live performance aspect of it actually for me is just a gesture. I see it as a marker to try and get the audience to engage with the histories of the original material and question the sense in which it is easy to think about aspects of popular culture and black culture as purely ephemeral or transient. The action of trying to create a moment when the audience re-engages — often I perform with the original image, I stand next to the original image and for me that is about a kind of 'pointing to', asking people for a moment of time to actually look at this image and give it time.

Figure 5. Harold Offeh (2015), *Covers Live: After Funkadelic, Maggot Brain*, 1971. Live Performance at MAC, Birmingham, UK 2015. Photo by Open Aperture UK.

I am interested in what you were just talking about there in terms of what is underpinning the *Captain Eko* project as a kind of co-opting of the academy into a very specific political aim in terms of giving recognition, and visibility and voice, and agency, ultimately, to these histories.

JH: Yeah, and we are doing that in a very practical way which has come up since, which might be interesting for you. In January 2016 we did two *Sound System Outernational* events.[3] They both gave recognition to the practice of sound-system cultures and popular street culture and brought some of the local sound systems and crews and followers into Goldsmiths for a whole series of seminars and workshops that allowed us to recognise what we are doing and how important that is. It was really about building the relationship between the research in the academy and the local community. It was also intergenerational. One of the speakers was Young Warrior who is the son of Jah Shaka, and Young Warrior brought his mum down. And the women sound systems, like "Legs Eleven" and "CAYA" (Come As You Are) and the pioneer "V Rocket" from Nottingham, who have a lot of experience. So there is a real practical engagement with the culture, which Goldsmiths is in a very good position to have an input on, to encourage. We had several local sound systems and the university supporting it, in terms of the College's goals of "outreach", in terms of their "impact". The university and higher education is under attack in all kinds of ways and the future is hardly rosy. But still it has a residual capital, a cultural capital that can be used in these ways to encourage the recognition of the value of popular cultures. Not just as entertainment, of course, they are that, but in terms of these deeper strands. Without an understanding of the popular street cultures and technologies we are going to have a distorted view of what technology itself is. So, this is really necessary mainstream stuff. No, seriously. If we have a mainstream that is deaf and blind to black culture, well then we get a kind of warping, in my view, an eviscerating of our humanity.

HO: Absolutely.

1. Evidence for this thesis has been traced in the financial records of slave ownership by the "Legacies of British Slave-ownership". See https://www.ucl.ac.uk/lbs/; accessed 20 September 2016.
2. This is discussed in detail in terms of the sonic logos in Henriques 2011: 242-74.
3. See our blog, https://soundsystemouternational.wordpress.com; accessed 20 September 2016.

Works Cited

Attali, Jacques (1985), *Noise: The Political Economy of Music*. Manchester: Manchester University Press.

Chude-Sokei, Louis (2015), *The Sound of Culture: Diaspora and Black Technopoetics*. Middletown: Wesleyan University Press.

Eglash, Ron (2007), "Broken Metaphor: The Master - Slave Analogy in Technical Literature", in *Technology & Culture*, 48.2: 360-69.

Foucault, Michel (1986), "Of Other Spaces", in *Diacritics*, 16: 22-27 (also available at: http://foucault. info/documents/heteroTopia/foucault.heteroTopia. en.html; accessed 20 September 2016).

Henriques, Julian (2011), *Sonic Bodies: Reggae Sound Systems, Performance Techniques and Ways of Knowing*. London: Continuum.

— — — (2014), "Rhythmic Bodies: Amplification, Inflection and Transduction in the Dance Performance Techniques of the 'Bashment Gal'", in *Body & Society*, 20: 79-112.

Williams, Eric Eustice (1964), *Capitalism and Slavery*. London: Andre Deutsche.

HOW MUCH THE HEART CAN HOLD

Annett Busch

Something alluring unfolds over three screens that is too enigmatic to speak of as a crisis, yet the crisis is clearly present. A lost space opens up in John Akomfrah's latest three channel installation, *The Airport* (2016). Bright warm light, a wide-angled viewpoint, a composition of straight lines. Figures in melancholic composure: walking, sitting, waiting. A female voice singing a song in Greek. The cinematic space opens onto a time of mourning and recollection. Fragments of newsreel dialogue connect these different "space-time" images with a present in which they have not yet arrived. The past, with its heavy burden, cannot impinge upon the claims of the future, so it seems. Present time comes into the image through direct sound, and while image and sound are technically disconnected, they merge in our perception.

The following text is based on a movement of thought that one can possibly imagine as a rollercoaster, a looping line that turns around at least twice and ends up slightly displaced: memory, in moments and fragments, passing through the "amorous organ of repetition" — the heart, as Gilles Deleuze puts it in his introduction to *Difference and Repetition* — to find a divergent form on the border of knowledge. Writing along the border of knowledge — of what is known, what can be known — is what Deleuze calls science fiction. "How else", he asks,

> can one write but of those things which one doesn't know, or knows badly? It is precisely there that we imagine having something to say. We write only at the frontiers of our knowledge, at the border that separates our knowledge from our ignorance and transforms the one into the other. Only in this manner are we resolved to write (1994: xxi).

Writing on, with and about film, and on the films of John Akomfrah in particular — less in the mode of film criticism than as an attempt to understand an arrangement of image, sound and voice — can become science fiction in this very sense. Not only as writing that skims the border of knowing and not-yet-knowing, but as a transcription of a future that evolves from an image arriving from the past, an image that is not evident and not necessarily visible. The image must be *seen through*. It is not so much about reading and deciphering the image, but more about discerning how its echo reaches us. Much has been written about the artist and filmmaker John Akomfrah in recent years, particularly since his filmic and sonic oeuvre (and that of his long-time collaborators from the Black Audio Film Collective era and after) began to circulate as multi-channel installations in galleries, biennales and museums. The strong presence of media coverage and the relative absence of the work itself can make it difficult to experience the adventure of ignorance and surprise, of not-yet-knowing. The discursive framing of the work can suggest that we have already seen it. Seen what? To avoid the trickery of depressive boredom — as audience, spectators, passers-by, as readers and writers — falling for the assumption that the media has already said it all — and to regain the possibility of writing, and seeing, we must first realise that we only know "badly".

Hope — A Form to Move On

"In the Shadows of the Real", a lecture given by Akomfrah in the context of a student-based project on Afrofuturism at the Art Academy in Trondheim in March 2016, slows down our assumption and reveals what we have not seen, what we have not listened to carefully enough. The lecture accompanies and informs this writing and unrolls as recurrent theme. Taking *The Principle of Hope*, the all-too-famous, yet little-read book by the German philosopher Ernst Bloch, as a point of departure, Akomfrah elaborates on the idea of the "utopian image". Written between 1938 and 1947 in exile in the United States and published in three volumes between 1954 and 1959 in the GDR, and only translated into English in 1986, Bloch's extensive history of utopian thought had a difficult career and seemed completely absent as a reference for many years, at least in Germany. The German edition gained momentum in the late 1960s and 1970s within the student movement, which Bloch, then already in his late eighties, was emphatically engaged in. People who once experienced Bloch debating always emphasised the importance of his rhetoric as an expression of lived theory, with concepts animated and renewed through spoken language. A decade later, after his death, Bloch's concepts of hope and utopia had already become popularised and emptied of meaning. He was further labelled as someone who bridged Christianity and Marxism; all before *The Principle of Hope* had even been published in English. What too easily resonates with the concept of hope is the association with Christian passivity. But Bloch rather suggested an affective methodology, a form and a movement: "The essential content of hope is anything but hope" (Zudeick 1985: 308). He defines hope as an emotion that "goes out of itself, makes people broad instead of confining them [...]. The work of this emotion requires people who throw themselves actively into what is becoming, to which they themselves belong" (1995: 3).

Following Akomfrah's take on these concepts also means going back to moments of departure, loaded and necessarily full of hope. Hope as the incitation of a new beginning can display a vast field of lost traces, liberating and challenging in their simplicity. Going back to Bloch through the reading and appropriation of a Marxist-informed Afro-British filmmaker to nourish a thought on the concept of the "elsewhere" with regard to image-making fundamentally shifts the perspective, context and tone of my own memories of Bloch's book being part of my parent's bookshelves. This also implies that I have more of a specific sentiment for that very book which recalls a sense of

Christianity, than a particular knowledge. For whatever reason, Peter Zudeick's biography, *The Devil's
Buttocks*, is one of the very few items from that time, a
kind of heritage, that survived all my relocations span-
ning twenty-five years, and now it is the first time I
had a reason to read it. Bloch, who "dropped out of the
race between his fellow Western Marxists like György
Lukács, Walter Benjamin and Theodor Adorno" — all
of whom were significantly missing from my parent's
bookshelves but became much more important for my
further education — got a second life.

The notion of an "elsewhere" that Akomfrah fore-
grounds in his talk does not merely mean off-screen,
or *hors champ*, a cinematographic term which goes
beyond the capacity and necessity of the lens to frame,
never capturing the whole picture. Rather it connects
to a reality of the picture, a resounding but invisible
experience of a person appearing in the image. An elsewhere effected through sound. Or as Akomfrah puts it:

> A voice of a woman comes in with pure form, within
> this form it brings a mood — that speaks to us and says
> three things: I am one with the image. I speak to you
> from the same space, the space of cinema, and so I am
> here, says the voice, to add what the image wants to
> say to you. Yes, I am here, but my domain is elsewhere
> and the manner in which I will speak to you within this
> frame, the way I will move you, owes its meaning to
> that elsewhere.

Bloch's futurity begins with daydreams as distinguished from one's dreams at night, which he leaves

to the psychoanalysts. He is mainly interested not in the unconscious, but in the "not-yet-conscious", the not-yet-settled, the potential and becoming, terminology which resonates with a Deleuzian understanding of a knowledge in the making. As such, Bloch does not question the origin of hope, but states its sheer existence and wonders where it may lead to. His concern is with the subject who is discontent with the present, open to revolt against his living conditions, who utters, imagines or desires a better future:

> Nobody has ever lived without daydreams, but it is a question of knowing them deeper and deeper and in this way keeping them trained unerringly, usefully, on what is right. [...] The desiderium, the only honest attribute of all men, is unexplored. The Not-Yet-Conscious, Not-Yet-Become, although it fulfils the meaning of all men and the horizon of all being, has not even broken through as a word, let alone as a concept. This blossoming field of questions lies almost speechless in previous philosophy. Forward dreaming, as Lenin says, was not reflected on, was only touched on sporadically, did not attain the concept appropriate to it (Bloch 1995: 3).

This again connects to Akomfrah's lecture where he emphasises the aspect of the *looking forward*:

> For Bloch, thinking means venturing beyond... [Everybody lives in the future, because they strive, past things only come later, and as yet genuine present is almost never there at all. The future dimension contains what

is feared or what is hoped for; as regards human intention, that is, when it is not thwarted, it contains only
what is hoped for.

Translated to the practice of cinema, Akomfrah turns
it into: "The future begins by making an image". By
the hope that leads to the agreement of being filmed,
of becoming part of an image that matters and will be
watched by an audience to come in the future.

A Refusal to Produce Knowledge...

Through a detour we come back to this promise of
image-making, but this leads us first to another beginning, namely to *Handsworth Songs* (1985). This was
the first film by the Black Audio Film Collective to
receive widespread attention, winning several prizes
and provoking a heated debate. *Handsworth Songs* is
a dense reflection on a couple of days of riots taking
place in September 1985 in a district in Birmingham,
where mostly families from the Caribbean found their
homes in the 1950s, struggling with youth unem-
ployment, education, poverty and racism during the
heyday of Thatcherism. The movie did face the challenge of deliberating form and politics of representation, image and image-making, story and storytelling.
There is a refusal of representation in *Handsworth
Songs*, and instead of narrating a kind of counter-story
the film unfolds these elements as being in crisis — a
new tactical approach to image-making which is not
easy to read. Salman Rushdie famously criticised the
film from the perspective of literature in *The Guardian*,
arguing that it failed to "give a voice to the voiceless":

There's a line that *Handsworth Songs* wants us to learn. 'There are no stories in the riots.' It repeats, 'only the ghosts of other stories'. The trouble is, we aren't told the other stories. What we get is what we know from TV.

Salman Rushdie's reproach still seems to hit a nerve, namely to satisfy a desire for the untold upsetting individualising story that allows us to feel good about our compassion, a feeling that helps for charity, but only tolerates a very thin line as to what can or should be politically possible. "Giving a voice to the voiceless" can be seen as a noble, well-meaning gesture, but it remains within a certain paternalistic logic of control — a voice given and not just taken. This can lead to the more difficult question of how we understand all these voices and how we deal with them. A long thread of responses by Stuart Hall, Paul Gilroy, Isaac Julien, Darcus Howe, Kobena Mercer and others provide an intriguing debate on the question of the politics of representation. Refusing the imperative to tell individual stories and thereby establishing a narrative evolving in and from the past, *Handsworth Songs* condenses the narrative within images that question time rather than index time. Time-layers start to blur between the footage from the 1960s and the 1980s. These images are not explained, they require their own translation, a reading that has to be invented and contains its own fiction. Archival images in black and white, glimpses of an everyday street life and work environments, all moments of encounters, and speaking also of a belief in the significance of making these images, for a time to come, in juxtaposition with then present scenes of street battles, of a youth that claim their future through their own struggle.

The image, the voice, the sound and the song, each element resonates with its own divergent form of storytelling and affection and requires its own recognition and knowledge. It marks a substantial aesthetic and political shift: to cut out the motive, the why, the reason of movement and migration as a justification. Reasons for departure are not in question. Taking the *arrival* as a given, time and place where hope once led to, demand an understanding of the image that contains past, present and future at once. A storytelling immanent within the grammar of cinema that does not use image and sound as a tool, but as a form that tells its own story, that refuses to be defined by any identitarian parameter as it refuses to produce ethnographic or sociological knowledge. The knowledge generated instead can tell us more about the production of images than it gives us information to classify phenomena of difference. Akomfrah underlined this notion in a 1989 interview with Gilroy and Jim Pines:

> You can't use the film to construct other knowledges about Handsworth, other than what you already know. Once you have done that, anything else that you get is purely a profilmic event. The film doesn't make any pretensions to know where Rastas are at in Birmingham, or where the 'unclubbables' hang out à la the police report. It seems to me that the missionary zeal with which black life is chased in this anthropological way, is precisely what is missing from *Handsworth Songs* (1988: 14).

... And How Image-Making Can Change the Notion of Knowledge

The images of the riots in Handsworth, of uprising, police brutality and anger, do not accumulate as riot-porn. They are constantly transitioning, stretching from significant symbolic images towards non-significant images of everyday life and detailed reflection, whether from the archives or as footage recorded in the then-present. The images bridge decades, in black-and-white and in colour only within a few frames. Like a panning shot through time around a few streets and a crossroad, while a female narrator whispers to us, talking with the images, not over them, adopting different voices:

On the 10th of September 1985 a journalist is pestering a middle-aged black woman on the road, he wants her opinion on the disturbances: 'Did you have a relative involved? Could we talk to one of them?' He is writing a story. She says to him calmly: 'There are no stories in the riots. Only the ghosts of other stories.' If you look there you can see Enoch Powell telling us in 1969 that we don't belong, you can see Malcolm X visiting us in 1965 and a Conservative said: 'If you want a nigger for your neighbour, vote Labour.' She remembered Malcolm strolling through Smethwick saying: 'If this is the centre of imperialism then we have a common struggle.' For a moment the voice of Malcolm swooned over the ashes of decline.

With these words the images arrive in 1965, after panning along unspectacular street sceneries, construction sites, people standing around watching policemen standing around on both sides of the barriers, most likely at the same corner we see now: Malcom X in front of Marshall Street, not talking, walking down the street, alone in the picture, even while surrounded by photographers, accompanied by an abstract sequence of tones — an echo — which summons up more black-and-white photographs, another protest. This sequence of non-melodic tones, sounds, echoes, compresses time and image and enters almost unnoticed into a new movement with an astonishing length. Leaving the photographs of young people reclaiming the streets, carrying slogans, the photographs arranged hanging in a dark room, the camera of this archival footage starts pursuing, pestering without any motivated reason two women carrying their small children, their thin wide trousers and false fur coats marking their difference from other passers-by wearing the tight British knee-length skirt. The two women, turning around visibly annoyed, start to almost run. The pursuit ends with a gesture, with one of the women attacking the camera with a handbag. Ghosts of another story we cannot grasp, but which arrives with quite an excess. "Something in the image always resists", Stoffel Debuysere suggests in his contribution to a special issue of *Black Camera* on Akomfrah and the Black Audio Film Collective. "Something that escapes the look of the beholder handling the camera and the powers guiding it, something that goes beyond the inherent inequality between those filming and those being filmed" (2015: 69).

The Future Begins by Making an Image

What remains important for a debate today? Why be so precise on a sequence of images and their background and not just summarise some key content? "To spell a suspicion of how images come into being, how they circulate and what sustains their circulation", Akomfrah argues, understanding the precondition of image-making as Benjaminian, anticipatory — that to consent to be filmed implies an agreement to appear as an image in the future. In his lecture he offers a multi-layered reading of one particular scene that becomes crucial to lay out the dimensions happening during this specific moment while making an image, the implicit contract for a future and the encounter between the person filming and the person being filmed, but also connects *Handsworth Songs* to *Nine Muses* (2010). It is a scene from a 1964 BBC documentary, *The Colony* by Philip Donnellan, "a fantastic pioneer of essayfilm who worked principally in television". And because Akomfrah's reading is very detailed, I will quote this part of the lecture at length, as it also provides an insight into an ethics of the archive.

Akomfrah describes a scene filmed one Sunday morning: people singing in a Baptist church in Birmingham, near where most of the footage of *Handsworth Songs* was shot. It now becomes the transcription of a viewing experiment. While reading this, one has to imagine what would have remained invisible while watching without knowing: the scene was shot during the first openly racist election campaign in Britain, which the female voice in the quote above of *Handsworth Songs* is referring to.

So, you are watching people who know that they are
the objects of racist division, it is not something you
can miss if you are a minority and this is the only news
about you around. [...] Everybody you have seen
in this scene has migrated from the Caribbean. They
might have had a few days in London, but all headed
straight to Birmingham, and to Handsworth. You are
watching people who had all arrived at the promised
land, where they wanted to be. But in 1964, the journey to the promised land will be caught and cut short
by some very specific historical events. All the people
you see in this film have become recently not British,
for the first time in their lives. The majority are from
Jamaica, some from Barbados, some from Grenada —
and when you look at their faces, you can see they are
all in their thirties upwards, so for thirty plus years
most of them had been British subjects. But between
1962 and 1964 their identities would have changed,
they became West Indians, very recently. Which also
means that they became coloured, very recently. It's
a group of people in a major transition in their lives,
singing in a hostile city, about to become a racist land-
mark. A place they had made their home, some of them
for a decade or more. And you are also in a very profound sense watching the place where most will die.
Most of the figures in that film never made their way
anywhere else.

This scene can also tell a story of how image and sound
can come into sync, two distinct itineraries unfolding
as fiction. "The scene which has been filmed on that
Sunday 1st of March 1964 also made it into a film by

Richard Marquand, *Home for Heroes*." *The Colony* does not exist as "a film one could show with great sound", and would have been lost, not interesting for puristic documentarians to restore. The sound, which has been synced by Akomfrah, comes from somewhere else, from an oral history recording made by Donnellan's friend and collaborator Charles Parker.

Charles Parker was a champion of oral history of ordinary working class folks narrating their own lives, he was a veteran BBC producer, radio producer who worked for the corporation between the early 1950s and 1970s. In 1958 Charles Parker along with the musicians Ewan MacColl and Peggy Seeger came up with this remarkable form of radio documentary called *The Radio Ballads*. *The Radio Ballads* became for Parker the default radio documentary mode. So, why was he in that church on that Sunday? [...] There was an existing set of radio recordings made on the 1st of March 1964, that day that maybe could help us to reconstruct *The Colony*, because until now *The Colony* doesn't exist as a film that you could show with great sound. [...] When you watch this now, you are not aware of that sophistry. You are not aware that *a fiction* is unfolding in front of you. [...]

Occasionally I come across an image or a sequence that reminds me of the key ethical claim behind what we do. And that is this injunction on us in a way we handle and relate to the image. As a double demand, a double burden, a double consciousness if you will, because first of all we are confronted with this implicit claim of mortality that such moments come with. We do what we do because we want partly moments like this, to live and not die, that is part of the utopian contract. But secondly, we do what we do because of something which is the opposite of mortality, the exact opposite, we do what we do because of the immortal yearnings of such moments. The ways in which they say to us: come to us, because with you and through you we will and want to be forever. Etched into every gesture of that performance. This is in fact the precondition of what we are watching. As you watch them you can almost feel them say to you: I can feel your look which is to come from somewhere not of this moment, from somewhere in the future. From a place which is not right here, right now, and I am consenting to this process in anticipation of that look. [...] We are here, they say, for you and with you. But this is not a mere service, in being here for you in this moment, we know you will be there for us in your moment. This is the utopian contract I'm talking about.

We have to imagine the editing room as social space, a space of collective decision-making and debate, and not of solitude. And that the process of choosing images is as complex as making them and finding them: "Through the absence of black lives documented, they come to us as pure utopic fragment that it both confirms and blurs". The era in which the images of *The Colony* (1964) found their way into *Handsworth Songs* was in many respects quite different from that of *The Nine Muses*. A fragile male broken voice speaks, bridging excerpts from *The Colony* with new images. A boat is moving.

Sometimes we think we should blame the people because it's we who have come to your country. On the other hand, we think if they in the first place had not come to our country and spread the false propaganda, we would never have come to theirs. If we had not come they would none be the wiser and we would still have the good image of England, thinking that they are what they are not. And the English would be ignorant of us.

Hangover: A Time for Recollection

Within the montage of the abstract frozen images of northern landscapes in clean High Definition, the lively urban, grainy analogue film excerpts from the 1960s interrupt with a different noise. They permeate and inform the abstract surface of the filmic landscape with traces of industrial labour, means of transport, kids playing and laughing, people descending from a boat, faces, heavy snow, pictures of an everyday life; and at the same time they go beyond, through another layer of imaginary abstraction, to a stream of European and Asian literature and poetry. Text samples of travel literature unfold into polyphonic narratives of drifting, travelling, working towards the inner states of consciousness: from Homer's *Odyssey* to Emily Dickinson, to John Milton, Matsuo Bashô, Li Po, Kabir, Rabindranath Tagore, Shakespeare, Zelda Fitzgerald, E.E. Cummings and John Berger. The self-contained images of these snowy northern landscapes, in greyish clear and constant twilight, seem designed to affect us with their beauty, along with various voices reciting, yearning and singing, and bits and pieces of music, from Schubert to the Gundecha Brothers. Arranged as a multi-layered hybrid score by long-time collaborator Trevor Mathison, they put us in a trance, enable us to fall out of time. Every image and every sentence speaks from a precise point in time, but we don't feel it, see it, decipher it at the moment of watching.

And yet within this dense aesthetic space full of indications and moving reflections we mainly see stagnation. Despite gestures of discontent from the past, there is a total absence of revolt in *The Nine Muses*; even the possibility seems absent. Human beings packed in snowsuits stand around and move like sleepwalkers in this forbidding place, seemingly incapable of action, confronted by compromised nature — heavy weather conditions, a heavily destroyed ecosystem (not visible as such). The third layer of images, recorded in the present, shows a man in an unspecified post-industrial wasteland, a former port and place of work for many immigrants. We see him lying down, sitting, his face lost in introspection, somehow absent. We see similar postures in Akomfrah's *Transfigured Night* (2013), an elderly man looking quiescently out of a vitreous skyscraper in Seattle, people walking in slow motion around state monuments. Fred Moten, in an introduction to *The Nine Muses*, called this downtime syndrome a hangover from the period of Black Power politics.[1] Akomfrah talks of a narcoleptic state, considering the example of Ghana, the disillusioning experiences of the collapse of post-independence politics and the unravelling of Pan-African networks. Re-collecting beginnings also entails recalling a range of unrealised possibilities. The accompanying and opposing archival footage in

Transfigured Night revives confident moments of state politics, of Kwame Nkrumah in his newly independent Ghana, followed by a state visit to the United States, moments of handshaking as expression and annunciation of a new era of international collaborations. There is quite a leap of time between these images, of more than fifty years, and a huge fatigue weighs on the present. Hope — to go back to Ernst Bloch —seems absent, invisible in these withdrawn faces and composures. But there is a sense of hope nevertheless, of an activation that only evolves within a period of recovery, a timeout — and in this sense, one might read what looks like stagnation as a state of re-covering. That standing still might be the precursor to moving on, making something new.

Bloch repeatedly defines the relationship of thinking and the beyond: "Thinking means venturing beyond. But in such a way that what already exists is not kept under or skated over. Not in its deprivation, let alone in moving out of it" (1995: 4). What evolves from this movement of venturing as something new is not imposed, not in front of us, not coming from outside. It comes into existence through a mediated reflection of what is already there, what has happened. Only an understanding of the past can lead to something new, but this needs the process of transition and transformation. Bloch writes against psychoanalytical procedures, against the danger of being caught in what he calls "contemplative knowledge", as this "knowledge can only refer by definition to What Has Become" (1995: 4). Instead he claims a "knowledge as conscious theory-practice" that "confronts Becoming and what can be decided within it" (1995: 4). The movement of venture seems to describe a double movement, a constant going back and forth between past and future, between recollecting, imagining, projecting. Filmmaking in this sense can be understood as a conscious theory-practice, while the cinematic can offer a space for affective recollection for an audience that allows itself a cinematographic experience, initiating a reflection.

> Over the years, I have worked with a variety of approaches to memory. And with 'Mnemosyne', I called on some of these. The first is an idea that you find in many writers and thinkers from James Joyce to Antonio Gramsci to *The Communist Manifesto*. And this is the idea that moments of crisis, moments of emergency are also at the same conditions under which new things emerge. So memory is a kind of crossroad, a junction, an intersection where the old and the new meet. The second idea is, again, one that you find in a range of writers. But the first indication that I got of it was from Aimé Césaire, one of the founding figures of the Négritude movement. You also see it in the work of Foucault, for example. And this is the notion of memory as counter cartography: memory as a map by which one re-navigates the present (Akomfrah in Scotini and Galasso 2015: 34-35).

An Unreliable Knowledge of Knowing Only Badly

Although *The Airport* eschews archival footage, Akomfrah's film creates a cinematic space that contains in itself simultaneously the absence and presence of the past. Trusting the surface, the landscape, the ruins to speak for themselves, the film is shot on the terrain of the defunct Ellinikon International Airport in Athens. An astronaut who fell off Kubrick's *2001: A Space Odyssey* (1968) is roaming around, revenants coming from Theo Angelopoulos' movies crossing his path. The place itself is full of history. Built in 1938, it was originally used mainly by the German Luftwaffe, after the Nazis had invaded Greece; and it became important again towards the end of World War II for the United States Air Force as one of its main bases to fight the fascist forces in the south of Europe. Closed in 2001, the area has since become a shelter for refugees, coming from other elsewheres. All this is information we can look for in other sources, but cannot see on-screen. The visual and acoustic space created resists the domain of information and communication, as well as the imagery of activism. A cinematic practice, not to be misunderstood as withdrawal, that activates a quite fragile, elusive, unreliable but resistant knowledge, close to affection, transmitting a foreshadow, but anything other than facts. The moment one tries to grasp and unfold what it contains exactly, the notion of knowledge has already dissipated and taken new shapes. A knowledge that might give us the sense of knowing only badly, absolutely needed to invent something new.

Towards the end of his lecture, Akomfrah speaks about Claude Lanzmann's *Shoah* (1985), a major work on recollection, which he says he revisits every year. Lanzmann as a reference has become nearly as uncommon and unpopular as Bloch, although for quite different reasons. His categorical rejection of archival footage, banning the image for its incapacity to illustrate the logic of fascism and the experience of the Holocaust, compels survivors to speak, to re-collect their memory, while the camera obsessively pans over places of extermination, creating an imagination between the resistance of nature and its strong presence and an activation of the past's traumatic ghosts.

Akomfrah, again, describes the moment at the beginning of an encounter, any encounter, when the interviewee starts searching for an answer, he or she is always turning the head away from the camera, and his or her eyes turn towards an elsewhere searching for an answer. "It is always like this", he says. Watching people recollecting. We are left with a space of recollection, of sound and image looping through the organ amorous of repetition. "Nobody has ever measured, not even poets, how much the heart can hold", whispers a voice in *The Nine Muses*, quoting Zelda Fitzgerald. The future has already begun by making an image.

1. Fred Moten introduced the double feature of *The Nine Muses* and *Archie Shepp in Algiers*, in Haus der Kulturen der Welt, Berlin on 4 October, 2013 during the conference *After Year Zero – Geographies of Collaboration*.

Works Cited

Akomfrah, John (2016), *In the Shadows of the Real*, lecture given at Trondheim Academy of Fine Arts (KIT), 16 March.

Black Audio Film Collective (1986), *Handsworth Songs*, DVD, SD Digital file by LUX, artists' moving image.

Bloch, Ernst (1995), *The Principle of Hope Volume 1*. Cambridge/London: The MIT Press.

Deleuze, Gilles (1994), *Difference and Repetition*. New York: Columbia University Press.

Debuysere, Stoffel (2015), "Signs of Struggle, Songs of Sorrow", in *Black Camera*, 6.2, Bloomington, 61-78.

Donnellan, Philip (1964), *The Colony*, on: *From Visions of Change Vol 1*, DVD by the BBC.

Gilroy, Paul and Jim Pines (1988), "Handsworth Songs: Audiences/Aesthetics/Independence – Interview with the Black Audio Collective", in *Framework* 35, ed. Jim Pines and Paul Willemen, London: Sankofa Film and Video, 9-17.

Rushdie, Salman (1987), "Songs doesn't know the score", in *The Guardian*, 12 January, available online: http://www.diagonalthoughts.com/?p=1343; accessed 28 October, 2016.

Scotini, Marco and Elisabetta Galasso (eds.) (2015), *Politics of Memory – Documentary and Archive*. Berlin/London: Archive Books.

Zudeick, Peter (1985), *Der Hintern des Teufels – Ernst Bloch – Leben und Werk*. Bühl-Moos: Elster Verlag.

LUXURY COMMUNISM

A Conversation between Mark Fisher
and Judy Thorne

Judy Thorne: Luxury communism[1] clashes together two concepts which change when they are juxtaposed. There are a set of meanings and associations with "luxury" and with "communism". Communism, what is communism about? It is about everyone dressed in overalls, working in factories, inefficiently producing machine parts and living in prefabricated concrete towers. It is possible, even common, to simultaneously believe that it would be better to dispossess the rich and organise production collectively, and to believe that such a system would involve reconciling yourself to a kind of grey penury and renouncing many of the pleasures of the present. A nice idea, maybe, that everyone could be equal. But look what happened in the end: the Soviet Union fell because people were envious of Western consumer goods, they stormed the Berlin Wall because the lure of Levi Jeans just became too much to bear. In the DDR Museum in Berlin, there is actually a pair of Levi Jeans hung up for you to fondle, to feel how soft and well-constructed they are, so you can understand how the people living under communism must have suffered, and how inevitable it was

145

for it to all collapse in the end. So that's communism.

What about luxury? When you are living in luxury, you have achieved the good life within capitalism. You have got a yacht with a helipad, an infinity-edge swimming pool, five large and glossy horses, and a watch so flash that people can see how important you are from across a business-class airport lounge. Luxury goods are luxurious precisely because they are exclusive; "exclusive" is basically a synonym of luxury.

Putting the concepts of "luxury" and "communism" together does not make much sense, and it is from this lack of sense that a new idea emerges. By clashing the concept of communism together with the concept of luxury, you create a kind of libidinal energy. Luxury communism provokes you to imagine what would be possible in a world where we held all wealth in common and applied it to advancing the joy of humanity as a whole; where everything was for everyone. "Luxury" and "communism" together point towards a system of value other than that of the commodity. Communist luxury is not going to be exclusive, decadent wastefulness. It is not about signifying high — that is, *higher than you* — status. Our luxury is not the pleasure of possessing exclusive goods, but rather the pleasure of *luxuriating*: the sensual joy of having to do less work, time to be unproductive, and the possibilities for more intense sociality, eroticism and adventure this opens up. I love the picture for "what we will" on the eight-hour-day movement image; as if we had time and energy after work to go boating together. After a three-hour day maybe, or as part of a two-day work week.

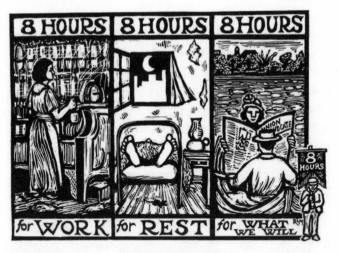

Labour Slogan Poster, 1908

As a way of imagining what public luxury would look like, I always start thinking of cities. A city which is truly beautiful, full of theatres, forest gardens, waterways, cafés, gorgeous buildings, curving arcades, life, art, is for me the clearest way to imagine communal luxury. As Kirsten Ross has described movingly in her discussion of communal luxury in the Paris Commune, communist luxury is art and beauty plundered from private salons, fully integrated into the public sphere, and elaborated and refined by this process. *Luxurious* public housing. There are some actually-existing places which feel prefigurative in this regard. In Berlin there are modernist housing estates built in the 1920s which reduced me to tears when I visited them, because they were simple, artful and beautiful, and built obviously with the idea of being the ordinary way housing would be built in the new century. When you are looking for an affordable flat in this country, it is rammed home to you how completely exceptional humane building is in Britain. Areas like the Barbican offer glimpses; the actually-existing Barbican is rendered almost irrelevant by its gross exclusivity, but imagine a whole city built like the Barbican, with its rhythmic concrete splendour, water gardens and tiled plazas, as well as a fully integrated free public transport system.

The Barbican, London (c) Judy Thorne

Park Hill in Sheffield is another place you can go and walk around and imagine what it would be like if cities were built for the pleasure of their inhabitants — much more modest, and obviously run into the ground by neglect, and now pretty much entirely depopulated and being turned into exclusive, private and unaffordable flats by Urban Splash.

Mark Fisher: The housing estates in Berlin, Park Hill, the Barbican — these belong to a popular modernist

Dieter Urbach image collage Large Hill House, based on a
design by Josef Kaiser, reproduced with permission from
Berlinische Galerie

moment whose ambition it is now difficult to imagine.
The installation of capitalist realism depended on making this popular modernist architecture and the vision
that underpinned it seem retrospectively impossible.
Partly, this is, as you hint towards, a question of libido
— the strange, science-fictional beauty of these housing projects belies the idea that left-wing initiatives are
inherently dreary. These examples make a powerful
case for the idea that beauty and pleasure are enhanced
by being shared. This brings out a further important
point, inherent in the idea of luxury communism: a
rehabilitation of the concept of the public. In neoliberal
propaganda, the public has been equated with a dreary
statism — which is one reason I think it is an urgent
task to distinguish between the public and the state.

The triumph of capitalist realism — the idea that there is no alternative to capitalism — has depended on not only a denigration of the public, but ultimately on a denial that anything like the public really exists. This was the intuition behind Thatcher's claim that there is no such thing as society: the idea that "society" is just some fiction that has no substantive existence. But the public — and the related idea of the public good — can both be fictional (in the sense that they are virtual, they do not have empirical existence) and real (once they are posited, they influence action and production in all kinds of ways). Park Hill, the Barbican, those housing estates in Berlin — they are all examples of the ways in which the concept of the public could inspire very tangible productions. These luxury communist spaces show how the positive fiction of the public can help to produce a future that contemporary capitalism is incapable of generating.

JT: The public as a space for vaunting ambition is certainly something that has faded since the end of the Cold War and the triumph of the private in every sphere, from the level of social atomisation to the agents of service delivery. There was a curious way in which the public was weaponised during the Cold War, not as soldiers but as more or less successful consumers of the material provision of their respective blocs. There was an exhibition in the summer of 2015 in Berlin about urban planning in the 1960s, showing how the East and West halves of the city competed with each other to demonstrate the superiority of their economic models, with the destroyed and partitioned city as their canvas. This led to extraordinarily science-fictional plans. One idea, to provide everyone in a growing population with fabulous living spaces, was for vast housing mountains with sloping sides, arranged amongst water gardens. The mountains would be oriented in such a way as to ensure every apartment was bathed in sunlight, with the core of the giant structure occupied by some acoustically sealed-off automated industry. Josef Kaiser, the architect of this vision, described the megastructure as "a friendly hill with hanging gardens, open and accentuated by a scattering of communal facilities such as gymnastic rooms, play areas or a snack bar, each on the various floors, easily reached via lift" (quoted in Köhler & Buttlar, 2015). Now it is not at war, capitalism's belief in, let alone ambition for, the public sphere has evaporated completely.

Part of reclaiming — or reinventing — the public also involves politicising the interiors of all these flats, and the work and social relations that take place in them. Luxuriant domestic space would also need to be deprivatised, so no one has to eat, spend an evening or raise children alone if they don't want to. Domestic work, as with industrial work, could be automated as far as is desirable, with vacuum cleaners which just get on with it by themselves and automated laundry systems, leaving us more time for care.

A word on automation: often luxury communism is paired with the demand for "full automation". Of course, we must automate all the work we have to do at the moment that is a drag, and which would still be a drag even if it was not alienated. The abolition of

151

work and the reduction of labour time towards zero have been demands of social movements across the history of capitalism. In the 1970s, 1980s and 1990s, workers' revolts in Italy, militant unionism and rave culture all took direct action to minimise the time actually spent at work. But even if work was entirely unalienated, and people did have genuine collective ownership and democratic control of the products of their labour, there would still be a lot of jobs that people did not want to do, that were boring, unpleasant or dangerous. These should be automated as far as possible, to free up as much of human time as possible for activity which is satisfying, delightful and sublime. But it is important to be clear that automation by itself never liberates, and can on the contrary lead to deeper oppression. The Job Centre excels at making time not spent in work even harder, more degrading and miserable than the worst job; and is, of course, preferable to starvation, the other alternative to employment in capitalism. The automation of laundry and chopping vegetables does not free women. What frees up human time is the construction of a society based on freedom, equality and mutual aid; and this is true under whatever mode of technology a society possesses, from Bronze Age to space opera. The abolition of gender requires a queer feminist revolution. But the collectivisation of domestic labour is part of the abolition of gender, and doing that labour, whether collectively or not, will be made easier and more pleasant by automating the boring bits.

One very early attempt to manifest the collectivisation of domestic labour architecturally was the

Narkomfin building in Moscow. The building was completed in 1932, by which time the explosion of the radical imagination that happened after the 1917 Revolution had been largely quelled by Stalinism, so Narkomfin was obsolete even before it was finished. But it was a wonderful architectural expression of early Soviet feminism, which in the 1920s was far in advance of any subsequent period. Narkomfin had communal kitchens, dining rooms, and laundry, a crèche, a gymnasium and a library. Its tall windows overlooked a park and flooded the rooms with light. Private space was visually and physically diffused out into the communal spaces of the building and the gardens beyond. The building was reserved for elite Ministry of Finance workers, and then for other specific categories of worker as the fashions changed and the building became less prestigious. But it still stands in Moscow, and the idea still serves as a jumping-off point to imagine feminist and luxury communist living spaces.

MF: This reminds us that, in Thatcher's notorious remark that I referred to above, she talked of there being "only individuals and their families". These experiments in collective living cannot but make us aware of the ways in which, under capitalism, and especially since the defeat of the counterculture, the family has re-asserted itself as a massive normative force. In her 1979 essay "The Family: Love It or Leave It", the late music and cultural critic Ellen Willis noted that the counterculture's desire to replace the family with a system of collective child-rearing would have entailed "a social and psychic revolution of almost inconceivable magnitude". Given the failure of that revolution, we are now faced with a situation aptly described by Helen Hester as "domestic realism", in which the fundamental structures of domestic organisation — physical as well as psychic and cultural structures — have become so embedded that it is difficult to imagine them ever shifting. Experiments like Narkomfin do the crucial work of reminding us that domestic space can be organised in very different ways.

J.G. Ballard's novel *High-Rise* (recently adapted for cinema by Ben Wheatley and Amy Jump) can be read as a parable about the thwarted desire to escape privatised luxury, and also about the pathologisation of the spaces beyond domestic realism. The inhabitants of the high-rise are all privileged, with the less wealthy living on the lower floors and the super-rich occupying the top of the building. The novel recounts the breakdown of the privatised luxury cells, and the emergence of tribalised groupings, as the high-rise becomes dominated by atavistic violence and Hobbesian struggle. I read this as an analysis of the bourgeoisie's simultaneous attraction towards, and abhorrence of, the possibilities of life beyond current forms of domestic privatisation. There is a discontent with the current repressions and boundaries, but any attempt to move beyond these strictures will only result in breakdown and savagery. Of course, this savagery is really only a projection of *current* social relations; it is just that the bourgeoisie is for the most part insulated from the kind of violent struggle that the novel describes. The light and serenity of Narkomfin breaks with the whole reactionary imaginary that *High-Rise* describes. The world beyond capitalist privatisation can simultaneously be orderly and playful, collective and creative.

But I suppose one obvious objection to luxury communism is that it is not the limits set by the bourgeois imagination which make it impossible, it is ecological limits: a society based around the principle of "everything for everyone" would, it has been argued, only be possible on the basis of practices that are simply not sustainable.

JT: Yes, within the capitalist conception of luxury, luxury for all would immediately lead to the destruction of life on Earth. Luxury communism does not tackle the ecological question directly, but it does invite us to think about the relationship between ecological devastation and human pleasure. Despite climate change being a profound threat to all life, the ecological movement has struggled with the problem of how to make resistance to climate change into a truly mass phenomenon. In meetings towards the end of Climate Camp, you would often hear people talking about the problem of sounding like we were preaching green austerity. There was a very strange period at the beginning of the Coalition government and the age of austerity, when the rhetoric of belt-tightening which they used was like a sick echo of ecological rhetoric. An anti-austerity communist ecology would need to be recast as part of the general project of the advancement of human pleasure. The intersection of Earth First! and rave culture in the 1990s was a version of this. There is also something quite luxury communist about part of the spirit of deep ecology; there is plenty about it which is really anti-human as well, but the idea that we should organise society in such a way as to prioritise the aesthetic and spiritual joy of forests and mountains is not alien to luxury communism.

Politicising the sensual pleasure of the natural sublime also links to the politicising of sensuousness generally. The queer liberation of sex from the dour capitalist constraints of binary gender and reproductive labour is also an aspect of any communist luxury. A wonderful embodiment of this principle is the work of Jack Smith, a filmmaker from the 1960s, whose work absolutely captures the luxuriating, voluptuous spirit of luxury communism. Jack Smith used B-movie tropes and images of sensual luxuriation to create visions of camp, surreal utopias. His films are pantheons of pleasures, inhabited by a bejewelled cast of gleeful queers. They are images of life beyond capitalism, beyond patriarchy; an Atlantis of luxuriant sex and camp splendour, which pushes at the limits of the aesthetic and political imagination. Smith's manifesto *Capitalism in Lotusland* (1977) outlines his project for utopian art:

Let art continue to be entertaining, escapist, stunning, glamorous, and NATURALISTIC — but let it also be loaded with information worked into the vapid plots of, for instance, movies. Each one would be a more or less complete exposition of one subject or another. Thus you would have Tony Curtis and Janet Leigh busily making yogurt; Humphrey Bogart struggling to introduce a basic civil law course into public schools;

infants being given to the old in homes for the aged
by Ginger Rogers; donut-shaped dwellings with sunlight pouring into central patios for all, designed by
Gary Cooper; soft, clear plastic bubble cars with hooks
that attach to monorails built by Charlton Heston that
pass over the Free Paradise of abandoned objects in the
center of the city near where the community movie sets
would also be; and where Maria Montez and Johnny
Weismuller would labour to dissolve all national
boundaries and release the prisoners of Uranus.

The excessiveness of luxury does raise the question of
whether the demand for "luxury for all" is much use
in a world where the first urgent steps a communist
project needs to take are the provision of solid housing, adequate food and healthcare for all. As you have
already touched on, Mark, I think the answer to this
is that utopian slogans and imaginary realities have
a role to play even in a present thrumming with the
dull roar of dystopia. The science-fiction and fantasy
author Ursula Le Guin has said that in order to con-
cretely create the future, we need to reach beyond narrow capitalist realism: we need poetry and visions of
a larger reality. We need to invent fictions about the
future, in order to then make them real. This is not just
about escapism, in the sense of creating an unreality to
take refuge in — though I would argue that escapism
is a legitimate, even necessary tool for psychological
and imaginative survival within capitalist realism. We
build counterpower simultaneously to end capitalism
and to survive within it whilst we fight against it; to
survive subjectively as well as materially. Our life sto-

ries and selves are spitefully measured by a capitalism which demands tireless emotional labour and perpetual performance improvement. Countering — or shooting high beyond — these demands with demands for the grandiose utopias of our imagination can be a way to emotionally renege on the pressure to internalise capitalism's assessment of ourselves, and refract disposability back onto the system itself.

MF: I think the provocative concept of luxury communism makes three important moves in the context of recent political struggles. Firstly, the positing of a positive concept — or two positive concepts — provides a break from the tendency to think of left-wing politics solely in terms of resistance and opposition. Framing what we are doing as a struggle for luxury communism rather than against capitalism moves us beyond the automatisms of anti-capitalism. One criticism that has frequently been made of left-wing politics in recent years is that it is clear about what it does not want — capitalism — but is less clear about what it does want. I think this criticism has been justified, and it is not always made by sneering right-wingers. Sometimes it is people who are sympathetic to the left-wing critique of capitalism who have made this point. Particularly after the financial crisis, those people understand all too well the problems with capitalism. What many who are discontented with capitalism cannot imagine is any alternative. This inability to even imagine an alternative is part of what I meant by capitalist realism, and moving beyond capitalist realism entails shifting the emphasis away from capitalism.

Positing something like luxury communism as a positive goal means that we can start to see capitalism as a force of resistance and obstruction. You could say that luxury communism names what capitalism must block in order for it to remain capitalism. This also allows us to reclaim the concept of communism. Perhaps even more so than it did in the Cold War, the concept of communism designates an outside, something which, according to capitalist realism, is as unthinkable as it is undesirable. Now that the Soviet system is a receding referent, there is the opportunity to both rediscover and invent a meaning for communism. At the simplest level, communism can be understood as a social system which maximises the collective capacity to share, care and enjoy: "Everything for everyone". The concept of luxury communism can help with this reclaiming of the concept of communism.

Secondly, I think the concept breaks what you might call capitalism's monopoly on libido. This is what the Levi's Jeans represented — the idea that only capitalism could produce desirable goods. In the 1980s, there was a UK TV advertisement that played on these associations, showing a teenager smuggling Levi's into the USSR. This led, quickly, to the conclusion that only capitalism is desirable. This was a mainstay of Cold War propaganda, and of the propaganda that was disseminated after the fall of the Soviet bloc. Ultimately, the reason that communism won't succeed is that nobody wants it. As you suggest, the concept of luxury communism disarticulates communism from the associations with anti-libidinal drabness. More than that, it invokes a wealth, a "red plenty", to use Francis Spufford's term, that makes capitalism's products seem somewhat tawdry. This is the point that the fictionalised Nikita Krushchev makes in Spufford's *Red Plenty* (an extraordinary work, which is very definitely a part of the luxury communist canon): yes, capitalism has produced all kinds of wonders, but it has done so in a chaotic and haphazard way. What would it be like if this wondrous production was managed in the interests of all?

The third important contribution that the concept alone makes is to shift us out of our current cognitive defaults. As you outlined, according to those defaults, "luxury" and "communism" are antonyms; their conflation does not make sense. So even beginning to think about what luxury communism might mean starts to unglue the habituated patterns of thought established by capitalist realism; it makes demands on the imagination, it already puts us into another world.

JT: Yes, that is exactly the function of the concept: it is nonsensical, and as such invites you to invent new meanings for "luxury" and "communism", which immediately sets you off imagining some form of utopia.

MF: I wonder if the emphasis on utopia is right here, though. I worry that the exiling of left-wing ambitions to a utopian space is the flipside of capitalist realism. Capital seizes what is realistic, what is pragmatically realisable, and we are left with the utopian. It seems to me that one crucial challenge implicit in the idea of luxury communism is the idea that, as you say, there is a sense in which this is actually possible now. The obstructions to an egalitarian reorganisation and redistribution of resources are not material or technological: they are political. So I would suggest that, rather than aligning with utopianism, we should develop a communist realism. Luxury communism is not only radically different from how we live now — it is also realistic, and realisable. It is only nonsensical from the point of view of a system that is itself a nonsense. It is only unrealistic from the point of view of a system which cannot be sustained, and which is prepared to risk everything in order to preserve its own fantasies.

JT: Formulating a hegemonic communist realism is exactly what we need to do! Ecological destruction, economic crisis, automation — the material conditions of the present show up the idea of business-as-usual as hopelessly unrealistic. We just have to knuckle down and accept that we are never going to be able to turn the clock back to the neoliberal heyday of the early 1990s! But what we as luxury communist realists need to pull off is the idea that, as the neoliberal status quo begins to melt, dystopia is not inevitable. And I think that unbridled utopianism can play a role in that, by permitting us to imagine versions of the future which are not just dystopias. We need to create a discursive space in which it is not just permissible, but necessary and realistic, to imagine futures we want. To outline them. Plan them. When I interview people about what they want for the future of the world, I often find that they are uncomfortable about expressing desire on a social, rather than individual, level, because it seems preposterous and unrealistic. Creating space for world-desire is the mode of utopianism which luxury communism gestures towards, I think.

MF: I suppose our disagreement here — which may only be terminological — is that you are seeing utopianism as compatible with (communist) realism, whereas I see utopianism as pointing to something quite different from realism, rhetorically and strategically. I absolutely agree that we have to generate possible futures that are not dystopian, but I do not think that utopia is the only alternative to dystopia. As you suggest, there is a kind of dialectical equivalence of the utopian and the dystopian in the current, collapsed form of neoliberalism. The attempt to save the neoliberal utopia is making dystopia more and more likely.

I think I would prefer to talk about hyperstition — which has been defined as the process whereby fictions make themselves real — than utopianism. Much of capitalism functions through hyperstitional processes. In fact, you could argue that capital itself is a hyperstition. At a smaller level, the various techniques of hype which capital uses — in which positing the success of a product helps to ensure that very success — are good examples of hyperstitional practices. I believe we need to think about what a communist hyperstitional practice would look like. You could say that the whole theory of class consciousness from György Lukács onwards was an attempt to do just that. Class consciousness would be a kind of self-fulfilling circuit, whereby the new revolutionary subject would produce itself. Class consciousness does not passively reflect an already-existing state of affairs: it actively intervenes to produce something new.

It is important to extend this kind of analysis to the more "molecular" level of consciousness-raising, something that I know we are both interested in. One problem that the left has had is convincing people that political activity will yield results in the immediate — or at least medium — term, not only in some impossibly distant future. Thinking of what we are doing in terms of consciousness-raising — which in one of its dimensions is the collective practice of dis-identification from dominant categories, concepts and forms of subjectivity — is one way of shifting that. The most important transformation of consciousness — and it has never been more important than in neoliberal conditions of compulsory individualisation — is the recognition that there are common causes for what we ordinarily experience as individual misery. It is not my fault — it is capitalist-patriarchy. We might "know" this, but such knowledge is empty if we cannot feel it and live it, and everything in capitalist culture is designed to make us doubt what we know, and to live and feel inside capitalist categories and concepts. It is only by being together in a particular way that we can break out of this.

One way of seeing neoliberalism — and the broader neoliberal culture — is as a set of practices specifically designed to obstruct consciousness-raising. Perhaps the most potent weapon in this struggle has been time poverty, and here we can return to the question of luxury. Thinking about having time to luxuriate makes us realise the extent to which time poverty is endemic now. Even the rich seem to lack this capacity for luxuriating. In fact, the rich seem to pride themselves on *not* having the time to luxuriate. CEOs and other capitalists enthusiastically embrace the domination of their lives by work. It is conspicuous labour rather than conspicuous consumption.

Time poverty obstructs consciousness-raising, because consciousness-raising requires time: a particular mode of time — a time of absorption and care — which it is extremely difficult to muster in current conditions of precarity and digital twitch. At the moment, there is a vicious circle in place. What we want is more time — time to go boating! But we need time now in order to be able to plan and struggle for the liberation of time in the future. The immediate challenge for luxury communism is to intervene in this vicious circle: to find ways of sharing and multiplying the meagre temporal resources we already have. How can we luxuriate now? How can we begin to re-train ourselves to experience time in a way that escapes capitalist imperatives and urgencies?

JT: My use of utopia is informed by the anarchist use of it, the idea of the propulsive utopia, which animates prefigurative action in the present, which creates space. So the creation of shared time to spend in consciousness-raising groups in which we have the luxury of absorption and mutual care, according to my gloss on it, is utopian. But the word famously is riven by this double-meaning (good-place/no-place), simultaneously signifying hope's ultimate realisation and its futility. So maybe hyperstition refers better to the luxury-communist-realist emphasis on the realisation of desire. None of this answers the question of time though, which I agree is the most pressing one to answer when considering how to build utopia now, or to hypersitise luxury communism.

MF: The question of time is difficult but fruitful — partly because time has been so depoliticised. Thinking of luxury communism in terms of superfluity of time can help to counteract this. First of all, it can begin to de-naturalise the current governance by anxiety, in which lack of time, or to be more precise, our constant immersion in a time of embedded urgencies, is a taken-for granted, and indeed libidinised. Much of what Jodi Dean calls communicative capitalism depends on the libidinisation of this sense of being "always on", of always being open to the flows of communication. I would like to think that luxury communism would take us out of this form of time. In capitalism, a smartphone used to be a luxury but in many areas of the capitalist world, it is closer now to being a necessity, something that has been made central to our work and subjectivity. The luxury of luxury communism would, by contrast, be about a liberation from many of the things that the smartphone currently stands for and facilitates. In *Eros and Civilization*, Herbert Marcuse wrote that

> the closer the real possibility of liberating the individual from the constraints once justified by scarcity and immaturity, the greater the need for maintaining and streamlining these constraints lest the established order of domination dissolve.

He goes on:

> In exchange for the commodities that enrich their lives,
> [...] individuals sell not only their labour but also their
> free time. [...] They have innumerable choices, innu-
> merable gadgets which are all of the same sort and
> keep them occupied and divert their attention from
> the real issue — which is the awareness that they could
> both work less and determine their own needs and sat-
> isfactions.

These passages strike me as extraordinarily prophetic,
especially in the light of the rise of communicative
capitalism and its technologies. Capitalist luxury is
always in the service of distracting us from the very
real possibility of liberation from work; communist
luxury would exactly be about the awareness that we
could work less and that we can determine our own
needs and satisfactions.

You referred a few times to rave culture, and it
might be worth thinking for a while about the role
popular culture might play in building the conditions
for luxury communism. Rave was the last example of a
popular psychedelic culture. I have started to thinking
about an "acid communism" — a fusion of the psychedelic and the militant that did bubble up in actuality at
particular moments (perhaps especially in the Italy of
the 1970s), but which was, for the most part, a haunting virtuality. Psychedelic cultures focus on consciousness in a different but potentially complementary way
to consciousness-raising practices. Consciousness in
psychedelic culture is always radically plastic and

mutable. This went alongside a certain — luxuriant, immersive — experience of time, which fed into a politics of the refusal of work. It is sad, catastrophically sad, that the mainstream left — whether social democrats or Marxist-Leninists — could not connect with the implicit or vernacular libertarian and anti-work politics in psychedelic cultures. But perhaps that previously missed fusion is one way of thinking about what luxury communism could be about now, and in the immediate future. The psychedelic returns us to the question of generative fictions, in that, in psychedelic culture from The Beatles through to rave, there is always a dreaming of a world governed by very different temporal rhythms: "stay in bed, float upstream" ... More time for boating!

1. A disclaimer: luxury communism, and the attendant slogan "luxury for all" are not my ideas. "Luxury for all" was a slogan associated with the German libertarian left, including ...*Ums Ganze*! in the mid-to-late 2000s, and was imported to the UK by *Shift Magazine*. The luxury communism Tumblr blog which was part of the popularisation of the concept was set up in 2012 by me and three or four other people, some of whom are part of Plan C. Parts of this conversation are inspired by the debates about luxury communism within Plan C; some people in Plan C like the idea, others hate it. Its popularisation was also hugely contributed to by Novara Media and their demand for Fully Automated Luxury Communism. The ideas that I bring into this conversation were put together from discussions with my friend Ian Childs. It is very much our personal take on the idea — if you listened to someone else talking about the idea, they would probably describe it quite differently.

Works Cited

Ballard, J.G. (2014), *High-Rise*. London: Fourth Estate.

Dean, Jodi (2005), "Communicative Capitalism: Circulation and the Foreclosure of Politics", in *Cultural Politics*, 1.1: 51-74.

Hester, Helen (2015), "Promethean Labours and Domestic Realism", https://www.academia.edu/11571359/Promethean_Labours_and_Domestic_Realism.

Köhler, Thomas and Adrian Buttlar (2015), *Radically Modern: Urban Planning and Architecture in 1960s Berlin*. Tübingen: Wasmuth.

Marcuse, Herbert (1972), *Eros and Civilization*. London: Abacus.

Ross, Kristen (2015), *Communal Luxury*. London and New York: Verso.

Smith, Jack (1977), "Capitalism in Lotusland", from a performance manuscript for "Irrational Landlordism of Bagdad", presented at the Cologne Art Fair.

Spufford, Francis (2011), *Red Plenty*. London: Faber and Faber.

Willis, Ellen (2012), "The Family: Love it or Leave it", in *Beginning to See the Light: Sex, Hope, and Rock-and-Roll*. Minneapolis: University of Minnesota Press.

EXTRATERRESTRIAL RELATIVISM

Stefan Helmreich

Peter Watts' 1999 science-fiction novel *Starfish* concerns a cadre of humans who have been physiologically engineered to live on the seafloor, near undersea volcanoes, where they do maintenance work for a multinational corporation mining the seabed. Their metabolisms are tuned to the high pressure and exotic chemical mixes of these settings so that they are fit to what, in contemporary scientific terminology, is called an "extreme environment". Partly adapted through technological prostheses, partly through more fleshly modification, these people might be called, after a term popular in recent biology, *extremophiles* ("lovers of extremes").

Robert MacElroy coined the word *extremophile* ("lover of extremes") in 1974 as a hybrid of the Latin *extremus* and the Greek *philos*. The word gathered together organisms — psychrophiles (cold lovers), halophiles (salt lovers), and more — that previously had little to do with one another classificatorily. Prior to 1974, if one spoke of these creatures in the same moment it was in the realm of food preservation; freezing, salting, drying, pasteurisation and irradiating are all methods of controlling the varied and resilient microbes that live in food. What brought these creatures under the same designation was the notion of the "extreme environment". While that phrase originated in clinical and personnel psychology and applied psychiatry in the 1960s to discuss communities of humans acting in isolated and intense social settings (Antarctic research stations, spaceships — the science-fiction setting of *Starfish* would fit perfectly), "extreme environment" by the 1970s came also to have a more ecological meaning. By the 1990s, extreme environments came to embrace extraterrestrial settings, and, in the early 2000s, there emerged the somewhat roomier concept of "extreme nature", the title of at least two popular science books in the first decade of the century (Curtsinger 2005 and Cowardine 2008, both titled *Extreme Nature*). In the contemporary moment, then, the "extreme" has become a frame for thinking about nature and its boundaries.

In this essay, I suggest that the shared semiotic terrain of the *extreme* and *extraterrestrial* now grounds a novel kind of relativism, where "relativism" describes a view that takes facts of existence and experience to be relative to conditioning situations, situations that themselves may require a certain suspension of judgment as to their absolute grounding. *Extraterrestrial relativism* is a relativism about "nature" over culture — and, more than this, a relativism about Earthly nature. It extends into the cosmos Eduardo Viveiros de Castro's (2009) concept of *multinaturalism*, an analytic he uses to describe interpretations of the world as made of creatures who all experience themselves as subjects (even "humans"), while also each summoning forth their own unique embodiment of "nature" (so, if for the Amerindian cases he discusses, "jaguars see blood as manioc beer [and] vultures see maggots in rotting meat as grilled fish" [470] — seeing all "food", in other words, as properly "cultural" — this encounter is clothed in different "natures" [jaguarness, vultureness][for a quick extraterrestrial analog, think of old *Star Trek* episodes in which even beings of pure light have "gender" and "morality"]). Extraterrestrial relativism as multinaturalism would track how different organisms summon different "natures" even as they share the enterprise of being "alive". But extraterrestrial relativism also has points of difference from Viveiros de Castro's experiential and phenomenological formulation of the multinatural. In some instantiations, extraterrestrial relativism is a *non-anthropocentric relativism* in which humans (as well as other creatures, and, at its limits, life itself) may be entirely absent. Such a relativism may evaporate residues of "culture" (as a contingent, symbolic system) that still reside in the very framing of relativism, forcing us not only to speak of comparisons that might be undertaken relative to different natures, but also, more expansively, to think about whether comparison might always require an agent to enact it and, if so, whether the limits of the concept of agency might then be coextensive with the limits of comparison itself.

In what follows, I develop the concept of extraterrestrial relativism by leaping off from ethnographic work I conducted among astrobiologists — scientists who consider Earthly extremophiles as analogs, stand-ins, for possible extraterrestrial life. Along the way, I suggest that extraterrestrial relativism be brought into conversation not only with multinaturalism, but also with a newly inaugurated conversation on "comparative relativism".

After *After Nature*

Toward the end of the twentieth century, Marilyn Strathern suggested that more and more people in the contemporary world were living "after nature", living simultaneously in pursuit of "natural" foundations for social relations as well as "post-nature", in a time when it had become clear that "nature" — particularly the biological — was a social category and one ever more amenable to cultural transformation. Following Strathern's cue, many anthropologists in the 1990s and early 2000s studied zones of cultural practice in which such conceptions of "nature" were in the making, from new reproductive technologies, to genetic engineering, to cloning. Indeed, my own *Silicon Second Nature* (2000), an ethnography of "Artificial Life", a field devoted to the computer modeling of living systems, concluded that Artificial Life — and particularly its key method, simulation — hinted at an undoing of the self-evidence of "life itself" as a natural kind, not least because nature itself had become multiple.

But "extreme nature" may be the new "after nature". Such certainly seemed plausible to me when I turned my attention from Artificial Life science to examine the work of biologists studying microbes living at deep-sea hydrothermal vents, at extremes of temperature and pressure (Helmreich 2009). Like Artificial Life scientists, these researchers were interested in stretching their concepts of living systems. Extremophiles like vent *thermophiles* (heat-lovers) pressed against the boundaries of what microbiologists believed living things could enact and endure. As Carl Wirsen, a microbiologist at the Woods Hole Oceanographic Institution in Massachusetts, told me in an interview in 2001, one might sensibly use vent microbes to think about the question: "What are the limits of life?" Wirsen's colleague, Andreas Teske, added that, "microbes have shown us many alternatives for living". And Mitch Sogin, a microbiologist at the neighboring Marine Biological Laboratory in Woods Hole, told me that many of his colleagues believed that marine extremophiles, like those at vents, might provide possible threads back to aboriginal life forms on Earth, which may themselves have been extremophilic microbes. As head of an astrobiology research group at the Marine Biological Lab, Sogin also suggested that such microbes might be pointers to life on other worlds, in other ecologies, analogs for extraterrestrial life. NASA's LEXEN (Life in Extreme Environments) project, I learned, was interested in precisely this question. The limits of life, the boundaries of vitality, may yet be unknown. Scientists are still chasing "after nature", but are now doing so by looking to the stars, for yet-to-be-characterised conditions, yet-to-be-known "extremes" relative to which life might be able to survive.

Extremophilic Relativism

I learned much more about such framings of extremophiles at a 2005 workshop on astrobiology I attended at the Marine Biology Laboratory. One intriguing presentation came from Lynn Rothschild, an astrobiologist from NASA who studies halophiles, salt-loving microbes that can survive extreme desiccation in suspended animation between waterings. With bacteriologist Rocco Mancinelli, she had in 1994 helped design an experiment for the European Space Agency in which halophiles were exposed to the extreme cold and unfiltered solar radiation of space. During a stint on a recoverable satellite these microbes survived for two weeks, a result that Rothschild argued supported the possibility that living things could be transited to Earth from such sites as Mars, if indeed Mars sports such life. That capacity could support the possibility that life originated on Mars and was ferried to Earth on, say, a meteorite. In this experiment, extremophiles become proxy aliens. The *extreme* and the *extraterrestrial* glide rhetorically into one another.

While the word *extremophile* has usually been taken to refer to microbial life forms, Rothschild pointed out that the term can apply to metazoans as well, and, more, that "extremophily" is a relative term. Humans might be imagined as aerophiles — air-lovers: an extreme from the vantage point of anaerobes. The "extreme", here, functions as a relativist rather than totalising operator. What this accomplishes is attention to environment; the ends of this kind of biology are about ecological context (itself in constant readjustment). The effect for many scientists in this discussion is further to displace humans as reference points for accounts of evolution and to place the whole conversation in a more cosmic setting (contrast Farman, this issue, on Singularitarians' vision of the universe as reaching toward a self-consciousness that has humans as a stop along the way; for Singularitarians a non-relativist "intelligence" displaces "life" as the object about which a cosmic account must be sought). The extreme — that which is outermost from any centre or which is opposed to the moderate (OED) — shades into extraterrestrial — that which exists or originates outside Earth. The fusion of extreme and extraterrestrial is also enabled by the scale at which each category operates — a scale that has zooming-out as its signature property and that has comparison built into it. The extreme and the extraterrestrial are also both relational categories, and perhaps relativist, at least in the canonical sense.

Comparative Relativisms

Such an articulation suggests extraterrestrial relativism as a possible data point for discussions of what social science and humanities scholars at a September 2009 meeting at the IT University of Copenhagen termed "comparative relativism" (Jensen et al. 2011). While "comparative relativism" is at first glance an oxymoron (how can relativism, the character of which is predicated on incommensurability, be a stage for comparison?), the question asked by the term becomes clearer if we think about the many uses and flavours of relativist claims. As the Copenhagen conveners put it:

Comparative relativism is understood by some to imply that relativism comes in various kinds and that these have multiple uses, functions, and effects, vary-

ing widely in different personal, historical, and institutional contexts; moreover, that those contexts can be
compared and contrasted to good purpose. [...] On
the other hand, comparative relativism is taken by
other[s] to imply and encourage a 'comparison of comparisons', in order to relativise what different peoples
— say, Western academics and Amerindian shamans
— compare things 'for' (Jensen et al. 2011).

In other words, comparative relativism can ask both
what knowledge or truth is being imagined relative
to and whether comparison always operates in the
"same" way — or with the same grounds or purposes
(e.g. shoring up the categories of culture, nature,
morality) wherever we find it.

For extraterrestrial relativism, knowledge or truth
about "life" (or even its "conditions") is imagined as
relative to a "nature" whose full character we do not
yet know, whose outlines may lead us toward comparisons we cannot predict. Take as a recent mani-
festation the announcement, in December 2010, by
geomicrobiologist Felisa Wolfe-Simon, of the possibility that living systems might use arsenic in place of
phosphorous in the making of DNA. Wolfe-Simon and
her colleagues isolated a microbe from California's
Mono Lake and cultivated a version in a lab that they
believed could live without phosphorus. Wolfe-Simon
put the significance of the finding this way: "This is a
microbe that has solved the problem of how to live in
a different way". In her reflections on the meaning of
her result, she suggested that she was "cracking open
the door and finding that what we think are fixed con-

stants of life are not" (quoted in Overbye 2010).

Such undoings of fixity, such agnosticisms about the ultimate anchors for life, may themselves go to extremes of meta-relativism. Physicists Alejandro Jenkins and Gilad Perez have argued in *Scientific American* that "Multiple other universes — each with its own laws of physics — may have emerged from the same primordial vacuum that gave rise to ours", and "may contain intricate structures and perhaps even some forms of life", which suggests that the cosmos as we know it may not be the only one hospitable to life (2010: 42). Such a framing offers a contrast with many discussions of human spacefaring, which pitch space as inhospitable to life as we know it. But astrobiological and astrophysical framings of space as hospitable resonate with some features of *multinaturalism*. Viveiros de Castro draws on his ethnographic work in Amazonia to suggest a way of apprehending the world that is not *multicultural* — "founded on the mutual implication of the unity of nature and the plurality of cultures" — but rather *multinatural*, supposing "a spiritual unity and a corporeal diversity" (1998: 470). For extraterrestrial relativism, a "spiritual unity" can be discerned in scientific faith in the universality of "life" as a category (which may itself be indicative of a wider epistemological moment in which the off-worldly has become a taken-for-granted point of reference. If in Vivieros de Castro's accounting, "jaguars see blood as manioc beer" where human people see blood as blood (as their natural, vital fluid), in an extremophilic relativist accounting, anaerobes may experience, say, air as a toxic pollutant created by plant life, where aerophiles experience it as a nurturing surround.

Of course, such relativism may in some instantiations actually underwrite a deep universalism, even absolutism. Witness in Jenkins and Perez's consideration of a multiverse a continued faith in "laws of physics" and "forms of life". Such trans-universe vitalism in view, it is not surprising that the Vatican has lately taken a keen interest in astrobiology (Pontifical Academy of Sciences 2009). For Vatican thinkers at a November 2009 meeting on astrobiology, the question was not whether God could create life beyond Earth or beyond Earth-like environments — of course He could — but whether humans might learn more about the Creation from knowing about such zones.

But extraterrestrial relativism may also be a tool for more thoroughgoing reframings of life on Earth. Another rhetorical move that an extraterrestrial relativism permits is a folding-back toward rethinking Earth "itself" (a theme iterated by Battaglia and by Valentine). Such bending-backs to think about alternative Earths in these days of environmental crisis tend, however, to unwind relativistic frames, asking humans to think about the uninhabitable Earths that may result from continued human depredation of the planet. In this way, extraterrestrial relativism is recuperated into more normative claims about life on Earth.

Extraterrestrial Earths

At the 2005 meeting on Astrobiology at Woods Hole, Philip Crane, who studies exosolar planets, described worlds that might support life as "other Earths". The phrase flummoxed many participants, who protested that *our* Earth is the only one there is; "Earth-*like* planets" might be a better term, they offered. But the framing also suggested its negative image: reimaginings of Earth as other than it is — a kind of speculative extraterrestrial relativism, bent back to respin "Earth". Interest in the extraterrestrial, after all, always comes with an attitude toward the terrestrial. Doom-and-gloom Cold War visions had escape from Earth as a necessity for survival in an apocalyptic age in which humanity was considered to be teetering on the brink of nuclear self-immolation (and persists these days in commercial NewSpacers' motivations for designing "exit strategies" for leaving a ruined Earth). More recent environmentalist attitudes have Earth as the only planet we have, one we must steward and love. The cautionary tales told in both narratives relativise Earth in the service of more absolute moralities.

Let me make a partial inventory of what I call "extraterrestrial Earths". I offer this historical list to point to the emergence of an extraterrestrial mode of thinking about the planet. After this detour, I return to the question of why an "extraterrestrial relativism" has come into articulation in the contemporary moment, what it might betoken, and how we might understand its limits.

In 1969, Buckminster Fuller argued in *Operating Manual for Spaceship Earth* that the modern world was first connected by those he called the Great Pirates, those mavericks who in traversing the sea comprehended how the globe could be connected and created through the lines of their repeated routes between nations and empires. Using such practices as triangulation — the taking of bearings from two sites such that a third can be fixed — they filled the world with imaginary triangles, shapes that wedged the earth into segments that could be mapped *to scale*, and that could therefore allow these agents to scale up their own traveling enterprises. Fuller's geometric and utopian vision of world history inspired his invention of the geodesic dome, a sphere constructed of triangles (though global Earth, of course, was also partially fashioned out of a more terrible, not unrelated, geometry called the triangle trade). Earth geometrised became an armature, a ship.

The famous Apollo image of Earth from space smooths that territory into something called "the globe". And for many viewers, the image of the Earth from space is not an image of Earth as ground, but an image of *Earth as sea* (famously so pronounced by Arthur C. Clarke: "How inappropriate to call this planet earth when it is quite clearly Ocean" [quoted in Lovelock 1990: 102]. This distant vision has been in the aid of a return to intimacy with the planet, what Donna Haraway calls a "yearning for the physical sensuousness of a wet and blue-green Earth" (1995: 174). Lifted above the ocean that Edmund Burke in 1757 named as the signature symbol of the sublime — that which overwhelms with terror and beauty — we embrace the blue planet as sensual home, as what atmospheric chemist James Lovelock called "Gaia". Earth not undone, but redone as Ocean. But the ocean also undoes Earth, too — and not only because of the uncanniness of an ocean as at once of us and not of us, but more, because the ocean becomes a metaphor for outer space. The sea

of space, the sea of stars, turns Earth into an island —
This Island Earth, as the 1955 science-fiction film had
it. But Earth is redone here, once more, for the idea of
the island suggests *other* islands and turns the space
between into a sea. Think only of the names of spaceships sent to Mars: *Mariner, Viking*. Here, astropoetics
is astronautics. For scientists who believe, with phys-
icist and astrobiologist Paul Davies, that life-as-we-
know-it may have originated as microbial life in an
ancient Martian ocean and then been ferried to Earth
on meteorites — the claim that Rothschild and Mancinelli sought, in part, to think through — the space
between Earth and Mars becomes very much like a sea,
with currents, eddies, pulls. Earth and Mars become
islands in an archipelagic ecology, ocean worlds in a
larger ocean. Space is not a "lifeless" sea in this imaginary (or, if it is, it is certainly not a space of calm —
nor, even, perhaps, a "space". These days, near-Earth
space is more like "an environment", or "ecology"
[Olson 2010]).

Mars and Earth have long been locked in relative
comparison — Lovelock's Gaia hypothesis, which suggested that one could read Earth's atmosphere as an
index of life, was first inspired by his meditation on
how one might look for life on Mars by seeking spec-
trographic traces of organically produced compounds.
These days, scientists looking for life on Mars scout for
microbes analogous to those archaebacteria on Earth
that live in such sites as deep-sea hydrothermal vents.
That project has the ricochet effect of making por-
tions of Earth into analogs for other worlds: turning
parts of the Utah desert into Mars, parts of the Arctic

into Jupiter's moon, Europa. Submerged in the sea of space, Earth acquires extraterrestrial characteristics. It becomes not only one planet among others, but also a planet that points to and even contains its others. Part-Martian Earth gathers to itself extraterrestrial relatives. An ocean world floating in a more capacious ocean turns Earth not into an ark, perhaps, but into a submarine, whose distinction from its outside is a differential, not an absolute. Not Buckminster Fuller's Spaceship Earth, but Submersible Gaia.

And Gaia is resilient. Less than an avatar of harmony, it is a cybernetic system, and it can do without humanity. This genre of extraterrestrial relativism does not care about humans. But humanity cannot do without a narrative about Earth, even a transformed one. In her dissertation on American astronautics, "American Extreme", Valerie Olson writes that

> Contemporary American ecologists imagine the future of life on Earth in astronautical terms as a kind of 'return' to an original planet, such as ex-NASA contractor James Lovelock's 'Gaia', or as an arrival to an utterly hostile one, such as Peter Ward's vengeful 'Medea'. There is also Bill McKibben's 'Eaarth', the title of his book predicting the human need to adjust to the permanent transformation of our planet. The book was released with jacket image featuring a small whole Earth rising — or setting — behind a giant black 'X' (2010: 9).

Recursively operated extraterrestrial relativism becomes a survival strategy, one that returns to humanity as the arbiter and measure of Earthly health. In this sense, this species of extraterrestrial relativism may have something in common with what Clifford Geertz (1984) described as "anti-anti-relativism" — not a double-negatived position that simply snaps back to relativism fullstop, but rather a position that indexes a commitment to understanding how conditions relative to which a phenomenon is to be understood are themselves arrived at.

The Objective Conditions of Extraterrestriality

Why is this materialising now, this extraterrestrial imagination? Olson writes that, for today's science, the "extreme" has come to be "regarded as a vital site (a place or condition) in which essential truths and proofs emerge", and that, more broadly, in American popular culture, the extreme is now used "to signify 'ultimate' generative, liberatory, alternative, and transcendental states of being; there are extreme sports, extreme foods, and extreme makeovers" (2010: 7). For Olson, the extreme is bound up with particularly American stories about limits, frontiers — and in that sense is not a relativist frame at all, but rather an argument for continued exploration in a neo-colonial key.

Sociologist Melinda Cooper suggests that life's newfound extraterrestrial elasticity is not only a function of work in the biosciences, but is also a function of capitalism:

the notion of life itself is undergoing a dramatic destandardisation such that the life sciences are increasingly looking to the extremes rather than the norms of biological existence. Importantly, these new ways of theorising life are never far removed from a concern with new ways of mobilising life as a technological resource (2008: 32).

Cooper argues that attention to extreme life forms is coincident with a capitalism anticipating and seeking to overcome its own ecological limits. In the wake of the Club of Rome's "Limits to Growth" report of 1972, which predicted environmental collapse if world industry and population continued to grow exponentially, capitalists began looking out for new modes of capital accumulation. Rejecting the geochemical finitude of Earth as the last word on limits, Reagan-era futurologists chided the Club of Rome for a failure of imagination for not anticipating the promise of biotechnology. Cooper detects in contemporary interest in extreme life forms — in researches into how biological systems continually redefine the limits of life — raw ideological material for fresh kinds of capital that burrow into the generativity of living things to create new fantasies of endless frontiers of surplus. That framing suggests that the "extreme" or "limit" may be, like the "mania" that Emily Martin (2009) finds valorised in popular culture and psychology, a sign not of biology unbound, but of its binding toward a political economic purpose (in this context, the appearance of the extreme in high-art worlds may also be a symptom, as with Eduardo Kac and Avital Ronell's 2008 bioart book, *Life Extreme*).

But I want to offer another reading. For many of the scientists I know, the "extreme" is not always about testing humans and their institutions — as in

Olson's excellent ethnography in which this is very much the case for her astronaut interlocutors — but is rather about relativising biology, and, by extension, "nature". This is not the "anthropomorphised cosmos" (127) Olson found in her research, but rather a kind of nonhuman — even post-human — relativism. It may intersect with the recent philosophy and art movement called "speculative realism", which seeks to produce philosophies and aesthetic objects that do not privilege or orient toward the human (Brassier 2007).

Still, yet another folding-back seems necessary to this analysis. Advocates of privatised space travel, of asteroids as destinations for exploration, and Sin-gularitarians often conjure their visions of extreme futures with respect to very human concerns. In some cases, such people speak from addresses of class and race privilege, and, in that sense, their extraterres-trial relativism represents not just a humanist point of departure, but an elite vanguardist one. Of course, even in less humanly oriented extraterrestrial relativ-isms — human locations and histories are ever-pres-ent. As indeed they are in speculative realism, which, for all its anti-humanism, actually posits a particular kind of nature (machinic, unyielding, sublime), and therefore, as Gayatri Spivak (1988) might have it, hosts within it invisible authors who deny their authorising and authoritative presence. Karen Barad's "agential realism" (2007), which posits that reality always man-ifests as such — comes to matter — with respect to an observing and participating agent, offers another use-ful query for speculative realism.

And for comparative relativism. The various flavors of extraterrestrial relativisms I have discussed here exist at the uneasy interface of speculative realism and agential realism, with "reality" at once abstracted away from human and organismic concerns and never quite achieving escape velocity. One might add to Casper Bruun Jensen et al's catalog of kinds of comparative relativism *speculative relativism* and *agential relativism*. In the hybrid of those two that is extraterrestrial relativism, the very nature of nature — as a space of the real, as a space of/for agency — may be becoming unmoored, something like the aquatic cyborg bodies in the novel *Starfish* with which I opened, working at the limits of categories and phenomena.

Works Consulted

Astronomy and Astrophysics Advisory Committee (2009), "Worlds Beyond: A Strategy for the Detection and Characterization of Exoplanets", Report of the ExoPlanet Task Force, Washington D.C. http://www.nsf.gov/mps/ast/aaac/exoplanet_task_force/reports/exoptf_final_report.pdf.

Barad, Karen (2007), *Meeting the Universe Halfway: Quantum Physics and the Entanglement of Matter and Meaning.* Durham: Duke University Press.

Battaglia, Debbora, (ed.) (2005), *E.T. Culture: Anthropology in Outerspaces.* Durham: Duke University Press.

Battaglia, Debbora (2012), "Arresting Hospitality: The Case of the 'Handshake in Space'", in Mattei Candea and Giovanni da Col (eds.), "Special issue—The Return to Hospitality: Strangers, Guests and Ambiguous Encounters", *Journal of the Royal Anthropological Institute*, 18.1: 76-89.

——— (2012), "Coming in at an Unusual Angle: Exo-Surprise and the Fieldworking Cosmonaut", in D. Battaglia, V. Olson and D. Valentine (eds.), *Extreme: Limits and Horizons of the Once and Future Cosmos. Special Issue. Anthropological Quarterly*, 85.4: 1089-106.

Brassier, Ray (2007), "The Enigma of Realism", in *Collapse II: Speculative Realism.* Falmouth: Urbanomic, 15-54.

Carwardine, Mark (2008), *Extreme Nature.* New York: Harper.

Choy, Tim (2011), *Ecologies of Comparison: An Ethnography of Endangerment in Hong Kong.* Durham: Duke University Press.

Cooper, Melinda (2007), "Life, Autopoiesis, Debt: Inventing the Bioeconomy", in *Distinktion*, 14: 25-43.

Cosgrove, D. (1994), "Contested Global Visions: One-World, Whole-Earth, and the Apollo Space Photographs", in *Annals of the Association of American Geographers*, 84.2: 270-94.

Curtsinger, Bill (2005), *Extreme Nature: Images from the World's Edge*. White Star.

Franklin, Sarah, (2007), *Dolly Mixtures: The Remaking of Genealogy*. Durham: Duke University Press.

Franklin, Sarah and Helen Ragoné (1998), *Reproducing Reproduction: Kinship, Power, and Technological Innovation*. Philadelphia: University of Pennsylvania Press.

Fuller, Buckminster (1969), *Operating Manual for Spaceship Earth*. Carbondale: Southern Illinois University Press.

Garb, Y.J. (1985), "The Use and Misuse of the Whole Earth Image", in *Whole Earth Review*, 18-25.

Geertz, Clifford (1984), "Distinguished Lecture: Anti anti-relativism", in *American Anthropologist*, 86.2: 263-77.

Haraway, Donna (1995), "Cyborgs and Symbionts: Living Together in the New World Order", in Chris Hables Gray (ed.) with the assistance of Heidi J. Figueroa-Sarriera and Steven Mentor, *The Cyborg Handbook*, xi-xx. New York: Routledge.

Harmelin, J.G., J. Vacelet and P. Vasseur (1985), "Dark Submarine Caves: An Extreme Environment and a Refuge Biotope", in *Tethys*, 11.3-4: 214-29.

Hartouni, Valerie (1997), *Cultural Conceptions: On Reproductive Technologies and the Remaking of Life*. Minneapolis: University of Minnesota Press.

Helmreich, Stefan (2000), *Silicon Second Nature: Culturing Artificial Life in a Digital World*, updated with a new preface (hardcover edition, 1998). Berkeley: University of California Press.

——— (2009), *Alien Ocean: Anthropological Voyages in Microbial Seas*. Berkeley: University of California Press.

Jasanoff, Sheila (2004), "Heaven and Earth: The Politics of Environmental Images", in Sheila Jasanoff and M. Martello (eds.), *Earthly Politics: Local and Global in Environmental Governance*, 31-52. Cambridge, MA: MIT Press.

Jenkins, Alejandro and Gilad Perez (2010), "Looking for Life in the Multiverse", in *Scientific American*, 302.1: 42-49.

Jensen, Casper Bruun et al (2011), "Comparative Relativism: Symposium on an Impossibility", in *Common Knowledge*, 17.1: 1-12.

Kac, Eduardo and Avital Ronell (2008), *Life Extreme: An Illustrated Guide to New Life*. Paris: Dis Voir.

Lovelock, James (1990), "Hands up for the Gaia Hypothesis", in *Nature*, 344: 100-102.

McGuirk, Kevin (1997), "A.R. Ammons and the Whole Earth", in *Cultural Critique*, 37: 131-58.

McKibben, Bill (2010), *Eaarth: Making a Life on a Tough New Planet*. New York: Times Books.

MacElroy, R.D. (1974), "Some Comments on the Evolution of Extremophiles", *Biosystems*, 6: 74-75.

Mancinelli, R.L., M.R. White and L.J. Rothschild (1998), "Biopan-Survival I: Exposure of the Osmophiles *Synechococcus Sp.* (Nageli) and *Haloarcula Sp.* to the Space Environment", in *Advances in Space Research*, 22.3: 327-34.

Markley, Robert (2005), *Dying Planet: Mars in Science and the Imagination*. Durham: Duke University Press.

Messeri, Lisa (2011), "Placing Outer Space: An Earth-Based Ethnography of Extraterrestrial Worlds". PhD

Dissertation, Program in History, Anthropology, and Science, Technology, and Society, Massachusetts Institute of Technology.

Martin, Emily (2009), *Bipolar Expeditions: Mania and Depression in American Culture*. Princeton: Princeton University Press.

Moulder, J.W. (1974), "Intercellular Parasitism: Life in an Extreme Environment", in *Journal of Infectious Diseases*, 130.3: 300-306.

Olson, Valerie (2010), "American Extreme: An Ethnography of Astronautical Visions and Ecologies". PhD Dissertation, Department of Anthropology, Rice University.

— — — (2012), "Political ecology in the extreme: asteroid activism and the making of an environmental solar system", in D. Battaglia, V. Olson, D. Valentine (eds.), *Extreme: Limits and Horizons of the Once and Future Cosmos. Special Issue. Anthropological Quarterly*, 85.4: 1027-44.

Overbye, Dennis (2010), "Microbe Finds Arsenic Tasty; Redefines Life", in *New York Times*, 2 December.

Pontifical Academy of Sciences (2009), Program for Study Week on Astrobiology, 6-10 November 2009. Vatican City.

Rabinow, Paul (1999), *French DNA: Trouble in Purgatory*. Chicago: University of Chicago Press.

Rapp, Rayna (2000), *Testing Women, Testing the Fetus: The Social Impact of Amniocentesis in America*. New York: Routledge.

Rothschild, Lynn J. and Rocco Mancinelli (2001), "Life in Extreme Environments", in *Nature* 409: 1092-101.

Spivak, Gayatri (1988), "Can the Subaltern Speak?", in

Cary Nelson and Lawrence Grossberg (eds.), *Marxism and the Interpretation of Culture*, 271-313. Urbana, IL: University of Illinois Press.

Strathern, Marilyn (1992), *After Nature: English Kinship in the Late Twentieth Century*. Cambridge: Cambridge University Press.

Valentine, David, Valerie Olson and Debbora Battaglia (2009), "Encountering the Future: Anthropology and Outer Space", in *Anthropology News*, 50: 11, 15.

Valentine, David (2012), "Exit Strategy: Profit, Cosmology, and the Future of Humans in Space", in D. Battaglia, V. Olson and D. Valentine (eds.), *Extreme: Limits and Horizons of the Once and Future Cosmos. Special Issue: Anthropological Quarterly*, 85.4: 1045-67.

Viveiros de Castro, Eduardo (1998), "Cosmological Deixis and Amerindian Perspectivism", in *Journal of the Royal Anthropological Institute* 4.3: 469-88.

— — — (2009), "The Nazis and the Amazonians, but then again, Zeno", in Simpósio "Comparative Relativism", Copenhagen, IT University, 4-5 September 2009. http://nansi.abaetenet.net/abaetextos/the-nazis-or-the-amazonians-but- then-again-zeno.

Watts, Peter (1999), *Starfish*. New York: TOR.

Woese, Carl R., Otto Kandler and Mark L. Wheelis (1990), "Towards a Natural System of Organisms: Proposal for the Domains Archaea, Bacteria, and Eucarya", in *Proceedings of the National Academy of Sciences* 87: 4576-79.

Wolfe-Simon, Felisa et al (2010), "A Bacterium That Can Grow by Using Arsenic Instead of Phosphorus", in *Science*, DOI: 10.1126/science.1197258.

SCAVENGING THE
FUTURE OF THE ARCHIVE

A Conversation between Henriette Gunkel
and Daniel Kojo Schrade

Henriette Gunkel: I would like to begin this conversation with a focus on the archive as a source for the future-oriented and the speculative since the archive was one of the first aspects we discussed in relation to your work. In your abstract paintings you tend to bring in otherworldly figures and narratives that inspire you and that seem to be familiar to an Afrofuturist canon, like Lee "Scratch" Perry or Jean-Michel Basquiat, for example. But you also focus on narratives and figures that reflect on your geopolitical positionings often ignored in the context of Afrofuturism — narratives and figures that are often hidden and out of reach of public knowledge, and in a way reference art practices that are not widely considered as part of black cultures. One example is your *Brother Beethoven* series for which you turned to classical music and researched the history of the Afro-European violinist George Bridgetower and the inspiration and challenges he posed for Ludwig van Beethoven. You understand this archival work as a retro-futurist approach, as a way of digging the future out of the archive — which also means that you look at archival material differently, as always already including the futuristic (either in terms of form or narrative) which seems to allow you a certain level of fictioning in your art practice.

Based on the conversations we had, and my engagement with your art practice, I began to rethink my own approach to Africanist science-fictional interventions and became increasingly interested in temporal strategies and the aesthetics of time, in forms of the futuristic that do not refer to typical science-fictional or Afrofuturist tropes, such as Martians, spaceships and hyper-technology, to name a few. I shifted my focus on forms and senses of otherworldliness that we could draw from the past and that would help us to develop a genealogy, if you wish, of futurist interventions in art practices on the African continent that do not necessarily announce themselves as such. Art practices that precede recent science-fictional interventions which received much attention on a global scale, such as Jean-Pierre Bekolo's *Les Saignantes* (2005), for example, or Wanuri Kahiu's *Pumzi* (2009), which are widely considered as the first African science-fiction films. So I invited you to the University of Bayreuth, Germany where I was working at that time and which has a long history of African Studies (with all its problematic implications). The idea was to visit an archive of African art, images and objects together and to explore, over a period of two weeks, what a genealogy of the futuristic could look like. We entitled these two weeks *Scavenging the Future of the Archive*.

Daniel Kojo Schrade: The idea of digging the future out of the archive has been around for a while, but continues to be an extremely relevant strategy. There is still a lot of material to dig out and to re-contextualise. Afrofuturism immediately has to do with research, bringing the future and the past together, while activating the space in-between. Claiming that space in-between is a very research-heavy endeavor. Looking backwards while imagining oneself in the future and being aware of the space in-between requires a lot of discipline.

The archive of the University of Bayreuth's IwalewaHaus consists of an art section, an audio and video archive, a poster section, and an ethnographic collection foremost from Africa. The main geographical focus of the collection is Nigeria, though some important pieces are from Sudan, Mozambique, Tanzania and the Democratic Republic of Congo. Our focus in the two weeks in the archive together was on collections of contemporary, popular and modern art, the audio archive, and selected pieces from the ethnographic collection. One of the reasons why the IwalewaHaus archive is a great research field is its lack of a consequent collecting strategy. The many sections of the collection have multiple nuclei, shaped by "collectors" with a wide range of capability. It was therefore exciting, specifically from my point of view, my artistic perspective, to dig into this extravagant collection. We had to work like foragers. We rummaged through the archive trying to find the courage that would matter on our mission to do fundamental Afrofuturistic research: *Scavenging the Future of the*

Archive. We first studied all the visual components we were able to find in the audio archive, which contains more than two thousand CDs, LPs, singles, MCs and tapes of the work of foremost African composers and musicians from the 1950s onwards. This rather unconventional engagement with the audio collection led to a four-minute, animated slide collage, which uses twenty of the LP covers and Arthur Russel's composition *The Platform on the Ocean* as the sound track. The graphic design of these selected covers depict space in a very futuristic way, whether this is a photographed or painted urban space, a landscape, an interior, or the light in the background of a portrait.

Figure 1. Ousmane Faye (1980). Painting on glass, 14cm x 12cm.

Back in the main collection we came across several works that were interesting for us, including a beautiful little 14cm x 12cm painting from the 1980s, on glass

by the artist Ousmane Faye. The digitised archive catalogue describes the piece as follows:

Portrait of male in front of white background. The
figure wears a yellow dress with white v-neck, which
merges into a blue triangular pattern, pointing one of
its edges downwards. In addition the figure wears a
red fez on their head.

While there is nothing wrong with the description,
which foremost aims to make the piece identifiable,
it misses out on equally relevant facts. Faye's painting additionally represents the most substantial basic
components of colour-theory and geometry. The four
geometric basic shapes — the circle, the rectangle, the
triangle and the square — are key to the composition
of the piece. The dress represents the circle, the fez
represents the rectangle, the triangular pattern represents the triangle, and a line surrounding the entire
piece represents the square. The colour composition
of the painting is just as consequent. Faye used the
basic colours Cyan (red), Magenta (blue), Yellow and
Key (black). Every imaginable colour can be mixed
based on the CMYK colour model. While Faye's colour
choice stands for the fundamentals of human visual
perception; circle, rectangle, triangle and the square
are the basis for the calculation of volumes and areas.
They are the basis for geometry and astronomy, central
for the calculation of shape, size, relative position of
objects (planets) and the properties of space; the foundation for the digitisation of space (Ehrhart-Polynom-
inal).

HG: The discussion we had around Faye's piece allowed us to think more specifically around the aesthetic forms of time. Time as a form. The futuristic. We came across, for example, images of the works by the late Congolese artist Bodys Isek Kingelez who built these fantastic utopian city models, which we can easily recognise as futuristic, as urban fabulations of a Kinshasa to come. Or the works of Méga Mingiedi, who in a way follows in the footsteps of Kingelez and creates large-format drawings of imaginary takes on Kinshasa that include elements of collage. In a way Mingiedi creates his own forms of skylines which can also be understood as urban timelines. In some of his drawings/collages you can find colonial figures like Leopold II next to Patrick Lumumba, or Mobuto Sese Seko next to skyscrapers and images and signs of capitalism and commercialisation/advertising. One of the works we looked at is Mingiedi's *Kin Delestage* from 2010, which is a drawing-collage in extreme landscape format (45cm x 245cm). In addition to the presence of historical events, Mingiedi maps out a potential future for Kinshasa represented by skyscrapers with antennas and satellite dishes on their rooftops. In the foreground his intense layering of drawn lines produces a multi-layered information highway that refers to futuristic tropes/concepts of speed and acceleration that he envisions for a city such as Kinshasa, while remaining committed to history and the struggles for independence and its aftermath. As such, the piece can be read as a "seismographic skyline". So of course, Kingelez and Mingiedi's art works were easier and more accessible than the image that you referred to by Ousmane Faye.

One of the most challenging moments was the interest in masks that the archival work triggered — which, as we know, occupy a rather problematic object of study in the field of African Studies, but also more broadly in white conceptions of "Africa". In the course of our workshop and through your reading I became interested in masks, for the first time, really, and in particular around the notion of fictioning in your reading of them. So we dared to ignore anthropological or religious knowledge production around those objects and produced our own reading. And maybe our focus on masks is not so surprising after all as it also developed out of our interest in the Dogon cosmology — the Dogon in Mali who understand themselves as descendants from Sirius B which they could astronomically reference correctly long before any Western technical devices could capture the star that was only photographed and hence "proven" in its existence in the 1970s. Every fifty years — this is how long it takes for Sirius B to complete its orbit — large-scale festivities take place in which the mask becomes an

Figure 2 and 3. Dogon Masks (West-Africa) and Bedu Mask, Nafana (West-Africa).

important element.

One image that we came across shows such celebration and ritual. The masks here, as you pointed out, are not only disguising the face but the main part of each mask extends above the head and as such extends the body and connects it with something broader. It can thus be understood as a communication device. As such this image and the masks resonate with Sun Ra's myth-science and how artists and performers re-create themselves — in Sun Ra's case in times of experienced oppression and discrimination. The Dogon masks further point to the fictioning aspect of technology, or an understanding of technology that moves beyond a common understanding of science and which refers to different, possibly spiritual ways of making use of the tools available. We can also find this approach in your own paintings in which you use analogue antennas, umbrellas, or even a flat iron.

DKS: Communication is indeed another key component in my reading of the masks of the archive we have studied. Masks are communication tools in a broad sense and some of them seem to have extensions for more sophisticated communication beyond the terrestrial space. You have already mentioned the Sirius B cult of the Dogon people of Mali. We also looked at a Bedu mask of the Nafana people, which are located not far from the Dogon, in north-west Ghana, Bukina Faso. The mask consists of three sections, a trapezoid lower part, a rectangular centre part and circular top. The geometric-abstract painting of the piece is limited to triangles and squares. Two holes in the lower section and support structures on the back indicate how the mask was worn. So the circular top, sitting on the rectangular central section, is actually in the position of an antenna. The mask turns into an emanation-tool, a receiver, a communication device.

I am applying this reading to many Senufo and Dogon masks, as well as to selected architecture, objects and two-dimensional works from West Africa. My Ghanaian background is not the only reason for my interest in the re-reading of these charged cultural key-stones. Through my own work, I permanently negoti-ate extended communication, the navigation of spaces and the complexity of time. One of the repeated motifs I am using in my painting, drawing and performance work is the umbrella. I read a lot into the umbrella. It is a mobile device and you can carry it. It is a communi-cation device as well because if you invite someone to walk with you under your umbrella, for example, you come into very close contact and can talk. It is a crafted space, with immediate exceptional conditions and it is a space that can travel. Also, if you flip the umbrella around, it could function as a satellite dish or a con-tainer, a vessel, so it has multiple meanings depending on how you position it.

HG: This focus on technology and communication devices in your art practice and your research is really intriguing — how you strategically repurpose existing technologies to re-engineer a collective understanding of politics and diaspora. In your work you seem to demand an investment in technological innovation irrespective of the market, consumerist needs and SF capital by focusing less on new forms of technology, but, more importantly, on new forms of using existing technology. I read your work as fictioning technology but also as pointing to a spiritual use. In that sense you seem to bypass the question of access and the techno-logical/digital divide, for example, and refocus our attention to what is already easily available to us.

What I could see from your research, though, is that you do not approach devices such as the umbrella naively, in that you conceptualise them as uncontested and unmarked devices. You seem to be aware of the violence and risks built into these devices, and their potentiality to create inequality and exploitation. In your research around the umbrella, for example, you trace their racialised uses and repurpose them from a theoretical and political diasporic position. In another conversation, you argued that these mutated technol-ogies tap into "survival strategies that were, and still are, existential in the depths of the (Black) Atlantic, in outer space, or in social spaces that aren't clearly defined — in spaces in-between". Maybe you could talk a bit more about these spaces in-between, also in relation to your own work.

DKS: As we all know, the dimensions of space and time are far from being set in stone. In our current, rather linear-functioning society, I am interested in concepts that have the potential to help shape important aspects of the future. The technological aspect of Afrofuturism is not so much of interest to me. I try to re-contextualise the past in order to better understand the challenging present, while considering future concepts.

Figure 4. © Daniel Kojo Schrade (2010), *Blueberry Hill*, video
still. Performance: Bayreuth.

I am an artist working mostly with mediums like the
body and paint. In many of my performances, I use
my body movements to spin a "net" throughout the
performance space. At certain locations they get tied
together and these intersections serve like synapses
where, instead of neurological signals, various sounds
get communicated by me talking, singing and creating
noise. The "net" then functions similar to the strings of
an instrument with the exception that its soundbox is
the space.

Devices such as the umbrella that I can literally attach to my body, and extend my body with,
are important within my work. As you mentioned,
socio-culturally the umbrella has a very rich and complex history and artists seemed to be interested in
them long before me. For example, the French painter

Jean-Baptiste Debret (1768-1848), who depicted colonial life in Brazil. When I discovered his lithographs, I realised that he included umbrellas in a substantial number of his works. It seems as if at some point the umbrella took over by becoming the main narrator in/ of his works. In one of the pieces there is a servant, holding a closed umbrella. He is not just carrying it for the "master"; he is wearing it. It is almost like a musket, a safety device, a weapon, and as such way more than just a service tool. Although the body of the servant is depicted as much smaller than that of the "master", extended by the umbrella and positioned in the centre of the print, the servant ends up being taller. We do not know whether this image composition means that Debret consciously considered the subtext of the piece, or whether he was rather a rapporteur, a witness of a moment. Besides its technical practicality — providing shadow, or shelter from rain — the umbrella is certainly a status symbol. Potentially extending the height of a body, marking and extending the space a body can claim while walking or sitting. The Ghanaian Aschanti people use umbrellas as such a signifier, to mark the social status of those who walk or sit within their space. So the dimensions of these umbrellas really matter.

For me painting was never just about depicting an object or a landscape. It is very important for me to go beyond that. So I start with information that comes from my own cultural archive and negotiate these complexities in a limited space, a canvas or a performance space. My work is heavily research-based and nurtured by a complex culmination of information stored in my own cultural archive. One would not necessarily be able to reveal all the layers of information that are present in most of my paintings and performances. Painting allows me to work with layers, I can take advantage of the synergy of multiple interacting layers. If I prime a canvas yellow and, after several layers, end up painting it blue, the yellow will still matter. A colour will generally have a very different presence depending on what other colour is underneath. This is true for all items that come from my archive, not only in relation to colour. All layers and their content, abstract or representational, simultaneously matter — independent from their materiality and position.

HG: I want to follow up a bit on this complex layering of paint in your work — which allows a colour to disappear and reappear elsewhere, to resurface differently, as you mention. In addition to the layers of paint, you include charcoal lines, defining scriptural fragments and figurative elements. The scriptural fragments are often visible as sequences of letters that refer to fragments of a word that we cannot see in full but can often still make sense of. It draws our attention to the idea of fragments, of what is left — the residue, in a way. This way you create this in-between space that you referred to earlier and that you relate to the diasporic experience which first and foremost means moving in and out of space differently, understanding space differently. An experience that in a way extends beyond the canvas and can be found in unlikely spaces, in the extraterrestrial, for example — or as Jared Saxton puts it: "Black life is not lived in the world that the world lives in, but it is lived underground, in outer space" (2011: 28).

So we clearly have this spatial dimension in your work. But your art practice, the conscious layering of paint, also produces a complicated temporality. Whether you use over-sized canvases or miniatures your work is created in stages. As Tobias Nagl has pointed out, your work is "separated by breaks, in which [Daniel Kojo Schrade] applies layer upon layer of paint, demarcates, sticks, modifies, scrapes away, or recontextualizes through added figurative or scriptural elements" (2010: 17). So you literally leave your work for days and weeks before you add another layer to the work, which brings in the element of duration (in a Bergsonian sense of conceptualising time) to your art practice, in itself a temporal process that allows the palimpsest of time to emerge in your art works. In addition to your use of archival material, your work produces its own force to think about and act upon time (not only on space) and hence provides a very specific form of time-travel — a time-travel that is not understood as moving between clearly distinguishable dimensions of time. In fact, your painting practice subverts the layers of time as clearly distinguishable between past, present and future. As such your abstract paintings operate similarly to montage and collage — both used as conscious temporal practices in Afrofuturist works, as the works of Wangechi Mutu or Ellen Gallegher, for example, show, or the essayfilms of John Akomfrah.

We have mentioned earlier the practice of collage in relation to Mingiedi's work which combines practices

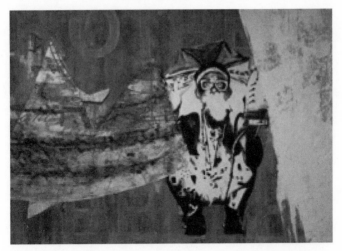

Figure 5. © Daniel Kojo Schrade (2008), *Afronauts (Brother Beethoven) 08C04*, oil-acrylic paint on canvas: 215cm x 380cm.

of cut-up of existing images, which also always means cutting the line of association, and the subsequent, at least partial re-assemblage of new associations, a form of montage of previously disparate fragments, that are reassembled into new worlds. Hence, we have an understanding of collage as possibly creating visual fictional spaces from fragmentation, as a form of world-making in mutation. It is this fictioning element of montage and collage that interests me and that I can also see in your art practice. You have elements of this in your painting — in your use of the archival figures, for example, in your inclusion of references to inspirational figures and texts, such as the crown as a reference to Basquiat, in your layering and reassemblage of fragments that provide a complicated temporal relationship between the different elements. Similar to the practice of collage, you also propose worlds within worlds while consciously working against a linear understanding of time by proposing a rhythm, in a way, that presents itself as an open-ended narrative that visually enters our historical consciousness.

DKS: The repeated stacking and overlapping of various layers within the painting above (*Afronauts 08C04*), indeed works like a painterly palimpsest. The viewer is asked to sense the content in-between the layers. My paintings provide space for multiple cultural dialogs in which the consideration of the conditions and options of such a dialogue is just as important as the dialogue itself. Icons, signs, letters and figurative fragments, which aggregated appear homogeneous, carry subtexts within multiple semantic levels. They allow a flip-flop between heterogeneity and ambivalence. Similar to Lee "Scratch" Perry, who confronts his vis-à-vis with mirrors, this painting holds a mirror up to whatever the viewer is able to decode and pigeonhole.

My non-representational painting is challenged by rather obvious icons, letters and figurative elements, while the painting as such refuses to be decisive. In 1999, after I had produced my first painting entitled *Afronaut*, I turned this title into a leitmotif for an ongoing series of *Afronaut* paintings. Although the Afronaut often appears as a figure that can be interpreted and read as human, carrying some kind of tool or device, Afronauts function as icons on the same level as symbols or written texts. Before the *Afronaut* series, other series entitled *Brother Beethoven*, *Du Bois*, *Gong Gong* or *StopLookListen* contributed and still contribute their leitmotif to my painting. A motif is something that is moved, like a locomotive, a place that moves. In painting, the motif is thus something that has been moved, maybe something that has been moved into the picture from a different context. There are not only motifs in painting, but also in songs, in music of course, but the accusation that motifs can deceive is mainly restricted to the visual arts, to painting — to the "icons" in pictures. The *Afronaut*, however, symbolises/stands for the stranger on the fringes of society, in-between cultures. The stranger who can use this position of exceptional strength to unhinge topoi, symbols and fragments; alienate them and present them beyond common rubrics.

So the multiple layers within the subject can be explored in many ways, beyond fascinating space travels outside of the solar system. Tricksters, similar to Afronauts, for example, are traveling space and time in different, actually more sophisticated ways. They are not limited to conventional measures of time and space. Tricksters are not restricted to conventional technologies; they are very creative in their traveling.

HG: I think you are right, your Afronaut is in a way a trickster and hence operates differently from the Afronaut figure proposed, for example, by Christina de Middel in her photograph essay book *The Afronauts* (2012) — in which she visually tells the story of Zambia during independence, alongside this historical moment's hopes and aspirations, hinged on the person of Edward Makuka Nkoloso. Nkoloso, founder and director of the Lusaka National Academy of Science,

Space Research and Philosophy, and an elementary school teacher with many futuristic visions, imagined a "space-age Zambia", which he formulated in a 1964 newspaper article with the title, "We're going to Mars! WITH A SPACEGIRL, TWO CATS AND A MISSIONARY". He trained ten men and a woman, who was supposed to be the first woman in space. The missionary was warned "not to force Christianity on the people of Mars if they didn't want it". Nkoloso's aim was to launch the rocket from Zambia's Independence Stadium — Zambia would have been on Mars only a few days after independence. Nkoloso's dream was never realised, because, among other issues, the *spacegirl* as well as the two cats had gotten pregnant, and the seven million pounds applied for to the UNESCO were not granted. This past future project is also taken up by Frances Bodomo in her film *Afronauts* (2014) — a still of that film is the cover image of this book.

de Middel, however, takes this narrative as a starting point and translates it into an imagery which uses familiar references to an astronaut figure into an "Africa" context by fabricating the space suit with supposedly "African" cotton textile and next to an elephant. In a way, there is a resemblance to Yinka Shonibare's *Space Walk* (2002), in which the space explorer is similarly identifiable as an Afronaut due to the "African" fabric used — and here it is important to remember that Shonibare was already working with African cloths in the 1990s, so long before de Middel. What is not acknowledged in *The Afronauts* photo essay — and what is so visible and compelling in your work — is the alternative ways of moving in and out of space. You do not seem to be really interested in space travel as such — or whether projects like the one by Nkoloso were in any way realistic or (rather) disillusional. This is not what you are interested in in your own conceptualis- ation of the Afronaut figure, as you have just pointed out. Your work points to a different conception of space altogether — acknowledging that the violence that constitutes blackness necessarily means moving in and out of space differently, which is also clearly articulated in your insistence on the in-between space. As such the normative dimensions of space — and time as we discussed earlier — do not hold any longer, and your work forces us to theorise and acknowledge both concepts differently. Your work insists on a sense of otherworldliness — in a temporal and spatial sense — that is always already implied in blackness — through movement, alienation, conscious mutation and prac- tices of disidentification in fabulation.

Works Cited

Nagl, Tobias (2010), "Afrolization (Blueberry Hill Dub)", in *AfroSat-1 Catalogue*. Bayreuth: Iwalewa Haus, 16-20.

Sexton, Jared (2011), "The Social Life of Social Death: On Afro-Pessimism and Black Optimism", in *InTensions*, 5: 1-47.

AUTOMATE SEX: XENOFEMINISM, HYPERSTITION AND ALIENATION

Luciana Parisi

The collective Laboria Cuboniks is a timely conjunction of artists, writers and computer programmers, who only came together two years ago, but since then have collaborated to write the "Xenofeminist Manifesto": a work in progress or scaffolding document (as the collective calls it) that addresses theoretical and practical efforts to think — and construct — political models with and through technology and science. As a manifesto, it lays out a series of claims whose axiomatic value is however ampliative or revisable to the extent that it presents itself as a continuous dialogue between entries: Zero, Interrupt, Trap, Parity, Adjust, Carry and OverFlow. Each of these entries can be read autonomously even if they evoke diffracting series of meaning as they accumulate together and pair up, or double to be followed in four verses or directions. The Manifesto is then written as sets of entries that can be expanded upon, added up — and yet each entry gives us specific constrains, directions, rules. What is offered here is a kind of mathematico-geometric architecture of reasoning that orders thoughts as sequences and vectors, but also exposes the dialogical dynamics of the entries, the collective quality of thinking marked by the guerrilla tone of their statements. In short, the Manifesto presents itself as both an axiomatic and experimental thought and indeed, read as a whole, it seems to repeat for us the mantra or question: how can experiments be turned into truths?

This question however is not rhetorical and is instead detonated or forcefully unleashed within and throughout the entries. The question is more an invite and not simply a remark to be raised and left. To pose this question already requires a collective effort to imagine which possible answers are here to be engineered, pushed forward, leaped into, bravely conjectured.

The question is thus posed in and through hyperstitional statements that have future consequences as they direct a political thinking aiming not simply to debunk norms and truths but also to invent structural and systematic models of alien feminisms that can speak to the historical complexity of gender, queer and sexual politics. This is to say that the Manifesto and its statements require us to use a "public key" to make explicit the encrypted data it contains and should not therefore simply be read lyrically, or from what it gives to us at face value. The Manifesto rather asks us to become abstracted from this or that political position. Simply said, it is not telling us to embrace one or the other position, include or exclude this or that gender politics, dismiss or embrace this or that practice. More fundamentally, it is an invitation to redirect our efforts to think together the question of how: how to force the localism of gender politics to construct general strategies for a trans-politics; how to develop models that address the specificities of practices and yet enable these practices to scale up towards common aims, extending out from physical and cognitive constraints; how to increase particular knowledge in order to increase collective action for the structuring of new truths.

The Manifesto should not be read as a declaration of intent, but must be addressed as an exercise in hyperstition: a thought experiment or an enabler of the future. Here the inexistent can be made explicit by and through a practical and theoretical enforcing or naming of truths in the face of indeterminacy, of engineering politics in the face of the relativism of positions. This hyperstitional exercise is, however, part of a wider history and shall be discussed here in relation to critical theory and the political propositions of Donna Haraway's "A Cyborg Manifesto" and the cyberfeminist writings of the 1990s.

Central to critical theory is the view that technoscientific epistemology — or knowledge generated through technoscientific rationalisation or conceptualisation of the real — determines the ontological condition of thought, thus reducing the possible configurations of political subjectivity mainly to what can be known, measured, calculated. If being is restricted to its technoscientific explanation, then it is argued that the political project for an autonomous thought beyond technocapitalism can be declared as defeated. This anti-technoscientific view that works to preserve the ontological truth of thought (that is, of political thought autonomous from the technoenvironment in which it operates) necessarily identifies technology with power on the one hand and separates the sacredness of human thought from the mechanical and automated systems invented by humans on the other. Whilst this sacredness is precisely what has become annulled by the neoliberal paradoxical condition for which the means of politics are the same as the means of profit (i.e. machinic and deterritorialised subjectivity), the cultivation of the human spirit in critical theory is at best idealistic as it assumes that the ontological condition of thought must remain immune from what humans actually think, do and make. The longing for a common state of immunity from the technoscientific instrumentalisation or artificialisation of thought constitutes, one could argue, the bedrock of critical theory.

Importantly, however, this argument for the separation of ontology from epistemology has been challenged by a feminist critique of technology, deploying a hyperstitional activation of material imaginaries (i.e. the future activation of material situations) that irreversibly breaks the equivalence between nature and woman on the one hand, and human and non-mechanical reasoning on the other. Hyperstition here concerns not the longing for a lost past or the wish for an impossible future, but the meticulous weaving of parts, enveloping the unknown in the present, gnawing at the futurities of the moment.

One cannot underestimate how Haraway's theory of the cyborg, so central to second-order feminism, profoundly challenged the naive view that nature is given and that technology can only mystify the operations of capitalism, that critical thought or the enquiry into the unexplainable is ultimately limited and shall resign itself to the ontological finitude of being. Instead, through a hyperstitial activation of the potentiality of machines, and against the naturalist rejection of technology as an extension of patriarchal logocentrism (and capitalism), the figure of the cyborg radically embraced the constraint of a historical situation in which "epistemology gives us ontology", to use Haraway's phrase (1985). The historical condition of the universality of information and communication systems declared by cybernetics had radically shortened the distance between the "what is" and the "how is" by challenging the biological ground of subjectivity but also pointing at the material becoming of thought.

There is no doubt that the cyborg figuration of the post-millennium has played a central role in the feminist critique of technology through its direct anti-essentialism and anti-naturalist propositions. By arguing for the constructed-ness of subjectivity and the artificiality of being, the cyborg figuration can be perhaps conceived as a radical hyperstitial attempt at exposing the alien or denaturalised fabrication of gender. Similarly, it can be argued that the cyborg as a political figuration was already able to reveal the paradoxical condition of neoliberal technocapitalism in which the (epistemological) making of subjectivity overrides the a priori form of being, and the presumption of an "all too human" thought. This co-existence of a double position in which the technocapitalist making of subjectivity absorbs the transcendental condition of being/ thought has defined the political situation of the late part of the last century in which the universality of the cyborg was politically contrasted with the situatedness of local — yet networked — configurations of subjectivity. In other words, by challenging the first order of feminism — and its essentialist ontology based on the claim for the biological difference of being — Haraway's cyborg manifesto pushed feminist critical theory of technology towards the unsettling ground of a denaturalised form of subjectivity, living off the artificial technoscientific constructions of a no-longer-given thought.

Following the cyborg critique of essentialist feminism and of the patriarchal alliance with technology, other gender strategies have focused on the performativity of language, signs and speech acts, arguing for a political production of meaning emerging from the specific use of signs. One can define this tendency in terms of a "culturalist" strategy of hyper-representation, aiming to radicalise the artificiality of culture by starting from the use of language. This strategy is part of a more general critique against normative discourses and, in turn, against the realisation of the rational project of the enlightenment in a double-edged architecture of governance. However, whilst this approach works to reveal the naturalisation of techniques and technologies of governance, the critical insistence on the cultural — or language-oriented — fabrication of gender also came to be questioned for its tendency to propose a relativistic and fragmented framework, in which the political question of gender became absorbed, as it were, by a neoliberal thirst for fluid signifiers.

The hyperstitional strategies proposed by the cyborg required both dismembering the unification of language whilst highlighting the materiality or the embodiment of language. However, this view had limited the material substrate of gender, i.e. sex, to just another conceptual variable in a linguistic system of signs. From this standpoint, the materiality of gender could only be historically — and thus cognitively — contextualised, showing that materiality is always already mediated by rule-bounded conceptual structures — that is a system of norms. Since here more than ever the semiotic matrix of epistemology allowed for a flexible deconstructing and reconstructing of ontological truths, the politics of the cyborg to some extent risked accelerating the cultural dissipation of the biophysical reality of matter, and of sexual difference. In particular, these semiotic strategies that characterised the feminist strategies in the early 1990s led to the conception of a hybrid form of subjectivity in which sexual difference became decentred from its privileged position in gender politics. The philosophy of sexual difference, and the work of Luce Irigaray in particular, had become particularly contested for its suspicious substantialism or essentialism.

Nevertheless, as the cyborg politics of signs merged with the neoliberal capitalisation of fluid signifiers, language became a cage for gender difference, risking a never-ending relativism of meaning springing from the emphasis on the plurality of local culturalisms. The semiotic exploration of postgendered alliances was questioned for its limits. Postgendered feminism was challenged by the emerging articulation of an imma-nent (and non-discursive) conception of matter, body and sex. Instead of explaining the materiality of sex through the semiotic chain of historically determined events, it became once again urgent to re-articulate the relation between the ontological and epistemological condition of subjectivity beyond representation, and the cognitive structure of meaning. In particular, the invisible plane of affects, the unmeasurable qualities of intensity, the corollary production of ideas, the numerical infinites between os and 1s, pushed cyborg politics further within the matrix of nature and the matrix of the machine. Here the hyperstitional activity involved not only a re-formulation of subjectivity as a human-animal-machine hybrid, but aimed to unearth the fluidity of matter and the infinity of numbers. In particular, Sadie Plant's book *Zeros and Ones* reclaimed the complexity of feminine sexuality, and by bringing together Continental with Anglo-American feminisms, she wrote of the history of computing with the histories of women, from Ada Lovelace's corollary coding for the Babbage machines, to World War II data inputters and phone operators. As women mediated the commu-nication between man and machine, the alliance with techne acquired a feminine tonality that would gen-der the very means of transmission. To claim the fem-inine materiality of the matrix also meant that matter and thought belonged to an immanent plane of multiplicity, instead of being caught in a dualistic mediation between matter and sign. Hence the connection between human and technology above all means that body and machine undergo affective encounters and intensive degrees of change. Here scientific epistemology coincides not with normative discourse, but with its experimental method of probing into the unknown and challenging the determination of truth.

By suspending the analysis of meaning and representation, Plant's cyberfeminism radicalised the political dimension of the body-sex-machine and worked through the speculative character of scientific epistemology (from chaos theory to quantum physics, from molecular biology to information theory) to argue for the indeterminacy of bio-physical materiality. Here sex is not filtered through the lenses of gender, but it is denaturalised, rendered alien from a specific biological bias. This involved not simply a rejection of nature, but the invention of a new philosophy of nature: a re-potentiation of what nature is and can be. If sex does not coincide with biological imperatives, so the body is not limited to the boundaries of the organism but becomes a plane of vectors stretching and curving together to generate assemblages of another kind. Sensation, or the elevation of sensibilities beyond sensori-motor and cognitive functions, enables the body to enter new phases of non-human becomings, a multiplicity of sexes for which new genders have to be invented. Here ontology is, as it were, plunged within the molecular dynamics of matter, offering a continuity of being in the process of becoming, whilst side-skipping the cognitive model of thought and its alleged representation.

Against the relativism of positions, cyberfeminism is committed to hyperstitial tactics to allow a continuous deterritorialisation from norms, rules, positions and pushes to the extremes of the immanent incompleteness of knowing and incompleteness of being. By embracing the Spinozian question, we do not know what a body can do, cyberfeminism had already sided with the promise of technology vis-à-vis becoming one with the dynamic mutations of nature. Here the nature/culture binary is not overcome by debunking the ideological construction of nature. On the contrary, the culturalist assumption about what nature is and can become is disentangled from the classic epistemological belief in a static nature that can be instrumentalised, subsumed and mastered. The cyberfeminist re-habilitation of nature rather addresses the untapped potentialities of matter, whereby molecular alliances across substances prefigure the Promethean qualities of a never-ending nature, claiming back its futurity. In other words, the realist and materialist approach to nature as a plane of becoming enables cyberfeminism to argue for the artificiality of the body-sex and to politically vindicate nature beyond the essentialisms. Here nature can be changed insofar as it is already machinic and open to becoming cultural, so as to affect the production of signs, meanings and representations.

Whilst there is no "given" nature, the invisible activities of natural processes are here taken as instances of the indeterminacies of knowledge and as sources of fictionalised praxis and tactics of becoming other than what one is. From this standpoint, the politics of representation is replaced by "low-grade" activities of becoming, where nature and culture are, as it were, in an auto-affective bifurcating loop, and the sex-gender alliance becomes open to the pragmatics of processes. In short, these alliances are to be determined and are not given by normative and biological truths. This is also the sense of a pragmatic or practical politics where gender and sex can be changed, mutated and re-artic-ulated. However, whilst the cyborg strategy embraces the pragmatic or performative activity of the sign, con-structing the world through the matrix of language, extending the body-sex to artificial manipulations, cyberfeminism rather makes of the body-sex-machine itself a hyperstitional praxis, embedding everyday living in the invisible potentiality of indeterminate nature.

These two political models of feminist emanci-pation contribute to shift the critique of technology beyond a mere debunking of patriarchal and capi-talist discourse. These models rather politically hack normative epistemology by exposing the challenges that technoscientific experimentalism poses to given truths. These two planes of critique have gone a long way to question scientific truism and have shown that science is itself an open affair, embedding wider cul-tural, political and economic consequences. Neverthe-less, whilst the cyborg strategy of hacking feminism involves a continuous mediation between matter and signs, the anti-representational immediacy of cyber-feminism as a micropolitics exposes an immanent con-tinuity between epistemology and ontology, whereby the infinite potentialities of nature are expressed as affects, percepts and concepts constituting lived experience as such.

One has however to pause here and recognise that the cyberfeminist embracing of the inexhaustible potential of nature has also risked becoming divorced from the material transformations of history. In particular, it has overlooked the implications of its hyper-stitional approach in the context of the cognitive/affective phase of neoliberal capital for which the immediacy of visceral response, and the appeal to a continuous transformation of being, have become the dominant motor of/for the abstraction of value. The consolidation of so-called cognitive capital embraces the scientific paradigm of scientific indeterminacy and has demarcated a shift towards the datification of the real, based on the assumption that there is no truth to hold on to, but only a sea of information from which truths can be fabricated. Paradoxically, the capitalisation of human intelligence has led to a capitalisation of affective responses working to neutralise — i.e. render null — the classic cognitive order of intelligibility (i.e. symbolic reasoning, reflexivity, logical implications). Within this cognitive phase of technocapitalism, ontology has become subjected to the epistemological claims about the indeterminacies of truths, leading to a form of visceral control where the amplification of affective responses has led to the systematic capitalisation of the intellect. The visceral modulation of the masses together with the stealthy incorporation of any form of desire into branding and marketing strategies aims not only to direct reactions towards pre-constituted goals, but to tap into the pre-cognitive pool of decision-making, short-circuiting the distance between emotion and cognition. At the core of cognitive techno-capitalism is a preemptive mode of power carrying out two main complementary activities: the harnessing of unknowns and the abstraction of non-conscious cognition. On the one hand, preemption involves the inclusion of indeterminacies in the calculation of chance. On the other, the epistemological formulation of a bodily-centred form of cognition points out that decisions can be taken at an increasingly fast speed and before self-awareness. In other words, the potential indeterminacies of many sexes or of a virtual plane of nature have come to coincide with the speed of non-conscious automated decisions, in which energy is transformed into information through the cybernetic machine of communication, command and control.

In this regime of contagious responses in which the immediacy of a certain kind of thinking replaces the critical capacity of self-reflection and causal awareness, affective politics risks remaining caught within the algorithmic culture of the programmed and the programmable. The paradoxical impasse between intelligent machines and corporeal intelligence urges us to shift the articulation of the relation between ontology and epistemology away from the mutual equivalence between being and doing, and concepts and objects. In other words, within the historical phase of cognitive technocapitalism, cyberfeminism shall not be limited to mirror the automation of affective thinking. One can argue that the limits of what Deleuze calls the "being of the sensible" are evidenced in how the promises to exceed technocapitalist control remain with cyberfeminism nonetheless caught within the paradoxical over-lap of visceral power and politics. But how to subtract from this paradoxical state perpetuated in neoliberal technocapitalism? How to turn the technocapitalist capture of the future into a hyperstitional activita-tion of collective desires able to invent a politics of the future? Can Xenofeminism offer us another entry point into the complicated mesh of affective capital, visceral governance and reactive control?

As with the cyborg manifesto and cyberfeminism, Xenofeminism claims a "fictive ideality" (an expres-sion borrowed from the collective) to discover and construct new conditions for the alliance between tech-nology-gender-sexuality. These conditions include for instance the temporalities of machines, whose asymmetric timelines are already imparting irrevers-ible de-naturalisations onto human's capacity to live in time. And yet the ingression of alien temporalities into human culture also delineates the opportunity for an alternative political subjectivity that can no longer appeal to the injustice of nature or natural laws. Com-pared to cyberfeminism however, Laboria Cuboniks's fictive ideality does not place trust in the promise of the unknown because indeterminacies have entered the hands of a free-falling capital disseminating molec-ular fragmentations under a hypersexist, hyperracist and hyperclassist governance. However, even if cyber-feminists' fictive ideality ended in the dissipation of structures and the political validity of indeterminacy, it does not mean that the alliance with technology that cyberfeminism proposed is to be simply condemned. Instead, Xenofeminism takes the challenge to further radicalise the alliance for the political promises that are already embedded in the logic of machines and the artificiality of knowledge. If the Xenofeminist Manifesto must be seen as contributing to technogender revolutions, then it seems important to bring back to its core the question of how to reclaim a fictive ideality of the future and enable political projects with and through technoscientific interventions.

According to Laboria Cuboniks, political projects shall not resign and leave the labour of inventing the future in the hands of a free-falling deterritorialising capital. As with the cyborg and cyberfeminism, Xenofeminists' fictive ideality is here an invitation to imagine, to orchestrate and to endorse the future even if it cannot be known in advance. Indeterminacy is not a limit to knowledge, but an incitement to gather collective intelligences and experiment with multiscalar modalities gathered amongst localised practices and their inferential connectives, so as to unite scales through the hypothetical construction of general meanings. The hyperstitional quality of the Xenofeminist Manifesto works not to extend localities to generalities aiming to represent feminist, queer and gender local practices in global political projects. Instead it requires the laborious invention and intervention in the creation of models that go up and across localities. Interventions are above all alienation not only from the natural order, but also from any given circumstance. Any given always contains an ideological infrastructure that would have to be made clear, worked through, and eventually overcome through the invention of other models, other abstractions.

This is a kind of alienation that requires the labour of reasoning, that begins with the social and collective imagination for building models or carrying out logical experimentations, enabling ideation to step forward into action, and work through local constraints in order to build a structure that can allow freedom. Not a freedom from constraints but a freedom towards the instrumental transformation of constraints for the collective endorsement of new ends. This is where alienation becomes a political possibility not only to destratify from the cognitive structure of habits and symbolic truths, but also to endorse material practices with new meaning, and allow the inferential implications of reasoning to re-assess truths, functions, behaviours and conducts.

One has to clarify however that this political possibility is not simply a performative exercise because alienation from human nature, as Lilith, the main character in Octavia Butler's *Xenogenesis* trilogy, is forced to learn, is an inhumane effort of collective re-engineering. The degree of inhumanity here concerns the traumatic qualities of being forced to change under the pressure of contingencies and the labour of re-commencing a dia-logical engagement with unfamiliar truths, rules and laws, surpassing the tendency of resigning in order not to risk, yet again, fallibility. Alienation therefore involves not an abandonment of the space of reason, but the claiming back of reasoning as inferential tools of emancipation, the labour of following a persistent direction towards thinking how to construct an *us* or a *we* with and through machines.

Indeed, technological mediation cannot be divorced

from the advancing of the automation of knowledge implying the formation of a new synthesis between reasoning, logic and calculation. If an alien language for sexual and gender politics through machine-thinking could be part of this new synthesis then the question for Xenofeminism could be how, and which experiments we need to embark on so as to scale up from within this new form of artificial knowledge. Xenofeminism has launched a mathematico-geometric format that affords new entries and experiments to change our nature. But to endorse the estranged consequences of a new synthetic reason would then also mean to automate sex. How Xenofeminists' fictive ideality might contribute to turn this dehumanising phase of transformation into a possibility for political emancipation is yet to be known, but the difficulty of this question can no longer be avoided.

Works Cited

Butler, Octavia (1987), *Dawn: Xenogenesis 1*. London: Popular Library.

Deleuze, Gilles and Félix Guattari (1987), *A Thousand Plateaus: Capitalism and Schizophrenia*, trans. Brian Massumi. London: Athlone Press.

Haraway, Donna (1991), "The Cyborg Manifesto: Science, Technology, and Socialist-Feminism in the Late Twentieth Century", in *Simians, Cyborgs and Women: The Reinvention of Nature*. New York: Routledge, 149-81.

Plant, Sadie (1998), *Zeroes and Ones: Digital Women and the New Techoculture*. London: Fourth Estate.

XENOFEMINISM: A POLITICS FOR ALIENATION

Laboria Cuboniks

ZERO

0x00 Ours is a world in vertigo. It is a world that swarms with technological mediation, interlacing our daily lives with abstraction, virtuality and complexity. XF constructs a feminism adapted to these realities: a feminism of unprecedented cunning, scale and vision; a future in which the realisation of gender justice and feminist emancipation contribute to a universalist politics assembled from the needs of every human, cutting across race, ability, economic standing and geographical position. No more futureless repetition on the treadmill of capital, no more submission to the drudgery of labour, productive and reproductive alike, no more reification of the given masked as critique. Our future requires depetrification. XF is not a bid for revolution, but a wager on the long game of history, demanding imagination, dexterity and persistence.

0x01 XF seizes alienation as an impetus to generate new worlds. We are all alienated — but have we ever been otherwise? It is through, and not despite, our alienated condition that we can free ourselves from the muck of immediacy. Freedom is not a given — and it's certainly not given by anything "natural". The construction of freedom involves not less but more alienation; alienation is the labour of freedom's construction. Nothing should be accepted as fixed, permanent or "given" — neither material conditions nor social forms. XF mutates, navigates and probes every horizon. Anyone who's been deemed "unnatural" in the face of reigning biological norms, anyone who's experienced injustices wrought in the name of natural order, will realise that the glorification of "nature" has nothing to offer us — the queer and trans among us, the differently-abled, as well as those who have suffered discrimination due to pregnancy or duties connected to child-rearing. XF is vehemently anti-naturalist. Essentialist naturalism reeks of theology — the sooner it is exorcised, the better.

0x02 Why is there so little explicit, organised effort to repurpose technologies for progressive gender political ends? XF seeks to strategically deploy existing technologies to re-engineer the world. Serious risks are built into these tools; they are prone to imbalance, abuse and exploitation of the weak. Rather than pretending to risk nothing, XF advocates the necessary assembly of techno-political interfaces responsive to these risks. Technology isn't inherently progressive. Its uses are fused with culture in a positive feedback loop that makes linear sequencing, prediction, and absolute caution impossible. Technoscientific innovation must be linked to a collective theoretical and political thinking in which women, queers and the gender non-conforming play an unparalleled role.

0x03 The real emancipatory potential of technology remains unrealised. Fed by the market, its rapid growth is offset by bloat, and elegant innovation is surrendered to the buyer, whose stagnant world it decorates. Beyond the noisy clutter of commodified cruft, the ultimate task lies in engineering technologies to combat unequal access to reproductive and pharmacological tools, environmental cataclysm, economic instability, as well as dangerous forms of unpaid/underpaid labour. Gender inequality still characterises the fields in which our technologies are conceived, built and legislated for, while female workers in electronics (to name just one industry) perform some of the worst-paid, monotonous and debilitating labour. Such injustice demands structural, machinic and ideological correction.

0x04 Xenofeminism is a rationalism. To claim that reason or rationality is "by nature" a patriarchal enterprise is to concede defeat. It is true that the canonical "history of thought" is dominated by men, and it is male hands we see throttling existing institutions of science and technology. But this is precisely why feminism must be a rationalism — because of this miserable imbalance, and not despite it. There is no "feminine" rationality, nor is there a "masculine" one. Science is not an expression but a suspension of gender. If today it is dominated by masculine egos, then it is at odds with itself — and this contradiction can be leveraged. Reason, like information, wants to be free, and patriarchy cannot give it freedom. Rationalism must itself be a feminism. XF marks the point where these claims intersect in a two-way dependency. It names reason as an engine of feminist emancipation, and declares the right of everyone to speak as no one in particular.

INTERRUPT

0x05 The excess of modesty in feminist agendas of recent decades is not proportionate to the monstrous complexity of our reality, a reality crosshatched with fibre-optic cables, radio and microwaves, oil and gas pipelines, aerial and shipping routes, and the unrelenting, simultaneous execution of millions of communication protocols with every passing millisecond. Systematic thinking and structural analysis have largely fallen by the wayside in favour of admirable, but insufficient struggles, bound to fixed localities and fragmented insurrections. Whilst capitalism is understood as a complex and ever-expanding totality, many would-be emancipatory anti-capitalist projects remain profoundly fearful of transitioning to the universal, resisting big-picture speculative politics by condemning them as necessarily oppressive vectors. Such a false guarantee treats universals as absolute, generating a debilitating disjuncture between the thing we seek to depose and the strategies we advance to depose it.

0x06 Global complexity opens us to urgent cognitive and ethical demands. These are Promethean responsibilities that cannot pass unaddressed. Much of twenty-first-century feminism — from the remnants of postmodern identity politics to large swathes of contemporary ecofeminism — struggles to adequately address these challenges in a manner capable of producing substantial and enduring change. Xenofeminism endeavours to face up to these obligations as collective agents capable of transitioning between multiple levels of political, material and conceptual organisation.

0x07 We are adamantly synthetic, unsatisfied by analysis alone. XF urges constructive oscillation between description and prescription to mobilise the recursive potential of contemporary technologies upon gender, sexuality and disparities of power. Given that there are a range of gendered challenges specifically relating to life in a digital age — from sexual harassment via social media, to doxxing, privacy and the protection of online images — the situation requires a feminism at ease with computation. Today, it is imperative that we develop an ideological infrastructure that both supports and facilitates feminist interventions within connective, networked elements of the contemporary world. Xenofeminism is about more than digital self-defence and freedom from patriarchal networks. We want to cultivate the exercise of positive freedom — freedom-to rather than simply freedom-from — and urge feminists to equip themselves with the skills to redeploy existing technologies and invent novel cognitive and material tools in the service of common ends.

0x08 The radical opportunities afforded by developing (and alienating) forms of technological mediation
should no longer be put to use in the exclusive interests of capital, which, by design, only benefits the few.
There are incessantly proliferating tools to be annexed,
and although no one can claim their comprehensive
accessibility, digital tools have never been more widely
available or more sensitive to appropriation than they
are today. This is not an elision of the fact that a large
amount of the world's poor is adversely affected by
the expanding technological industry (from factory
workers labouring under abominable conditions to
the Ghanaian villages that have become a repository
for the e-waste of the global powers) but an explicit
acknowledgement of these conditions as a target for
elimination. Just as the invention of the stock market
was also the invention of the crash, Xenofeminism
knows that technological innovation must equally
anticipate its systemic condition responsively.

TRAP

0x09 XF rejects illusion and melancholy as political
inhibitors. Illusion, as the blind presumption that
the weak can prevail over the strong with no strategic coordination, leads to unfulfilled promises and
unmarshalled drives. This is a politics that, in wanting
so much, ends up building so little. Without the labour
of large-scale, collective social organisation, declaring
one's desire for global change is nothing more than

wishful thinking. On the other hand, melancholy — so endemic to the left — teaches us that emancipation is an extinct species to be wept over and that blips of negation are the best we can hope for. At its worst, such an attitude generates nothing but political lassitude, and at its best, installs an atmosphere of pervasive despair which too often degenerates into factionalism and petty moralising. The malady of melancholia only compounds political inertia, and — under the guise of being realistic — relinquishes all hope of calibrating the world otherwise. It is against such maladies that XF innoculates.

0x0A We take politics that exclusively valorise the local in the guise of subverting currents of global abstraction, to be insufficient. To secede from or disavow capitalist machinery will not make it disappear. Likewise, suggestions to pull the lever on the emergency brake of embedded velocities, the call to slow down and scale back, is a possibility available only to the few — a violent particularity of exclusivity — ultimately entailing catastrophe for the many. Refusing to think beyond the microcommunity, to foster connections between fractured insurgencies, to consider how emancipatory tactics can be scaled up for universal implementation, is to remain satisfied with temporary and defensive gestures. XF is an affirmative creature on the offensive, fiercely insisting on the possibility of large-scale social change for all of our alien kin.

0x0B A sense of the world's volatility and artificiality seems to have faded from contemporary queer and

feminist politics, in favour of a plural but static con-
stellation of gender identities, in whose bleak light
equations of the good and the natural are stubbornly
restored. While having (perhaps) admirably expanded
thresholds of "tolerance", too often we are told to seek
solace in unfreedom, staking claims on being "born"
this way, as if offering an excuse with nature's blessing. All the while, the heteronormative centre chugs
on. XF challenges this centrifugal referent, knowing
full well that sex and gender are exemplary of the fulcrum between norm and fact, between freedom and
compulsion. To tilt the fulcrum in the direction of
nature is a defensive concession at best, and a retreat
from what makes trans and queer politics more than
just a lobby: that it is an arduous assertion of freedom
against an order that seemed immutable. Like every
myth of the given, a stable foundation is fabulated for
a real world of chaos, violence and doubt. The "given"
is sequestered into the private realm as a certainty,
whilst retreating on fronts of public consequences.
When the possibility of transition became real and
known, the tomb under Nature's shrine cracked, and
new histories — bristling with futures — escaped the
old order of "sex". The disciplinary grid of gender is in
no small part an attempt to mend that shattered foundation, and tame the lives that escaped it. The time has
now come to tear down this shrine entirely, and not
bow down before it in a piteous apology for what little
autonomy has been won.

0x0C If "cyberspace" once offered the promise of
escaping the strictures of essentialist identity cat-

egories, the climate of contemporary social media has swung forcefully in the other direction, and has become a theatre where these prostrations to identity are performed. With these curatorial practices come puritanical rituals of moral maintenance, and these stages are too often overrun with the disavowed pleasures of accusation, shaming and denunciation. Valuable platforms for connection, organisation and skill-sharing become clogged with obstacles to productive debate positioned as if they are debate. These puritanical politics of shame — which fetishise oppression as if it were a blessing, and cloud the waters in moralistic frenzies — leave us cold. We want neither clean hands nor beautiful souls, neither virtue nor terror. We want superior forms of corruption.

0x0D What this shows is that the task of engineering platforms for social emancipation and organisation cannot ignore the cultural and semiotic mutations these platforms afford. What requires reengineering are the memetic parasites arousing and coordinating behaviours in ways occluded by their hosts' self-image; failing this, memes like "anonymity", "ethics", "social justice" and "privilege-checking" host social dynamisms at odds with the often-commendable intentions with which they're taken up. The task of collective self-mastery requires a hyperstitional manipulation of desire's puppet-strings, and deployment of semiotic operators over a terrain of highly networked cultural systems. The will will always be corrupted by the memes in which it traffics, but nothing prevents us from instrumentalising this fact, and calibrating it in view of the ends it desires.

PARITY

0x0E Xenofeminism is gender-abolitionist. "Gender abolitionism" is not code for the eradication of what are currently considered "gendered" traits from the human population. Under patriarchy, such a project could only spell disaster — the notion of what is "gendered" sticks disproportionately to the feminine. But even if this balance were redressed, we have no interest in seeing the sexuate diversity of the world reduced. Let a hundred sexes bloom! "Gender abolitionism" is shorthand for the ambition to construct a society where traits currently assembled under the rubric of gender, no longer furnish a grid for the asymmetric operation of power. "Race abolitionism" expands into a similar formula — that the struggle must continue until currently racialised characteristics are no more a basis of discrimination than the colour of one's eyes. Ultimately, every emancipatory abolitionism must incline towards the horizon of class abolitionism, since it is in capitalism where we encounter oppression in its transparent, denaturalised form: you're not exploited or oppressed because you are a wage labourer or poor; you are a labourer or poor because you are exploited.

0x0F Xenofeminism understands that the viability of emancipatory abolitionist projects — the abolition of class, gender and race — hinges on a profound reworking of the universal. The universal must be grasped as generic, which is to say, intersectional. Intersectionality is not the morcellation of collectives into a static fuzz of cross-referenced identities, but a political orientation that slices through every particular, refusing the crass pigeonholing of bodies. This is not a universal that can be imposed from above, but built from the bottom up — or, better, laterally, opening new lines of transit across an uneven landscape. This non-absolute, generic universality must guard against the facile tendency of conflation with bloated, unmarked particulars — namely Eurocentric universalism — whereby the male is mistaken for the sexless, the white for raceless, the cis for the real, and so on. Absent such a universal, the abolition of class will remain a bourgeois fantasy, the abolition of race will remain a tacit white-supremacism, and the abolition of gender will remain a thinly veiled misogyny, even — especially — when prosecuted by avowed feminists themselves. (The absurd and reckless spectacle of so many self-proclaimed "gender abolitionists'" campaign against trans women is proof enough of this.)

0x10 From the postmoderns, we have learnt to burn the facades of the false universal and dispel such confusions; from the moderns, we have learnt to sift new universals from the ashes of the false. Xenofeminism seeks to construct a coalitional politics, a politics without the infection of purity. Wielding the universal requires thoughtful qualification and precise self-reflection so as to become a ready-to-hand tool for multiple political bodies and something that can be appropriated against the numerous oppressions that transect with gender and sexuality. The universal is no blueprint, and rather than dictate its uses in advance, we propose XF as a platform. The very process of construction is therefore understood to be a negentropic, iterative and continual refashioning. Xenofeminism seeks to be a mutable architecture that, like open-source software, remains available for perpetual modification and enhancement following the navigational impulse of militant ethical reasoning. Open, however, does not mean undirected. The most durable systems in the world owe their stability to the way they train order to emerge as an "invisible hand" from apparent spontaneity; or exploit the inertia of investment and sedimentation. We should not hesitate to learn from our adversaries or the successes and failures of history. With this in mind, XF seeks ways to seed an order that is equitable and just, injecting it into the geometry of freedoms these platforms afford.

ADJUST

0x11 Our lot is cast with technoscience, where nothing is so sacred that it cannot be reengineered and transformed so as to widen our aperture of freedom, extending to gender and the human. To say that nothing is sacred, that nothing is transcendent or protected from the will to know, to tinker and to hack, is to say that nothing is supernatural. "Nature" — understood here as the unbounded arena of science — is all there is. And so, in tearing down melancholy and illusion; the unambitious and the non-scaleable; the libidinised puritanism of certain online cultures, and Nature as an un-remakeable given, we find that our normative

anti-naturalism has pushed us towards an unflinch-
ing ontological naturalism. There is nothing, we claim,
that cannot be studied scientifically and manipulated
technologically.

0x12 This does not mean that the distinction between
the ontological and the normative, between fact and
value, is simply cut and dried. The vectors of normative anti-naturalism and ontological naturalism span
many ambivalent battlefields. The project of untan-
gling what ought to be from what is, of dissociating
freedom from fact, will from knowledge, is, indeed,
an infinite task. There are many lacunae where desire
confronts us with the brutality of fact, where beauty is
indissociable from truth. Poetry, sex, technology and
pain are incandescent with this tension we have traced.
But give up on the task of revision, release the reins
andslacken that tension, and these filaments instantly
dim.

CARRY

0x13 The potential of early, text-based internet culture
for countering repressive gender regimes, generating
solidarity among marginalised groups, and creating
new spaces for experimentation that ignited cyberfeminism in the Nineties has clearly waned in the twenty-first century. The dominance of the visual in today's
online interfaces has reinstated familiar modes of
identity policing, power relations and gender norms
in self-representation. But this does not mean that
cyberfeminist sensibilities belong to the past. Sorting

the subversive possibilities from the oppressive ones latent in today's web requires a feminism sensitive to the insidious return of old power structures, yet savvy enough to know how to exploit the potential. Digital technologies are not separable from the material realities that underwrite them; they are connected so that each can be used to alter the other towards different ends. Rather than arguing for the primacy of the virtual over the material, or the material over the virtual, xenofeminism grasps points of power and powerlessness in both, to unfold this knowledge as effective interventions in our jointly composed reality.

0x14 Intervention in more obviously material hegemonies is just as crucial as intervention in digital and cultural ones. Changes to the built environment harbour some of the most significant possibilities in the reconfiguration of the horizons of women and queers. As the embodiment of ideological constellations, the production of space and the decisions we make for its organisation are ultimately articulations about "us" and, reciprocally, how a "we" can be articulated. With the potential to foreclose, restrict or open up future social conditions, xenofeminists must become attuned to the language of architecture as a vocabulary for collective choreography — the coordinated writing of space.

0x15 From the street to the home, domestic space too must not escape our tentacles. So profoundly ingrained, domestic space has been deemed impossible to disembed, where the home as norm has been conflated with home as fact, as an un-remakeable given. Stultifying "domestic realism" has no home on our horizon. Let us set sights on augmented homes of shared laboratories, of communal media and technical facilities. The home is ripe for spatial transformation as an integral component in any process of feminist futurity. But this cannot stop at the garden gates. We see too well that reinventions of family structure and domestic life are currently only possible at the cost of either withdrawing from the economic sphere — the way of the commune — or bearing its burdens man-yfold — the way of the single parent. If we want to break the inertia that has kept the moribund figure of the nuclear family unit in place, which has stubbornly worked to isolate women from the public sphere, and men from the lives of their children, while penalising those who stray from it, we must overhaul the mate-rial infrastructure and break the economic cycles that lock it in place. The task before us is twofold, and our vision necessarily stereoscopic: we must engineer an economy that liberates reproductive labour and family life, while building models of familiality free from the deadening grind of wage labour.

0x16 From the home to the body, the articulation of a proactive politics for biotechnical intervention and hormones presses. Hormones hack into gender sys-tems possessing political scope extending beyond the aesthetic calibration of individual bodies. Thought structurally, the distribution of hormones — who or what this distribution prioritises or pathologises — is of paramount import. The rise of the internet and the hydra of black-market pharmacies it let loose —

together with a publicly accessible archive of endo-crinological knowhow — was instrumental in wresting control of the hormonal economy away from "gate-keeping" institutions seeking to mitigate threats to established distributions of the sexual. To trade in the rule of bureaucrats for the market is, however, not a victory in itself. These tides need to rise higher. We ask whether the idiom of "gender hacking" is extensible into a long-range strategy, a strategy for wetware akin to what hacker culture has already done for software — constructing an entire universe of free and open-source platforms that is the closest thing to a practica-ble communism many of us have ever seen. Without the foolhardy endangerment of lives, can we stitch together the embryonic promises held before us by pharmaceutical 3D printing ("Reactionware"), grass-roots telemedical abortion clinics, gender hacktivist and DIY-HRT forums, and so on, to assemble a plat-form for free and open-source medicine?

0x17 From the global to the local, from the cloud to our bodies, xenofeminism avows the responsibility in constructing new institutions of technomaterial-ist hegemonic proportions. Like engineers who must conceive of a total structure as well as the molecular parts from which it is constructed, XF emphasises the importance of the mesopolitical sphere against the lim-ited effectiveness of local gestures, creation of autono-mous zones, and sheer horizontalism, just as it stands against transcendent, or top-down impositions of val-ues and norms. The mesopolitical arena of xenofemi-nism's universalist ambitions comprehends itself as a mobile and intricate network of transits between these polarities. As pragmatists, we invite contamination as a mutational driver between such frontiers.

OVERFLOW

0x18 XF asserts that adapting our behaviour for an era of Promethean complexity is a labour requiring patience, but a ferocious patience at odds with "waiting". Calibrating a political hegemony or insurgent memeplex not only implies the creation of material infra-structures to make the values it articulates explicit, but places demands on us as subjects. How are we to become hosts of this new world? How do we build a better semiotic parasite — one that arouses the desires we want to desire, that orchestrates not an autophagic orgy of indignity or rage, but an emancipatory and egalitarian community buttressed by new forms of unselfish solidarity and collective self-mastery?

0x19 Is xenofeminism a programme? Not if this means anything so crude as a recipe, or a single-purpose tool by which a determinate problem is solved. We prefer to think like the schemer or lisper, who seeks to construct a new language in which the problem at hand is immersed, so that solutions for it, and for any number of related problems, might unfurl with ease. Xenofeminism is a platform, an incipient ambition to construct a new language for sexual politics — a language that seizes its own methods as materials to be reworked, and incrementally bootstraps itself into existence. We understand that the problems we face are systemic and interlocking, and that any chance of global success depends on infecting myriad skills and contexts with the logic of XF. Ours is a transformation of seeping, directed subsumption rather than rapid overthrow; it is a transformation of deliberate construction, seeking to submerge the white-supremacist capitalist patriarchy in a sea of procedures that soften its shell and dismantle its defenses, so as to build a new world from the scraps.

0x1A Xenofeminism indexes the desire to construct an alien future with a triumphant X on a mobile map. This X does not mark a destination. It is the insertion of a topological-keyframe for the formation of a new logic. In affirming a future untethered to the repetition of the present, we militate for ampliative capacities, for spaces of freedom with a richer geometry than the aisle, the assembly line, and the feed. We need new affordances of perception and action unblinkered by naturalised identities. In the name of feminism, "Nature" shall no longer be a refuge of injustice, or a basis for any political justification whatsoever!

If nature is unjust, change nature!

SONIC UTOPIAS: *THE LAST ANGEL OF HISTORY*

A Conversation between Kodwo Eshun, Ayesha Hameed and Louis Moreno

Louis Moreno: I thought we could begin by talking about our reactions to seeing this film tonight, as for many this might be their first contact with *The Last Angel of History*[1], and for others seeing it again it could have triggered different ideas and thoughts about what they thought the film was about. For my part, I realise that for all these years I'd seen a different film. When it was first shown on Channel 4 in the mid 1990s, *The Last Angel of History* was called *The Mothership Connection* and it was a sort of bastardised version, because — and I've only just realised because it's the first time I've seen the film since the 1990s — they removed the crux of the SF narrative and the explanation of the "Last Angel". So in my memory, *The Last Angel of History* exists as TV doc about SF, techno and jungle called *The Mothership Connection* circulating on a VHS tape around twenty years ago. But watching it this evening what seems clear is that *The Last Angel of History* is not some artefact of rave culture and cyber-theory lost in the midst of the 1990s. It's not as a historical document that gives the film its power, but that it's engaged in a "live" project. So watching it today, right now, even though the tech and visual FX may date it, its structure of feeling still seems extremely vibrant. It still seems to engage with its original project, which as you say Kodwo at the end of the film, is to "get out of right now", "to bring the future into the present". So, if we could start with you, Kodwo, as somebody who was involved in making the film, what's your sense of the project?

Kodwo Eshun: *The Last Angel of History* is a film much more discussed than screened. It might be useful to reconstruct the conjuncture from which it emerged and to which it contributed. *Last Angel* was conceived by the Black Audio Film Collective as an intervention into a number of academic debates taking place in Britain and in the UK in the early 1990s around the question of black popular culture. Within the US, there was a con- sensus that hip-hop epitomised the organising princi- ple of black popular culture. It was the point around which all black popular culture converged. You will notice that there is not a single mention of hip-hop throughout *Last Angel*. That was a polemical exclu- sion on our part. It was not that we disliked hip-hop. Far from it. Rather, we, that is, myself, director John Akomfrah and scriptwriter Edward George of Black Audio Film Collective, disagreed with the canonical claims made in the name of hip-hop by the majority of American academics. It seemed to us that the cul- tural mutation from rave to hardcore techno to jungle techno to jungle to drum 'n' bass from 1990 to 1995 in

Britain rendered those claims insufficient. This ongoing exclusion of what Simon Reynolds would later call the hardcore continuum compelled us to challenge the consensual account of black popular culture, to question its premise and its parameters. Instead we argued for an unblack unpopular culture that took the role of jungle and drum 'n' bass seriously, that elevated techno to its critical role from which it was habitually expelled and which affirmed dub as a critical sonic process throughout Afrodiasporic musics.

Throughout 1994, Edward George, who narrates and also plays the role of the Data Thief in *Last Angel*, would travel to my flat in Kensington. We discussed the relations between music, science fiction, futurity and theory. These ideas of music as a vehicle for the affirmation of alienation and extraterrestriality whose implications extended far beyond music emerged years later in the publication of *More Brilliant than the Sun: Adventures in Sonic Fiction*. Edward and John wrote the scenario for *Last Angel* and then travelled to Detroit and New York to film interviews. In September 1995, Channel 4 broadcast the thirty-minute version of the film entitled *The Mothership Connection*. At the same time ZDF broadcast the forty-five-minute version entitled *The Last Angel of History*. *Time Out* reviewed *The Mothership Connection* with predictable hostility. By contrast, *Last Angel* was well received by *Spex* magazine in Cologne. In 1997, Diedrich Diederichsen organised the *Loving the Alien* conference at the Volksbühne in Berlin. In the US, techno musicians such as Mike Banks of Underground Resistance immediately expressed appreciation for the film; academics proved somewhat slower.

Figure 1. © Smoking Dogs Films. John Akomfrah (1995), *The Last Angel of History*. Courtesy Lisson Gallery.

LM: Ayesha, as a writer and theorist, why is *The Last Angel of History* so crucial to your work? We've heard Kodwo say that the film was made as a vehicle to counteract the "future shock absorber" effect of mundane cultural criticism at the time. But in teaching and thinking about contemporary culture, how does it connect with your work and research today?

Ayesha Hameed: As you might know, one crucial difference is that I'm not from the UK, so I didn't see *The Mothership Connection* on Channel 4 like you did. I encountered this film only a half-dozen years ago. I use it to teach, and I refer to it in my own work. As Kodwo just said, a lot of people don't necessarily watch the film as much as it has become a reference point. That said, there's something incredibly relentless and uncompromising about the film itself. So in a way, you can jump into it *in medias res* without knowing its broadcast history and the context of its production and just start watching it and try to follow all the clues it leaves. The density of the narrative is uncompromising in its theoretical richness, its contextualisations and its philosophical bent. On top of all that, there's the audio and the sequence of images which are also incredibly complicated.

So I thought it would be nice to create a taxonomy of what is actually in the moving image itself. Every time I see this film, I see and hear something new. This is a list of props that I saw. The first and one of the most striking props is the Data Thief's reflective metal spectacles, the presence of which is interesting because the film is all about sound. You see the Data Thief wearing these glasses when he is sitting beside the two computers, one of the "lenses" of these spectacles is saturated with light. The Data Thief is also holding a blackbox. When the Data Thief refers to this contraption as a blackbox it reminded me of this lecture that Matt Fuller gave at Goldsmiths where, drawing from Bruno Latour, he talked about blackboxes. He described how Latour talks about how the blackbox as an object that you put everything you don't know about into. It becomes a cipher for the ways in which things work: that you put these incomprehensible things into the blackbox. What goes into it is transformed by the blackbox into what comes out of it. So you use the blackbox without understanding what has happened in between. Matt contrasted that with what

W.R. Ashby was doing much earlier than Latour in trying to think about the blackbox. Ashby said that it becomes a cybernetic thing because it implicates us as subjects. I was thinking about this when I wondered why the Data Thief is holding a blackbox. And wondered too, why is he holding these glasses?

The Data Thief also has a block of wood and a giant nail. He's constantly proffering the block of wood out. I don't know what the nail is for. He also has this bent stick. This was interesting to me when I was watching it, wondering what the point of these props was. The bent stick is initially introduced after a B-roll image of a solar flare, and the shape of the stick mirrors that flare. So the shape of the stick anticipates the arc of the solar flare.

KE: What you are pointing to is the performative dimension of speculation. *Last Angel* begins with Robert Johnson's "Me and the Devil" from 1937. Robert Johnson sings, "Me and the devil, walking side by side" in his unsettling voice. The Data Thief, played by Edward George, wearing special sunglasses, then says, "Flash forward 200 years" to the year 2137. The Data Thief is a time-traveller that navigates what he calls "the internet of black history". Everybody he visits is a historical figure and every prop he picks up is a techno fossil. What is mundane to us is enigmatic to him. His role is to excavate fossils and to narrate these fragments. Edward George also plays the role of the narrator that comments on the epistemological enquiries of the Data Thief. The complexity of the film has to do with keeping those roles distinct.

Figure 2. © Smoking Dogs Films. John Akomfrah (1995), *The Last Angel of History*. Courtesy Lisson Gallery.

LM: Let me ask you both a speculative question: if the film was being made today, how would it engage with contemporary music? One thing that gives the film its "periodicity" is the compartmentalisation of sonic genres — techno, jungle, house, primarily. Also electronic music still exists as an underground culture. But if the film was being made today, music seems much more compressed and hybridised, almost all forms of popular music have been compressed into one universal electronic dance music genre. But back in the 1990s there seemed a more tangible separation between sonic forms of dance music, which gave an opportunity to infiltrate and subvert the mainstream, or provide fusions with science fiction, philosophy, politics and so on. So I'm just wondering if you think there are the same opportunities in contemporary sonic culture to recombine sound, space and thought in order to re-engage this sense of futurity?

KE: As you watch A Guy Called Gerald and Goldie speaking, you begin to hear the ways in which the music they are making presupposes a theorisation of its conditions of production. That is the case for all the other musicians as well. But with drum 'n' bass, there is a special urgency that emerges from the producers being asked to articulate the music they are inventing. When Gerald says that jungle represents a world that is "changing from the analogue to the completely digital", today's viewer recognises that she or he lives on the other side of that change. You can hear that music producers of the 1990s were living through this change. The ability to articulate this shift, to narrate this epochal passage in all its contingency takes on a specific poignancy at this moment. When Greg Tate states that "all eras of black music are collapsed onto a chip", it is possible to hear the entire film as a dramatisation of the possibility space opened up by Afrodiasporic avant-gardes as they transition and transform sonic practice from analogue scarcity to the digital abundance in which we live.

What I see and hear now are the absences. Missy Elliot's "The Rain (Supa Dupa Fly)", which announces the arrival of herself, Timbaland and Hype Williams, is still two years in the future. There is no way for *Last Angel* to register her existence as yet. Musics like kuduro or Shangaan Electro are not available for *Last Angel*. What animates *Last Angel* is the sense that the producers and novelists and writers are grappling with vast technosocial processes that instantiate themselves in musical form much earlier than other artforms. Jacques Attali's *Noise: The Political Economy of Music*, which we all read at the time, proposed such an argument in 1985. By 1995, we all experienced that sense which Goldie describes when he states that "we are the future". 1995 is also the year that I met Mark Fisher, Steve Goodman, Luciana Parisi, Nick Land and Sadie Plant of the Cybernetic culture research unit or Ccru, who were all based at Warwick University. The questions around Afrofuturism articulated by *Last Angel* converged with questions of Cyberfeminism and the Cybergothic formulated by the Ccru at Warwick. There was a real sense of asymptotic intensity that compelled a desire to invent forms that combined digital abstraction with concrete reality.

AH: People being interviewed in the film were saying these really positive things about the future: that the future is under your nose, we are the future. But I think the conversation that *The Last Angel of History* would have now would be quite different if it responded to music coming out now. In my opinion, albums like Kanye West's *The Life of Pablo* or Future's track "Codeine Crazy" are exciting in their over-saturation and their sense of dissolution. It's a very uncompromising look at anxiety, addiction, the emptiness of fame; a kind of failure of the future really, played out in exciting ways.

But I'm still thinking of Kodwo's response to Louis' previous question, around the idea of relics and time.

How this film does not seem to have aged very much and still seems very relevant. And a part of it I think has to do with its own relationship between the past and the future. As Kodwo has just mentioned the relics that the Data Thief who is not the Data Thief, the Data Thief who is separated from himself, is finding. Apart from that the images of technology in the film don't seem to have aged either. I mean obviously the computers are old and the images are old, but these obsolesces are built into the film. The images are already pixelated and the computers are already outdated. The film is already acknowledging the passing of the moment of its own production. We might notice that the computer looks old, and that the images are pixelated, but the film is already in on that secret, isn't it? I think that the film is constantly doing that.

Figure 3. © Smoking Dogs Films. John Akomfrah (1995), *The Last Angel of History*. Courtesy Lisson Gallery.

The quick scroll of images on the computer screen form an archive that the Angel is constantly going through, repeatedly. At one point in the film there's a great interview that Nichelle Nichols, Uhura from the *Star Trek* movies, is giving. But after she speaks the film then cuts to a scroll of the Data Thief's archival images and she's *in* that scroll of images. Her *present* becomes a part of that archive, which I think is really interesting in a way as a kind of response to when Samuel Delany talks about how science fiction is a distortion of the present. They are distorting the present to accommodate the past that is simultaneously the present. The scroll of the archive is the presentation of the present and the past in one moment.

KE: You are right to point to the interviews that are continually interrupted by rapid-eye montage. Whenever Octavia Butler speaks, a recurrent musical motif recurs and yet I cannot quite say if I ever actually registered its elusive insistence. These visual and musical interruptions perform the circulation of images in different ways. In the tableaus in which the Data Thief sits at a high chair, we can see three computers that scroll through imagery and the same imagery of planets and mathematical equations scroll within the slits of his sunglasses. These images travel at speeds too great to be grasped as anything other than fleeting moments. Slowed down, they begin to reveal themselves as depictions of Pharonic statues, the interiors of mosques and formulae that allude to the ancient algorithms from the Islamic Golden Age. We see black-and-white photographic portraits of Ghanaian bourgeois families and African-American soldiers. These accelerated images constitute the internet of Black Culture that is entirely readable for the Data Thief. He is processing data and reading images at post-human speeds. What we see in this scene is a staging of the act of streaming in which the computational temporality and planetary trajectory of images are as important as their content. *Last Angel* dramatises the streaming of culture in the form of the circulation of images.

AH: I think it's interesting that you started off with responding to Octavia Butler's clip and then you went to the rapid scroll of images, because one of the things I was interested in with all these interstitial moments are the ways in which this scroll of images becomes more and more of a character, more and more of a presence that, as you say, this Data Thief is processing. But I think it's also interesting because really the film is about sound and music, and yet the Data Thief is wearing glasses and what we see is this scroll of images. And then you have this distorting audio background to Octavia Butler speaking.

Actually the more I watch the film, the more I think about the audio in the film and one of the things is that when John Akomfrah made the film and Trevor Mathison did the sound design, that they worked together at the same time. It's not like they laid down the visual track and then Trevor Mathison just scored it. So in a way the sound is performing a very similar archival gesture as the visual scroll, which is quite interesting because it's predominantly his soundtrack. There are some very tantalising snippets of Sun Ra and

A Guy Called Gerald and Kraftwerk. But the sound doesn't keep you with them. It keeps you with these other sounds like a kind of tide of wavey music, and then this kind of rapidly moving scrolling sounds. And the sound that lingers at the end of the film is that of birds, except that they are not real birds, they are synthesised birds. And why did the birds predominate after you've had the last word in the film, Kodwo? What is happening? I think what is so compelling about the audio is that it doesn't call attention to itself at all, but it's just as complicated as the visual elements of the film itself.

LM: Could we develop this a little? Aside from the direct engagement with music producers like Juan Atkins, Underground Resistance, Goldie, amongst others, the film's soundtrack, ambient patches, glitches, are of course crucial. And it's interesting because there's a feeling of bliss in the film. But it's a weird bliss. It's not some kind of Buddhist introspection. It's not the kind of utopian future where all conflict is neutralised. But there is a sort of power to the film which comes precisely through its original soundtrack, an ambience that's cut through with all these shards of noise, these intense cuts and audio intersections. The sound of the film gives us a sense of a different, altered relationship to technology. But what is going on here, is it a signal of the kind of new anxious and paranoid relationship we have to social media, networked tech today?

KE: The sounds that Ayesha describes have different roles. Ambient synthetic sound soothes and reassures and bridges and cradles. At other times, sound intrudes, interrupts and escalates. You can hear the tantalising opening passages of A Guy Called Gerald's "Finleys Rainbow (Slow Motion Mix)", of 4 Hero's "Parallel Universe" and Rhythim is Rhythim's "Kao-tic Harmony". All of these tracks fade into and emerge from the ebb and surge of Trevor Mathison's synthesisers, which continually modulate the affective tone of *Last Angel* in relation to its colour, its pace, its space and its syncopation. The scenes of the Data Thief that are filmed in the Mojave Desert introduce a digital chiaroscuro composed of burnt orange shadow. These chromatic temperatures were quickly imitated on British television throughout the 1990s to the extent that they now look thoroughly clichéd. It's important to note that Akomfrah and the cinematographer Dewald Akeuma invented this aesthetic as a deliberately digital response to the overt digital drum 'n' bass produced by A Guy Called Gerald, Goldie and 4 Hero. The oversaturated colour creates an afterimage that is picked up and modulated by specific musical sequences. The artificial colour and synthetic music enter into a co-constitutive relation of synthetic sensation and artificial emotion that lingers with the spectator as an emergent structure of feeling that is never quite verbally articulated as such.

AH: The film starts and you're suddenly in the desert, you are hearing Robert Johnson, and everything is in this sepia tone. One of the things I noticed was that the anticipatory futuristic images were in sepia, which is normally a kind of nostalgic colour. It's in the past. It's

Figure 4. © Smoking Dogs Films. John Akomfrah (1995), *The Last Angel of History*. Courtesy Lisson Gallery.

also the colour that images of Mars are suffused with. In contrast the archival images are a cold blue. So there is a kind of switching of the kind of semiotics of what you would associate with these colours. Usually it's the archival images that are the sepia-toned, brownish, receding, fading. Whereas here it's the landscape of the desert, which is sepia-toned and looks like Mars. The dust that floats in the air is what makes all these images from Mars that kind of colour. So the anticipatory images look nostalgic. And the archival images are not even a warm blue. There's something that's not nostalgic, that's not soothing about that quality of blue. Or more accurately, it's soothing, but in a kind of non-empathetic way. There's a sense of distancing that is built into it. And you can see this as well in the black-

and-white archival images of the Ghanaian families. In this context, why are these photographs in black and white? And what kind of distancing, auratic quality is being created in this code-switching of colour?

There's always another layer to jump out at you. We tend to focus on the narrative provided by the voiceover. It is hard and rich enough to follow the narrative of the development of these three musical genres in light of Afrofuturism, but in addition to that there are these ancillary almost non-narrative elements. And all of these elements create a way to think about the future in a way that is code-switched with history, that creates a kind of remembering that is shot through with the future.

KE: In *Last Angel*, you hear the narrator Edward George speaking about navigating the "land of African memory" and entering "the internet of Black culture". It is at that point that you glimpse the figure of Kwame Nkrumah, first President of the Republic of Ghana, in black and white and in colour. George's voiceover speaks of defeats and successes, failures and promises. For me, the critical reason to screen and to discuss *Last Angel* today is to situate the aesthetic-political project of Afrofuturism in a broader genealogy that extends beyond the 1990s and out into the Promethean Pan-Africanisms formulated throughout the twentieth century. At the same time, it is critical to direct Afrofuturism's affirmation of alienation towards the range of contemporary cultural practices that have emerged and continue within and between the diaspora and the continent.

Many contemporary artists and critics within the

continent object to the perceived Americocentricity of Afrofuturism. They argue that Afrofuturism fails to account for the preoccupations that inform practices produced in the past and the present throughout the cities of the continent and the Caribbean. In Johannesburg, Nairobi, Lagos and Accra, novelists, theorists, bloggers, photographers and filmmakers are debating "the planetary turn of the African predicament", which Achille Mbembe argues "will constitute the main cultural and philosophical event of the twenty-first century". Watching *Last Angel* confronts contemporary viewers with the urgency of speculation and the necessity for extrapolation in order to navigate the dangers of the present and the threats of futures that will be continental, oceanic and archipelagic in their scale and their scope.

1. Thanks to UCL Urban Laboratory's Jordan Rowe, Andrew Harris and Rafael Schacter of A (b) P, for helping to organise the screening and discussion of *The Last Angel of History* on Sunday, 20 March at Somerset House, London.

Works Cited

Akomfrah, John (dir.) (1995), *The Last Angel of History*. London: Black Audio Film Collective, C4/ZDF.

Attali, Jacques (1985), *Noise: The Political Economy of Music*, trans. Brian Massumi. Minneapolis: University of Minnesota Press.

Dent, Gina (ed.) (1993), *Black Popular Culture*. Seattle: Bay Press.

Diederichsen, Diedrich (1998), *Loving the Alien: Science Fiction, Diaspora, Multikultur*. Berlin: Id Verlag.

Eshun, Kodwo and Anjalika Sagar (eds.) (2007), *The Ghosts of Songs: The Film Art of the Black Audio Film Collective*. Liverpool: Liverpool University Press.

Eshun, Kodwo (1998), *More Brilliant than the Sun: Adventures in Sonic Fiction*. London: Quartet Books.

Fuller, Matthew (2016), "Black Sites and Transparency Layers", Inaugural Lecture Goldsmiths, University of London. 15 March.

Mbembe, Achille, (2015) "Africa in the New Century", in Lien Heidenreich-Seleme and Sean O'Toole (eds.), *African Futures: Thinking about the Future in Word and Image*. Bielefeld: Kerber Verlag.

Plant, Sadie (1998), *Zeroes and Ones: Digital Women and the New Technoculture*. London: Fourth Estate.

Reynolds, Simon (1998), *Energy Flash: A Journey through Rave Music and Dance Culture*. London: Picador.

Tate, Greg (1982), *Flyboy in the Buttermilk: Essays on Contemporary America*. New York: Simon & Schuster.

FLICKER-TIME AND FABULATION: FROM FLICKERING IMAGES TO CRAZY WIPES

Bridget Crone

Introduction

A single flash! A cut of light!

This essay explores the flicker or flicker-image as a flash of light that has the potential to disrupt the mechanics of vision. The most elemental of images, the flicker is at the very basis of both vision and mechanical image production; it is the flash of light that makes an image possible, and it is the continuous flickering of light across the eye (or lens) that connects visual perception with time perception through the operation of critical flicker frequency: the speed at which the brain joins those flashes of light together and thus perceives the movement of time. Yet when isolated or disaggregated from continuous movement, the flicker-image disrupts the smooth space of both image production and time perception. The flicker-image therefore refers to a correlation between analogue cinema practice in which a frame of film runs flickering through the projector and the physiological mechanics of image production in which flickering light is perceived by the brain. To think of images in this way is to understand images as single elements, as flashes of light, frames of film, individual pixels — individual units that are joined together. Image. Followed by image. Followed by image. Yet to insist on the flicker-image as a single flash of light — a "cut" or "point cut" as Gilles Deleuze does in his writing on experimental artists' films — is to isolate an image from the constant movement of images, and, in doing so, to break into the flow of time: interrupting, disrupting or re-routing time's movement (Deleuze 2005: 207).

Taking cue from Tony Conrad's 1966 film *The Flicker*, aspects of Manuel DeLanda's films produced approximately ten years later, as well as Russell Hoban's novel *Fremder* (1986), the essay addresses the way in which radical editing techniques that cut or break the linear continuity of image movement offer the means for escape outside of existing space-time parameters. This escape from linear, chronological time is the time of the flicker; it is a time broken into a gazillion pieces, each with the potential for another as yet unknown or unmade relation. Each piece, each jump-cut, splice or broken edit, interrupts the flow of time as we know it and calls forth time anew. The particular form of time produced by the operations of the flicker-image (the image cut from movement) has much in common with the time of Aion or the instant, as that which cuts into the linearity of chronological time. In this way, flicker-time takes us out of the "no-time" and "no-space" of our continuous present, and thus from the continuity of time that is dominated by demands for constant productivity and progress on the one hand, and an entropic, unending present on the other, as Jonathan Crary observes in his book *24/7: Late Capitalism and the Ends of Sleep*: "A 24/7 world is a disenchanted one in its eradication of shadows and obscurity and of alternate temporalities" (Crary 2014: 19). The flicker-image is therefore a resistant technology that breaks and remakes the relationship between time and the image in order to both occult the world and produce it anew, and flicker-time is a "fabulated" time-space. Here fabulation suggests an estrangement that is rooted in conditions of the "real" (that occur in real life; IRL) yet also gestures towards a form of speculative thought: the telling of stories, the weaving together of forms of speculation — the might be, could be, possibly. Fabulation is thus at the heart of an art practice that provides the means to "project — into things, into reality, into the future and even into the sky" (Deleuze 1997: 118). And so, focussing our attention on the operation of the flicker as a single flash of light — a single flash that cuts or breaks into linear time and space — rather than a continuum of flashes, enables us to explore the way the flicker acts as a launch-pad that takes us out of time into a fabulated time and space. This is a time-space that couldn't possibly exist, might exist, probably doesn't exist, could perhaps exist through another understanding of time and space.

There are three distinct operations of the flicker in the work of Conrad, Hoban and DeLanda. These are summarised as, firstly, an expansion of time and space;

this is the case in Conrad's film, where the operation of the flicker produces a journey into a world beyond the image, a world of psychedelic experience. Here the flicker acts as a launch-pad for entering into another dimension. In contrast to Conrad's freedom *through* the flicker to a space outside of it, Hoban's novel *Fremder* proposes that liberation might be found in the space between the flickering images that make up perception. In *Fremder*'s world, perception of so-called "reality" — a "reality" produced by the continuous flickering of light across the eyes — is controlled by a sinister organisation referred to as "The Corporation". The potential for freedom therefore can only be found *outside* of the image. In a move that mirrors Crary's remarks made twenty-five years later, Hoban's novel proposes that in order to resist control we must enter into the world of "shadows and obscurity" (Crary 2014: 19), and where Crary explores sleep as the last bastion of resistance to the demand for constant production, Hoban proposes that this is to be found by slipping into the space (the darkness) between images. The forced conjoining of images that is imposed through continuity editing techniques and enforced by capitalist institutions is also addressed by Manuel DeLanda in his little-known films from the mid-to-late 1970s, and informs the third operation of the flicker. In the films, DeLanda uses radical editing techniques to produce a new relationship to time by completely severing the correlation between images and the continuities of time and space. Conrad, DeLanda and Hoban's works acknowledge the potential of the flicker-image to re-forge our perceptual relationship with time (thus producing a form of time that is non-linear) and undermine or question the shared certainties of this so-called "reality". This is to say, more explicitly, that the flicker-image harbours the potential for disobedience and resistance so that the forging of discontinuity is a resistant act that seeks to open up the possibilities for different inhabitations and understandings of time through its fabulation.

Figure 1. Tony Conrad (1966), *The Flicker*, screening at
Film Exercise, Arnolfini, December 2010.
Photograph: Sam Nightingale.

Flickering Jewels

A flash that breaks into and transports us out of time is what Tony Conrad sees when he first observes the myriad points of flickering light cast by the performer: Mario Montez's sequinned dress at a party held by the artist-filmmaker Jack Smith at the apartment that the three of them shared. It "created an incredibly luminous effect and froze Mario Montez when it was shone

Figure 2. Tony Conrad (1966), *The Flicker*, screening at Film
Exercise, Arnolfini, December 2010.
Photograph: Sam Nightingale.

onto her" (MacDonald 2006: 65), Conrad recalls, and
his words create a vivid picture of an image snatched
from movement and multiplied into an array of flickering points of light, each projecting and refracting
their own polyphony of effects. Conrad's first encounter with Montez's flicker then led to experiments that
involved Montez dancing in front of the beam of light
emitted from a lensless projector. Again, the image that
Conrad paints of this is so evocative that it is easy to
imagine being entranced by the magical array of lights
emanating from Montez's sequins amidst other similarly glamorous invitees — particularly knowing the
beauty and dream-like qualities of Smith's films such
as *Flaming Creatures* (1963), which he had dedicated to
the film star Maria Montez, Mario's namesake. Seeing
the potential in Montez's flickering sequins, Conrad
goes on to play with the frequency of light that shines

upon Montez; "fiddling with the knobs" of the projector is the phrase used in one account, although the
origins of Conrad's subsequent film, *The Flicker*, have
become somewhat mythologised (Shirley 2009). In
Smith's version of the story "Mario and the Flickering
Jewel"[1], he himself also dangles a piece of green costume jewellery in front of the lens, causing the light to
"refract erratically from the green jewel, flickering violently across the room" (Shirley 2009). Yet what is clear
is that for Conrad the flicker-image immediately opens
the possibility for the expansion of experience through
the flickering points of light, which he goes on to liken
to journeying into another world or dimension.

Conrad has stated that his intention in making *The
Flicker* was to create an event that the audience would
understand as "going on — not just passing by" (Mac-
Donald 2006: 70). This sense of event is partly enacted
by a rather long seizure warning for epileptics, which
is beautifully rendered in cursive-style handwriting
and accompanied by a music-hall-style piano number, rather cheerful in mood — and referencing the use
of such devices in early film screenings, which were
often referred to as the "flicks" and again highlighting the important role of flickering light. Interviewing
Conrad, Scott MacDonald enquires whether the long
duration of the warning is a deliberate gesture towards
creating some kind of suspense at the start of the film.
Conrad denies this, speaking of his concern to allow
those who might fear having a fit time to leave the
room, but later admits that it was intended to create
the screening as a space set apart from the everyday; a
space to enter into as well as creating a sense of com-

pliance, commitment and surrender in the viewer, as Conrad notes. And he further emphasises this sense of entering into another time-space, stating: "I wanted people to lose themselves and to understand they had lost themselves in that world" (MacDonald 2006: 66). Conrad's emphasis on the spatial dynamic of an event "taking place" highlights his intention to create a different temporal experience — "not just passing by" but entering into a distinct space and time which is not only produced by setting the space of the film screening apart from the everyday (through the inclusion of the long credits) but also, most importantly, through the operations of the flicker-image itself.

This space that is created by the operations of the flicker image is produced through a double movement of expansion and contraction at once — contraction into the image as a point of light that is cut from movement, on the one hand, and, on the other, the expansion outside of the image into another dimension. Thus we are transported away from the image via its excessive effects into a hallucinogenic experience of multiplying images and after-images, and at the same time the world contracts to the experience of the single points of light, not light, light, not light. Here the "cut" refers to interruptions and breaks that contrast to the continuity of film in which images are propelled through their relationship to each other. Here, the flicker-image can be considered both in the instant of its illumination — that is the little events of the individual flashes — and in relation to the *incorporeal* optical effects that the flicker-image produces. In this way, it is the *freezing* of Montez in the light of the projector and the visible breaking of the image into a series of tiny individual points of light of that is of the most interest to the development of the flicker-image.

To articulate the flicker-image as a "point" is to highlight its interruptive and disruptive aspect and to further emphasise the image that arrests or holds out against movement itself. This means that rather than considering the image as always connected and in movement, or as a form of montage in which the dynamics between images produce meaning, as in Deleuze's movement-image, the flicker-image acts more like a singular point in time. It is a moment of projection that occurs in time but disrupts the ongoing, linear movement of time. Here the flicker-image operates as a kind of insistent point-like *now* that is inserted between the past and future. It is a *now* that is defined by its impossible limits rather than duration, and which breaks into the present which is fleeting and almost ungraspable: a point or prick in the movement of time rather than space, a single flicker of light, a single point appearing fleetingly upon a screen and crucially opening up a space that we might enter into. Yet at the same time, this singular image projected in the instant is expansive, producing a series of effects that emanate outwards from the point itself. We can visualise this as the psychedelic flashing of light that results from a strobe, for example, where each point or flicker of light produces a doubling or tripling of the image. It is this multiplication of the effects of the flicker-image that is so fascinating, especially considered in relation to Montez's sequins and, later, Conrad's film. This is because there is a possibility of transportation in and away from this single point of light towards what Conrad calls the "experiential excess" of the flickering light, an excess that transports, that produces other worlds. As Conrad has stated: "I've always thought of *The Flicker* as a bizarre science fiction movie, as a space that you can enter [...] and go floating off into some weird dimension and then come back" (MacDonald 2006: 66).

The question of perception and its limits is inherent to the composition of *The Flicker* and connects the film with early twentieth-century experiments in neurology, particularly those concerning the treatment and diagnosis of epilepsy, and most particularly Conrad's interest in the visions experienced by epileptics during a fit. Therefore while *The Flicker* draws upon parallels with musical composition and mathematics, the experiment with patterning and repetition — and the *disruption* of these patterns — that is explored in the film is also a crucial aspect of this neurological research. As W. Grey Walter points out in his book *The Living Brain* (1953), which was influential to Conrad's work, there is a "synchronisation between the flicker and the brain rhythms" (Walter 1961: 92). Walter describes how the scientists made a type of flicker-film themselves by projecting light through a turning wheel. The compositional structure of *The Flicker* speaks directly to the correlations between the mechanics of film and of visual perception by addressing the frequency at which the eye can detect light, which differs according to the structure of the eye, the type of light falling upon the eye (colour, black-and-white, moving or still) and the point of the eye upon which the light falls (frequency differs across the eye). This is seen most obviously in Conrad's piecing together of single frames within the overall movement of images, and his consideration of the role of rhythm, patterning and repetition in the processes of perception.

After his initial experiments with Smith and Montez, Conrad went on to work on what becomes *The Flicker* on his own, and while the basis of the film seems so simple, so basic to film, and the image, itself — that movement between light and darkness, between white and black and black and white film frames, its planning and execution were complex and diagrammatic. Beginning from questions of composition, harmony and rhythm, Conrad, who was also a musician, ponders upon the "frequencies [of image movement] you would have to use in order to get flicker", and he pursues this question in a highly systematic way, working through calculations of frame rate, film speed and, finally, through an intensive editing process that involves splicing hundreds of pieces of black-and-white film. The initial problem that Conrad recounts in the making of the film is the question of how to shoot white frames. He recalls that Jonas Mekas brought him a number of rolls of old negative film, and that shooting the black frames was simply a matter of covering the camera lens. However, exposing for the white frames so as only to get "projected light" proved more difficult than simply removing the lens of the camera as hoped. Finally, on a borrowed 16mm Bolex camera, Conrad succeeded in shooting forty-seven variations of black and white frames. Ten copies of this film were subsequently printed, which Conrad then cut and spliced into the final film, which contains five-hundred splices. Working with the constraints of twenty-four frames per second, the projection speed of a 16mm projector dividing the film strip into variations that will produce between three to twelve flickers per second, depending upon the length of blocks of black-and-white frames used. *The Flicker* therefore develops through a mathematical structure (which, in itself highlights music's indebtedness to mathematics) in order to determine and to experiment with the limits of vision — that question of how many flickers of light per second the eye can see.

Montez's flickering sequins enabled Conrad to recognise the expansive effects of the flicker. As Conrad has noted, this is a moment of expansion and contraction at once, as, on the one hand, time is reduced to the instant of flickering light and, on the other, a new experience of time and space opens up. This can be understood as the intensity of experience that Conrad asks the viewer to enter into through the space of the film, but also most importantly it is the breaking and remaking of time that takes the viewer on a journey from the myriad of individual flickering points of light in Montez's dress or Conrad's film to a new experience of time and space. Here the points of light act as a form of transportation by contracting time to the instant of illumination and then expanding it into other visuals effects. This is a space that might be called hallucinogenic, that might be attributed to a form of image referred to as a noosign (an image that exists only in our head) or likened to what Deleuze refers to as the Crystal Image of Time — a place in which the actual and virtual are drawn close together and time dominates (Deleuze 2005: 95-121). The domination of time over image-movement highlights another more mechanical aspect of the flicker that is suggested by Conrad's experimentation with projection speed and the inter-spacing of the film-frames. Here there is a direct link to neurological research in which the pace of the flickering light is observed acting to stimulate brain activity such that the experience of time is altered relative to the speeds of flickering light (or images). It is therefore the rhythm and speed of the points or flashes of light and crucially the distance between these flashes measured by the duration of darkness between them that produces this sense of time passing.

Flicker Time and Crazy Wipes

Excavating the relationship between flickering light, brain activity and the experience of time enables an opening up of the limits of chronological time that results in a time that is dependent upon the speed and frequency of flickering light; what we might term, flicker-time. Early neurological studies, such as those discussed by W. Grey Walter (and read by Conrad), note a connection between the flickering of the eye-lids, the stimulation of light and brain activity and the perception of time. And indeed, Walter reports on experiments to alter the rhythm or frequency of this flickering light: "Sometimes the sense of time is lost or disturbed. One subject said he had been 'pushed sideways in time — yesterday was at one side, instead of behind, and tomorrow was off the port bow'" (Walter 1961: 98). Here the disaggregation of time from its usual linear arrangement hints towards what might be recognised as a form of time-travel. René Thoreau Bruckner addresses this possibility in the essay "Travels in Flicker-Time (Madre!)", proposing that the flicker enables a form of time-travel by extending upon the neuro-scientific notion of critical flicker frequency to understand the moment in which the mind gives way to the breakdown of chronological time — or gets "pushed sideways in time" (Walter 1961: 98). We also see this concept explored in Hoban's novel *Fremder* through the notion of the flicker-drive — the (fictional) means of travelling through vast distances of time and space by manipulating the brain of surgically conditioned people, called flickerheads.

If we recognised that chronological time is, first and foremost, time arranged spatially and dominated by a linear trajectory or progression, the flicker is the breaking up of this ordered forwards movement. In this way, the flicker is then the repeated transmission of light broken up and constantly interrupted by moments of darkness, such that time is experienced not as duration nor as linear movement but as the "palpitation" of points of light (Bruckner) or the "pulses of cognition" that are inherent to the individual's ability to "self organise time perception" (Vimal and Davia 2008: 108). Thus consciousness is not experienced as continuous but as a series of successive pulses. We might relate this then to critical fusion frequency — the rate of flicker or the "palpitation" of light upon the eye that produces images. For example, in a scientific report on the relationship between phenomenal (or experienced) time and quantum (or measurable) time, Ram Lakhan

Pandey Vimal and Christopher James Davia note that yoga practitioners and those that practice meditation develop a higher critical fusion frequency than others, suggesting that they may synthesise images at a faster rate; this further highlights the mutability of the experience of time.

Bruckner postulates that it is the operation of critical flicker frequency that is at work in time-travel insofar as it can control the disruption of linear, spatially well-organised (chronological) time. He gives two examples to support his case for time-travel in this manner. Firstly, he cites the twelfth-century fable of the wolf and the animals, in which a wolf circumvents his two-year ban on hunting by speeding up time through the opening and closing of his eyelids to evoke the darkness of night and the brightness of a new day with each successive blink. "The Wolf's trick, his invention, is a device for moving things along by blinking, producing for himself a proto-cinematic, flickering picture", Bruckner notes (Bruckner 2008: 63). Secondly, Bruckner addresses H.G. Wells' novella *The Time Machine*, in which the protagonist, simply referred to as the Time Traveller, invents a machine that allows him to travel through time and space. Wells' novella, published shortly after the Lumière Brothers first revealed their cinematograph and R.W. Paul demonstrated his theatrograph, can be seen to refer directly to the invention of these cinematographic devices that transport the viewer/operator out of the present in a way that is akin to jumping through time and space. In both examples, Bruckner suggests that time-travel is the result of a "merging of glimpses" — the wolf rapidly opening and closing his eyes to speed up time, and the Time Traveller in Wells' novella travelling through the neurological operation of critical flicker frequency and the mechanical operation of film projection. What is significant in this "merging of glimpses" is the breaking down of a continuity of smooth image-movement to individual glimpses or pulses; these are akin to what I have referred to elsewhere as flashes, points or flickers of light. Similarly, the linear movement of time is disrupted and replaced, not by an extended present, but with a non-linear version of time dominated by a succession of accelerated instants, glimpses, flickers, points, flashes of light that is suggested by the theatrograph, cinematograph and film projector. Again, there is a correlation here between the mechanics of visual perception and that of film projection in the connection made between the manipulation of vision in terms of the wolf opening and closing his eyes more quickly than normal to evoke the passing of day and night more quickly, and in the movement of film through the projector gate — it's mechanical eyelid.

In Hoban's novel *Fremder*, transportation through time and space via the image produces a world of flicker space, a world that is produced through the alternative "stilling" and movement of (frozen) images. Fremder, the novel's protagonist, is known as a flickerhead or a deepspacer — travelling via the flickering image. These journeys, which exceed what is possible in a regular human lifetime, are made possible by the implanting of an oscillator in Fremder's head. This enables Fremder's projection through time and space through what is termed, in the novel, "the jump" — the instant of projection into another time-space. This is fast-forward on a massive scale and echoes Bruckner's notion of time-travel through altering the speed of critical flicker frequency: speeding through time, driven by the flicker, flicker, flicker. However, in a sinister twist, the oscillation of the flicker is co-opted into the smooth space of Corporation control. This is a world that flickers constantly, a world in which the world pulse rate (WPR) governs the appearance of things and freedom itself might lie outside of this flickering appearance. As Fremder's mother, Helen Gorn, suggests, or hopes, it is perhaps not the flickering of images that provides the real disruption to the smooth co-joined space of the horizontal plane (the Corporation's absolute control in the novel) but, rather, the obverse space that is opened up by the appearance of the flicker — that is, the space *between* the appearance of images, *between* the flickering points of light and through the disentanglement of their relationship to time.[2] Helen has been obsessed with the question of escape, and she experiments with the idea of escaping in the gap between the images, that is, escaping between the pulses of the world in its appearing. While she ultimately fails in her endeavour (she is unable to escape the totality of Corporation control), her research is useful for us because it suggests that rather than focussing upon the appearance of images — the moment of illumination or flicker — we could, instead, consider what lies outside of the image: what lies outside of the frame of the visible? Therefore, rather than the point of light and its relative speed of transmission and reception, it is perhaps the surrounding points of not-light, or not-image, that provide a real rupture or disruption to the continuing flow and appearances of the image.

Both Hoban's novel and Bruckner's postulations on time-travel and critical flicker frequency tie the experience of time to the mechanics of perception so that time might be slowed down or sped up, or even frozen, yet these interruptions are still predicated upon an idea of chronological time, time that moves forward or backwards in a linear manner — easy to envisage as a strip of film running through a film projector either fast-forwards or in reverse. Particularly in Bruckner's example, time-travel is analogous to the action of fast-forwarding through images to get through time more quickly. Contrary to this, Fremder also speaks of the "jump" as the act of being launched into an entirely non-contiguous time and space. This could be seen to link with another film technology or, in this case, editing technique: the jump-cut, where time is advanced — or jumped forward — through the use of a non-continuous but still linked shot. DeLanda takes this even further in his film work through the violent refutation of continuity editing techniques that seek to question and ultimately *break* the relationship between image-movement and continuous, chronological time. Through his use of radical editing techniques in films such as *Incontinence: A Diarrhetic Flow of Mismatches* (1978), DeLanda creates a disjunction between image and the narrative movement of time by using editing techniques that will destroy the link between image and image, image and reaction or response, and the spatialisation of time.

In *Incontinence*, any sense of linear time, or, indeed,

the groundedness of being-in-time, is completely ruptured, as time is cut up into a series of pieces that seem
to be randomly pasted together. DeLanda's approach
focuses upon a single form of editing, in this case
sightline or eyeline matching, matching in which the
protagonist looks out of the frame in the direction
of the next scene, thus producing continuity from
one scene to the next. Through the use of repetition,
DeLanda exaggerates and subverts the construction
of a unified space and time to the point of the ridic-
ulous, thus defying the homogenising possibilities of
the technique and returning the "life" and "energy"
to what he calls "film's wet body", suggesting film's
own slippery mutability (Halter 2011). The result, for
the viewer, is a nauseating sense not of groundlessness
but of being forcefully and constantly *ungrounded* from
any stable connection with time and space: the notion
of the "jump" therefore seems highly appropriate to
explain this experience — although in film editing the
jump-cut does involve a sense of connection, often
through continuity of subject or only very slight variations of camera angle. *Incontinence*, however, violently
disrupts the spatialisation of time through the misuse
of matching techniques — that is, through emphasis
on image-to-image movement, refusing the spatialisation of time by breaking the cause-effect relationship
that links action in the present to that of the immediate
future. The fact that this film is composed from scenes
from the well-known play and film *Who's Afraid of Virginia Woolf?* means that an even greater sense of narrative confusion and structural incontinence is achieved.
Recognisable scenes from the play are enacted repeat-

edly — with actors switching roles and locations, dialogue is fragmented during each replay of the same scene — undoing the expectations of gender, role and script. This fragmentation emphasises time as a series of ruptured moments.

DeLanda works through a repertoire of "crazy wipes", pixelated transitions and other "fancy optical transitions" in his films in order to create this discontinuous time-space (Rosenbaum 2009). Mapping DeLanda's use of these editing techniques is to understand the manner in which he approaches frames of film (he was working with 8mm, then mostly 16mm film and later video) as singular units to be pieced together in no predetermined order, and film itself as a mutable form to be freed from the constraints of an enforced linearity. Many of the effects that DeLanda uses, particularly in the early work, involve hand-painted wipes, effects that are drawn onto the film strip and which create the sense of DeLanda himself reaching into the space between images (or between frames) or of entering into the spaces between the flickering reality that Fremder experiences. *Incontinence*, for example, is organised into eight separate scenes, taking pieces of dialogue from Albee's play, dialogue that is repeated within each scene (as mentioned previously). The disruption to the continuity editing technique of sightline matching is also played out through the breaking up of space and time within each scene and in the transition between scenes. This is achieved through shifting gender roles, replay, reversal and mirroring of space (people drop in and out of the frame from above and below, they speak to interlocutors in a previous or an ensuing scene and so on), and through intervention into the film strip itself in the form of the removal of frames (creating a flickering effect), as well as the use of DeLanda's "crazy wipes" (vertical, horizontal and diagonal transitions across frames).

Slippery Pixels and Flicker-Points: Final Fabulations and the GIF

To exit time's flow, to disrupt the continuous movement of time through a flicker of light or through the imperceptible shadows between flickering images is an impossibility for many of us in our current psycho-physical form; it is therefore what I would term a type of fabulation — a possible-impossible. Fabulation is a term often associated with literary analysis to describes forms of narrative and their relationship to time, yet here I evoke the term as an operation of possibility that is not yet possible, an action that is intimately bound up with time itself — an action that projects *out of* time. In this understanding, fabulation is bound up within the technical operation of the flicker to create a new time and space, and in this way the flicker-image enables a time and space that exceeds and evades the possibilities available to it and to us, and that calls forth a new understanding of time and the image that is not simply bound by the limits of "real" or already-existing. Yet fabulation, and by association, the flicker or flicker-image, is bound up with questions of "political meaning" (Bogue 2010: 14, quoting Deleuze); for to question the possibilities for an escape *through* time is to evoke the form of control that is inherent to a state of constant productivity and "the ends of sleep" (that Crary invokes in the title of his book), and to find a time that resists or at least disrupts the entropic space of time's flow.

We live amidst an accumulation of now-times — live broadcasts, snapchats, insta-everything trapping us in an ever-expanding present — the "illumination" "beyond clock time" and "duration without breaks" of which Crary speaks (Crary 2014: 8-9). This is a present that is governed by the linear logic of accumulation of "now" and "next", of moving forward and going nowhere. What then would be a contemporary equivalent for the flicker-image that updates the mostly analogue technology (both human and machine) of the flicker to the digital? And could the flicker-image with its focus upon a time-space of "points" and "cuts" offer any potential for resistance today in a world that is saturated by a constant present? Born as a marketing device at control central, the GIF is a hybrid format composed of a series of still images put into motion. The GIF's composition and the fact that it can be broken down — *slowed* — to reveal its constituent parts (single still images) opens up possibilities for escape into the "black between images" or the spaces between a controlled "reality" as in that proposed by Hoban (Hoban 2003: 9). Crucial here too is the element of time and its relationship to the image, because in order to be coherent as a moving image the GIF requires a consistent run speed, therefore to slow down the run speed is to open up the spaces between the individual images from which the GIF is composed and thus undo the smooth continuity between images. Perhaps, then, entering into the time-space of the GIF — if such a world were possible — would be to enter into the discordant space of the stuttering freeze-frame (of VHS technologies) and other flicker-images in which time and time perception are remade in a way that contrasts with the constant movement and seamless flow of images.

Could the GIF offer an additional operation for the flicker-image, for the way in which it offers an alternative time-space that differs from the constantly expansionist attitude of the corporate (Corporation, in Hoban's novel) production of images? For example, in a recent article, neuroscientists have reported that the rate at which the human eye can process flickers of light is much higher than previously thought — operating at a rate of up to 500hz in relation to certain forms of image display. HD screens have been working at progressively higher and higher speeds (currently operating at average speeds of 120hz), yet the demand for a higher and higher flicker fusion rates (also known as "refresh rates") to avoid "the flicker" suggests a process of adaption and co-option across all fronts — flesh, image and digital. Similarly, GIFs, which were initially imbued with a "poor" aesthetic through their commonality and accessibility (as in what Hito Steyerl has termed the "poor image"), have become increasingly finessed — a process that has involved closing the gap between the single still images that make up the GIF and thus removing the potential for flicker and further co-opting spaces of resistance. Within contemporary imaging technologies the so-called intrusion of a flicker at the edge of a screen or through variegated transmission rates is termed an *artefact*; *artefact* suggesting the intrusion of a lag, a past time or an alter-time into the endless expansionist present of corporate control. This immediately reinforces the alternative time-space of the flicker-image, if we were to think of the flicker as this undermining of the smooth spaces of control, by introducing a more complex temporality. So while digital technology works on the gathering of pixels at faster and faster speeds and smoother accumulations, the flicker-image (whether GIFs, freeze-frame or single film-frame repeated or dropped) provides us with an alternate time-space. This is a time that we might enter into and occupy through flicker-points and their multiplying effects, or through the opening of the dark matter between flickering points of light.

1. Included in volume 2 of the CD collection of Smith's work *56 Ludlow Street 1962-4* but also recounted by Conrad in interview with MacDonald (MacDonald 2006).

2. Despite, the multi-temporalities and the inter-galactic travel that occurs in the novel, *Fremder*, there is an overriding sense of the containability of time and space. Although written before the advent of HD digital technologies, this rendering of time and space as smooth and containable (despite time-travel), is reminiscent of the flatness of the HD image in which there is no space outside of the frame but, instead, a continuing stream of image-code. The hyper-reality of the HD image is the result of a process of constant augmentation — the perfect of code and coding — into an ever-more seamless presence of images — a hyper horizontal state perhaps.

Works Cited

Bogue, Ronald (2010), *Deleuzian Fabulation and the Scars of History*. Edinburgh: Edinburgh University Press.

Bruckner, René Thoreau (2008), "Travels in Flicker-Time (Madre!)", in *Spectator* 28.2, Fall: 61-72.

Conrad, Tony (1966), *The Flicker*, 30 minutes, 16mm film, black-and-white, sound.

Crary, Jonathan (2014), *24/7: Late Capitalism and the Ends of Sleep* London and New York: Verso.

Davis, James, Yi-Hsuan Hsieh and Hung-Chi Lee (2015), "Humans perceive flicker artefacts at 500hz", in *Scientific Reports* 5, Article number: 7861.

DeLanda, Manuel (1973), *Incontinence: A Diarrhetic Flow of Mismatches*, 18 minutes, 16mm film, colour, sound.

Deleuze, Gilles (1997), *Essays Critical and Clinical*, trans. Daniel W. Smith and Michael A. Greco. Minneapolis: University of Minnesota Press.

— — — (2005), *Cinema 2: The Time-Image*, trans. Hugh Tomlinson and Robert Galeta. London and New York: Continuum.

Halter, Ed (2011), "Abstract Machines: Nonlinear dynamics and the films of Manuel DeLanda", in *Moving Image Source*. Accessed via: http://www.movingimagesource.us/articles/abstract-machines-20110304; accessed 13 February 2013.

Hoban, Russell (2003), *Fremder*. London: Bloomsbury.

MacDonald, Scott (2006), "Tony Conrad: On the Sixties", in *A Critical Cinema 5: Interviews with Independent Filmmakers*. Berkeley and Los Angeles, CA and London, England: University of California Press: 55-76.

Metzinger, Thomas (2003), *Being No One*. Cambridge, MA and London, England: MIT Press.

Pisters, Patricia (2015), "Temporal Explorations in Cosmic Consciousness: Intra-Agental Tanglements and the Neuro-Image", in *Cultural Studies Review*, September, 21.2: 120-44.

Rosenbaum, Jonathan (1983), "Manuel DeLanda", in *Film: The Front Line*. Denver, CO: Arden Press. Accessed via: http://www.jonathanrosenbaum.com/?p=16037; accessed 29 August 2016.

Sellars, John (2007), "Aion and Chronos: Deleuze and the Stoic Theory of Time", in *Collapse*, 3: 177-205.

Shirley, David (2009), "Jack Smith, Les Evening Gowns Damnées and Silent Shadows on Cinemaroc Island (Table of Elements 1997)", in *The Brooklyn Rail*, 7 May 1997.

Vimal, Ram Lakhan Pandey and Christopher James Davia (2008), "How long is a piece of time? Phenomenal Time and Quantum Coherence, Towards a Solution", in *Quantum Biosystems*, 2: 102-51.

Walter, W. Grey (1961), *The Living Brain*. Middlesex, England and Ringwood, Australia: Penguin Books.

SURFACE FICTIONS

Theo Reeves-Evison

One of the most popular exhibits in South London's Horniman Museum is a dead walrus. Perched atop its blocky iceberg, the walrus cuts a smooth and unusually bulbous silhouette against the surrounding natural history displays. This is because the nineteenth-century taxidermist who worked on the specimen did so with neither a photograph of a walrus nor personal experience of seeing one in the flesh to help him. When others might have stopped, this taxidermist kept stuffing — not realising that a walrus' skin usually has deep wrinkles folded into its surface. For lack of a visual comparison, the result may not have seemed unusual to visitors of the Colonial and Indian Exhibition in South Kensington in 1886, where the walrus was first exhibited, but now its appearance is a source of notoriety and humour, to such an extent that the walrus has a dedicated museum guard, as well as its own personal Twitter account.

The morbid science that delivers such stuffed pleasures begins in the taxidermy workshop, where the insides of the animal are replaced by a non-perishable model that imitates the shape of the living specimen. The skin is carefully applied to this model, treated with a preservative, and the eyes are replaced with glass copies. Of all of these components, it is only the skin — the envelope of the body — that remains of the original animal. Despite its indexical link to the living beast from which it came, this surface nevertheless deceives the eye. All traces of the animal's death are erased, and the skin is pulled into a shape that seeks to resemble the animal's mortal pastimes: birds swoop, polar bears fish, badgers burrow. Sight is our primary mode of experiencing taxidermy, and since the eye cannot penetrate beneath the skin (unless transparent), all of the craftsman's skill and energy are channelled into marshalling its deceptive power, thereby galvanising an age-old association between deception and an object's visual appearance. Looks, according to this tradition of thinking, always have the capacity to deceive.

That an object's ability to deceive the eye has a great deal to do with the way in which its surface communicates its interior is a fact both well-known and equally well-documented. Well before modern camouflage, forms of *trompe l'oeil*, or *faux bois* painting effects, in the first century AD, Pliny the Elder was already exploring the theme in his *Naturalis Historia* (1991: 330). The Greek naturalist and philosopher documents a painting competition that supposedly took place several centuries earlier between Zeuxis and Parrhasius to determine who could create the most convincing illusion. As the story goes, Zeuxis painted grapes that were so life-like that birds flew down to peck at them. However it was Parrhasius who won the competition by tricking everyone into thinking that his painting was concealed behind a curtain. When asked to uncover it for the judges, he revealed that it was the curtain itself that he had painted.

The painting competition between Zeuxis and Parrhasius was a competition to create an illusion, which is to say, a competition to find out who was best at deceiving the eye. The account hinges on a link between the appearance of a surface and its power to deceive. While taxidermy also embodies this link, I want to argue that the Horniman walrus is part of a small class of objects that create a link between the appearance of a surface and its status as an object of *fiction*, rather than deception, and that fiction can be layered both spatially and temporally.

One distinction between fiction and deception pivots on their respective claims to the truth. According to this dichotomy, deceptive utterances (taken in the widest sense of the word) lay claim to the truth, which may subsequently be revealed to be false. For their part, fictive utterances are accompanied by a disclaimer that relinquishes their truth claims. This may be explicit, in the case of books and films that bear the legal disclaimer that "any resemblance to actual persons, living or dead, or actual events is purely coincidental", or it may be implicit. The way in which this disclaimer acts in the world is worked out in a dialogue between an author, an artwork and its audience according to a shifting set of conventions that change over time. Needless to say, sometimes a gap emerges between the way in which the artist intends the work to be read and its actual effects. Upon publishing his foundational work *Utopia* in 1516, one can presume that Thomas Moore only ever intended for the book to be read as a work of fiction. However this did not stop some earnest members of the Church from discussing the possibility of sending missionaries to convert the population of the imaginary island he described (D'Is-raeli 1973: 23). It would be difficult to imagine this confusion resulting from the publication of a modern work of fiction, even if by some librarian's blunder it were shelved in the non-fiction section. This highlights the fact that an artwork's status as an object of fiction can change over time. Lies can be misread as fictions and vice-versa, depending on the conventions of the milieu in which they act, have influence, and become affective.

A provisional definition of fiction could therefore be "a lie revealing itself as a lie" (Scheibe 1980: 21), with the added proviso that the revelation in question might only take effect in a particular context. Both fiction and deception peddle untruths, but fiction scuppers its own ability to deceive. In the case of the Horniman walrus, this dynamic plays itself out in the tensions between the interior and the surface of the mammal. The skin of a taxidermied walrus helps us to suspend our disbelief that the specimen we are looking at is in fact nothing more than a hide stretched over a sub-strate. This attempt to deceive the eye, however slight, is sabotaged not through some fault in the skin itself — some tear, transparency or discolouration — but through the interior — the substrate (too much stuff-ing as it were) — creating surface effects and distorting its "natural" appearance. Like a cartoon character who attempts to hide behind a lamppost quite obviously smaller than their body, the substrate of the walrus undermines the deception of the surface. However, the walrus's substrate only renders itself visible *through* the surface of the animal, shattering the illusion the taxidermist works hard to create. To use another metaphor, the dynamic between the surface and the interior operates like a blush that unmasks the most accomplished of liars through the sudden rush of blood to the face. If surfaces can deceive the eye, this does not mean they are immune to an internal agent contradicting their truth claims. Objects in which this occurs operate on the basis of fictions rather than deceptions.

To subsume this curious object under the category of fiction, is, given the above definition, to claim that it operates as a lie that reveals itself to be a lie. With most works of fiction, this act of revealing is deliberate rather than accidental. With the Horniman walrus however, there is an internal agent that (at the risk of anthropomorphising the dead animal) "speaks" with a different voice than the one emanating from its surface. One need only consider the category of self-deception to realise that lies need not be spoken univocally. The same, I would claim, holds true for fiction. Since intentions can be elusive at the best of times, it is better to focus on the effects of fiction and deception, effects that can by turns be dazzling, confusing and deeply seductive.

Each of these effects hold true for an alternative definition of fiction, a definition which in many ways overruns the very notion of a definition, if we take the latter's etymology as a boundary-setting activity at face value. For fiction is not always the equal partner in a stable relationship with fact. Sometimes fictions can operate outside of codifications of true and false. This is not a fiction that is opposed to fact, or even to deception, but one that builds up a series of surfaces so thick that notions of interiority and exteriority are thrown into question.

Essential Claims

For now let us dwell on the seam that separates the surface from its interior, which is a seam that has been mined by a great variety of artists, both living and dead. It has also proved to be a popular theme in philosophical thought. A theoretical preoccupation with surfaces and superficiality reached its zenith in the 1990s following the publication of Jean Baudrillard's *Simulation and Simulacra*, which famously lamented the meaninglessness that inheres in a social sphere dominated by simulacra. Around the same time, Fredric Jameson proposed that one of the supreme formal features of postmodernism was a new kind of depthlessness. Staging a confrontation between Vincent van Gogh's painting of a peasant's boots with Andy Warhol's *Diamond Dust Shoes* (1980), he argued that the latter was symptomatic of a change in the way artworks encouraged us to read them, replacing a hermeneutic search for a larger meaning "behind" the work with a superficial fetishisation of the surface. Meanwhile Gilles Deleuze developed a more philosophically rooted conception of simulacra, grounded in a reading of Plato, or to be more precise, an interpretation of Friedrich Nietzsche's rallying call to "overthrow Platonism" (45). It is not my intention to retrace any of these arguments in any detail, but rather to conduct something of a raiding of Deleuze's argument, insofar as it marshals an entire vocabulary of interiority, exteriority, falsehood and mimesis in order to redefine the concept of simulacrum.

Deleuze's argument proceeds from the platonic distinction between essence and appearance, which in turn rests upon their respective proximity to transcendent *Ideas*. As Deleuze shows, the Platonic dialogues are replete with occasions when the philosopher is required to distinguish the true from the false, the pure from the impure. This activity touches on a range of subjects and involves a number of conceptual persona, from the best lover to the most abominable sophist. In each case, the philosopher's task is to measure the truth claims of a particular person, object or event. And how does (s)he measure such truth claims? How does (s)he dismiss the false claimant and admit the true? It is, according to Deleuze, by measuring their proximity to a transcendent *Idea*, which is in turn grounded in myth, insofar as the latter is understood as a set of foundational archetypes rooted in the past, that carry symbolic weight in the present. This *Idea* cannot be embodied fully — the claimant is always only proximate to it — but it is nevertheless sufficient to bestow a certain degree of legitimacy on the claim, enough at least to protect the honour of a philosophy that sees itself as the arbiter of Truth.

A key aspect of this process is that for a claimant to be deemed legitimate, their resemblance to the *Idea* must go beyond surface appearances. They must carry their mimetic adherence to their core. For example, a legislator who lays claim to embodying the *Idea* of

Justice must act in such a way that goes beyond the external appearance of being just. They must embody justice in all they say and do, regardless of how this might look. External resemblance is not enough to legitimise a claim for Plato. It must be backed up by an interior continuity with a transcendent *Idea*.

Armed with this philosophical rule of thumb, Plato is able to distinguish a valid claim, which is essentially a *copy* of the *Idea*, from an invalid claim, which is its *simulacrum*. Deleuze writes of the distinction as follows: "Copies are secondhand possessors, well-grounded claimants, authorised by resemblance. Simulacra are like false claimants, built on a dissimilitude, implying a perversion, an essential turning away" (1983: 47). The difference between the two is fundamental, and can be mapped onto the gulf that separates external appearance from interior essence. This is not to say that simulacra exist as pure surfaces, void of any interiority. As Deleuze makes clear, "the simulacrum implies great dimensions, depths, and distances which the observer cannot dominate" (1983: 49). In other words, the simulacrum allows for a discrepancy to creep in between the interior and the exterior. The simulacrum does not "do what it says on the tin", in fact, its contents might be in total contradiction to the label. The simulacrum is founded on a principle of difference both between its interior and exterior, and between its interior and the *Idea* against which the philosopher tries to measure it.

As you might expect from a thinker well-known for his sustained critique of representational thought, Deleuze is quick to affirm the simulacrum over the copy, insofar as the copy derives its power from *re-pre-*

senting an original. However, he does so not on the basis of a simple reversal of the Platonic position, but because the simulacrum abolishes the very distinction between the simulacrum and the copy. "The simulacrum is not a degraded copy", Deleuze writes, "rather it contains a positive power which negates both original and copy, both model and reproduction" (1983: 53). In other words, the simulacrum should not be understood as a copy of a copy, and therefore belonging to the same series as the *Idea* against which it is measured. Such a series would be founded on a hierarchy of more or less mimetic forms, and would therefore still be representational. The simulacrum destroys such hierarchy; there is no commonality between the simulacrum and the original, or even a position from which to judge this commonality. In contrast to the copy, the simulacrum is founded on a principle of difference.

The example Deleuze gives of this is Pop art, which, needless to say, had an enduring concern with the mass (re)production of objects and images. On the face of it, the Campbell's soup cans, Brillo boxes and Coca-Cola bottles reproduced in Warhol's work would seem to constitute straightforward duplications of the imagery of mass-produced consumer items. However the resemblance for Deleuze is only external, and the significance of Pop art lay precisely in its ability to push the mimetic principle so far that it changes not simply in degree, but in nature, turning from a copy into a simulacrum. Such an example is moot, given that many Pop artists not only mimicked the external appearance of consumer culture, but also actively embedded its logic of production into their artistic methodologies.

The resulting artworks, it could be argued, were similar both in degree and in nature to the cultural artefacts they copied, in so far as they passed through consumer culture without causing much friction along the way. Perhaps a less debatable example can be found in practices associated with camouflage.

Contrary to a popular misconception, camouflage is not simply a practice of copying the background environment into which one wants to blend. If the skin is an exterior border between the subject and their environment, camouflage, or to use the more technical term, "protective colouration", does not seek to erase this border altogether. This is true both in human and non-human uses of camouflage. At the same time that camouflage enables a subject to become imperceptible within their environment, most often through visual means, it also enables an act of individuation to go undetected. This can happen on the scale of a single organism, for example a caterpillar that individuates and turns into a butterfly hidden inside a cocoon that resembles a dried leaf, or it can occur on an evolutionary timescale, where a species slowly individuates itself in relation to other elements in its background environment, while coming to resemble these elements ever more closely as time goes by. The potential for difference to emerge between the morphological (how plants and animals look) and the behavioural (how they act) shows that human visual perception can only ever scratch the surface of natural complexity.

In his uniquely heterodox work on mimicry, the surrealist writer Roger Caillois claimed that mimicry in the natural world "is necessarily accompanied by a decline in the feeling of personality and life" of the animal in question (1984: 30). If we look at camouflage from a vitalist perspective, this could not be further from the truth. Animal camouflage is not merely a form of adaptation to the background environment in which the animal lives. Nor is it simply a visual pattern or aesthetic effect. As Hannah Rose Shell points out, camouflage is "meaningful as a way of seeing, being, moving, and working in the world. It is a form of cultivated subjectivity" (2012: 19). Shell makes this point in relation to human uses of camouflage, but I would claim it also holds true for non-human animals. The idea of cultivation hints at the presence of a self-reflexive agent modifying their appearance in relation to their surroundings, a ubiquitous process in nature, albeit one that may occur on a different timescale to the strictly human. In the natural world, a process of cultivation adds to the animal's armoury of tools and techniques for defence, but also for doing battle with other animals, giving them a strategic advantage in a field layered with manoeuvres and counter-manoeuvres. What appears to be a process of copying disguises another process of individuation. An apparent invisibility masks the roar of a species fighting for its ability to flourish. To borrow a term from Félix Guattari, we could say that such an operation proceeds by means of an "existential cut out" (2013: 63), which is to say, a territory established on the basis of an organism self-separating from a background that nevertheless sustains it.

Figure 1. Abbott Handerson Thayer (1918), *Cut Out Silhouette*.

In quite a different context, it was through the use of physical paper cutouts that Abbott Handerson Thayer, an American artist and naturalist who challenged nineteenth-century ideas about animal colourings, conveyed his discoveries to anyone who cared to listen.[1] Such cutouts are one example in a long line of tools, techniques and technologies that have been used to expose the separation between exterior appearances and interior processes, from didactic collages to the military instruction videos and surveillance footage used today. These examples raise an interesting question regarding the visibility of simulacra in relation to the background of expected behaviours, objects and events with which they bear a resemblance. Namely, in order for the power of difference embodied in a simulacrum to make itself felt, must its ability to resemble that which it imitates momentarily be relinquished?

Put otherwise, for us to recognise that someone is wearing a mask, must it momentarily slip, if not to reveal the face behind it, then at least another mask?

See Shells

In order to answer this question, let us take a detour through an artwork by Goldin+Senneby, an artist duo who have explored the murky world of "shell" companies in their collaborative practice. This example serves the additional purpose of shifting the emphasis from the visual to the discursive, allowing us to see that surfaces can operate in all manner of semiotic regimes, not only those apprehended through sight.

Goldin+Senneby's longest running project to date, entitled *Headless* (2007-2014), is a complex conceptual object to describe, involving multiple exhibitions, a commissioned documentary, meetings in pay-per-hour office spaces, interviews with appointed delegates, a lecture performance in a forest near Paris, another outside the macaque enclosure in London Zoo, and a murder-mystery novel dramatising the project's development as a whole. The project hinges around a forced connection between the secret society set up by George Bataille in the 1930s (*Acéphale* — a French transliteration of the Greek for headless) and Headless Ltd., an offshore corporation registered in the Bahamas. Goldin+Senneby test the theory that Acéphale did not disband, as is generally assumed, or end with the eventual death of its members, but instead migrated into the secret world of offshore finance. This initial conceit for the project is ultimately rather implausible, and when we learn that Headless Ltd. is registered with The Sovereign Group (an international company that provides "wealth management services"), anyone who is familiar with Bataille's work on sovereignty is likely to let out a small groan. Rather than focusing on this aspect of the project and the issue of sovereignty, it will be more useful to see what the work can tell us about the link between surfaces and fictions.

Figure 2. Goldin+Senneby (2009), *Headless Symbol*. Designed by Johan Hjerpe.

In the *Headless* project, the springboard that launches the work into the realms of fiction is again based on mimicry. Goldin+Senneby mimic the operations of the offshore financial companies they investigate by receding out of view as a proliferating cast of delegates and specialist contractors comes into focus. For example, when asked to give an artist talk at a gallery or university, they invariably send a spokesperson or emissary (the economic geographer Angus Cameron has played this role on a number of occasions); when asked to mount an exhibition, they employ curators or set designers to generate didactic displays. For part of their exhibition at The Power Plant in Toronto they screened a self-reflexive documentary in which two young filmmakers were hired to interview an investigative journalist about how they should go about investigating Headless Ltd. These working methods are central to the project as a whole, and they in effect create a "shell" of objects and actors that come into focus as Goldin+Senneby themselves recede from view, in the process mimicking similar practices of withdrawal in the world of offshore finance. The novel, also entitled *Headless*, mimics the genre conventions of a murder-mystery novel, and features a cast of real, made-up and slightly indeterminate characters and events. It has an almost telescopic structure of authorship, in the sense of a telescopic ladder where one section slides inside the next. Not only does *Headless* have a ghostwriter, John Barlow, but this ghostwriter himself has a ghostwriter, K.D., who seems to have been written into the plot against her own wishes.

Mimicry is what allows deception to go unnoticed, both in the *Headless* project and in the world of offshore finance. In the latter, a shell company mimics the operations of a normal company, in some cases inventing shareholders, nominating a fake director and fabricating transactions. These actions and persona are what constitute the shell, or surface of the company. But what lies beneath this shell? From one perspective, shell companies are essentially hollow, which is to say empty of the usual functions of a company: selling goods or services. And yet from another perspective they mask an extended network of operations, often illicit, that hide within the interior of the shell. Exposing the discontinuity between the two is the unenviable task of financial investigators; rarely do shell companies undermine their own ability to deceive from within. By contrast, the deceptive surface of the *Headless* project is constantly threatened by the artwork itself. In fact, we could say that its very status as a work of art already casts doubt on the credibility of its authors' claims. With both real shell companies and the *Headless* project there is a discrepancy between external appearance and an internal process, which involves the production of simulacra. However, it is only the *Headless* project, just like the Horniman walrus, that exposes the play between interior and exterior, and this is what allows the project as a whole to assume the status of a fiction.

This status depends on a certain degree of visibility. When real shell companies are successful, they blend into a background of expected behaviours, appearances and events, and the illicit activity they cover remains invisible. The significance of the *Headless* project is in its ability to *stage* an act of mimicry, for if it were effectively mimetic we would not know the names of Goldin+Senneby in the first place, nor recognise the project as a work of art. This performative dimension of the project is arguably what allows us the space to reflect on its critical function in respect to the structures it mimics, a critical function that rebounds back into the art world itself, which is no stranger to strategies that euphemistically fall under the category of "wealth management". *Headless* creates a discourse on mimicry, rather than mimicry itself. To translate this into the terms of our argument, the deceptive surface of the project is threatened, and ultimately rendered fictional, by the project itself. It's not so much that the shell reveals a deeper truth within. Rather, the shell highlights its very status as a shell, it scuppers its claims to being a truthful discourse not through revealing the truth, but making a spectacle of its artificiality. To paraphrase Michael Taussig, what is at stake is a deft display of deception's deception, skilled revelation of skilled concealment (2008: 108).

Battle Buses and Post-Truth Politics

The *Headless* project is one of a number of recent artworks that experiment with truth, fiction and superficiality, which have in turn given rise to a growing theoretical discussion about the stakes involved in such practices. This discussion gains the most traction when it is grounded in a consideration of wider socio-political conditions. Taking this approach allows us to see that artists who use 'fiction as a method' do not simply tread the same path as their Eighties and Nineties predecessors — a long list of artists that includes such names as Jeff Koons, Thomas Demand, Sherrie Levine, Jeff Wall and Gretchen Bender.[2] Their work is not a recapitulation of the "the new depthlessness", a term that Timotheus Vermeulen associates with such practices. It is a repetition with a difference.

The perennial interest in all things superficial occurs against a backdrop of what has come to be known as "post-truth politics". In itself, post-truth politics is nothing new. It is what gave a sense of urgency to earlier artistic and theoretical explorations of fiction and deception, particular those of Baudrillard and Paul Virilio. Over twenty years later the work of these authors is not referenced half as much as it once was, and yet the urgency that animated it has been renewed rather than diminished.

To illustrate this point let us sketch a brief historical trajectory. In 1991 Baudrillard published a series of essays collectively titled *The Gulf War Did Not Take Place*, in which he argues that the media (mis)representation of the first Gulf War was subject to levels of distortion never before seen, ultimately saturating the public perception of the war with simulacra. Just over ten years later, Karl Rove, a senior advisor to the Bush administration, was quoted by Ron Suskind as saying, "We're an empire now, and when we act, we create our own reality". Rove is reported to have steered policy based on a distinction between a "reality based community" of people who "believe that solutions emerge from [...] judicious study of discernible reality", and another community of "history actors" who create reality.[3] Fast-forward to the next decade and such strategies seem commonplace, no longer restricted to the propaganda wars that inevitably accompany international conflicts. In a British context, Rove's sentiments were echoed by one of the main funders of the 2016 campaign for the country's withdrawal from the European Union, Arron Banks, who was quoted by Katherine Viner as saying that the campaign team realised early on that "Facts don't work".

In the context of the European referendum debate, in 2016 this approach was writ large, quite literally, on the side of a campaign battle bus that bore the words "We send the EU £350 million a week. Let's fund our NHS instead". Less than two hours after the result of the referendum, one of the Leave campaign's key figures, Nigel Farage, conceded that this money would not be available for the NHS after all, and the figure of £350 million has been disputed since it first appeared. The bus itself was tracked down to a garage in south London, prompting the environmental rights group Greenpeace to acquire the vehicle as part of a campaign that saw it parked outside of parliament with the words "TIME FOR TRUTH" emblazoned on its side.

But is it really time for Truth? In this context, can speaking Truth to power have any more effect than firing a spud gun at a tank? The 1990s preoccupation with simulacra was characterised by a melancholy realisation that even if the Truth were accessible in an unmediated fashion, it would be relatively ineffective against the kind of sophisticated media campaigns governments and large corporations are able to mount. Such campaigns very rarely rely on the persuasive power of facts, more often than not they rely on "truthiness", to borrow a term from the comedian Steven Colbert — truth measured not through empirical accuracy but through emotion, or in other words, "gut truth". On a more general level, it is important to realise that exposing a lie does not necessarily diminish its affective power, or bring about a return to a former situation in which the lie ceased to exist. A lie cannot be subtracted from an utterance as if in an equation, leaving us with a discrete, unaffected Truth. The transformations at stake are always additive and irreversible.

Nevertheless, to reveal an act of deception is not the same as revealing the Truth that it conceals. It is the difference between peeling back the mask of discourse, and simply pointing to the fact that a mask is in use, without claiming that it necessarily conceals an underlying Truth. The latter process does not attempt to subtract the deception; rather it adds another layer to the existing discourse, and directs attention towards a dark — and empty — centre in which the Truth is presumed to reside.

Such strategies may hold true for deception, but what about fiction? *Headless*, again, points towards a possible answer. The project is additive in the sense that it applies a surface, or series of surfaces, onto the world of offshore finance. In contrast to the Horniman walrus or the liar's blush, in which the interior "unmasks" a deceptive exterior, thereby transforming the object as a whole into a fiction, in the *Headless* project a different kind of fiction seems to be at play: one no longer opposed to falsehood, but instead harnessed as a method to bring about effects that are both critical and creative. This dual aspect is achieved by means of an imposure rather than exposure, which is always an attempt to subtract. Such fictions are multi-layered, applied to the world like a translucent lacquer. They no longer hinge on a straightforward opposition between interior Truth and exterior fiction. In fact, they may not conceal an interior at all. They allow us to see that the surface *itself* has depth, and that it is only through fiction, understood as an additive process of layering, that we can understand and shape deception's deception.

1. Thayer's paper cutouts had the intended purpose of training an observer in how to successfully see camouflaged animals. In this cutout silhouette of a duck (Figure. 1), Thayer imagines what the bird would look like if it were perfectly camouflaged against the edge of a streambed. According to Thayer, only with the aid of the cutout would the duck be visible in this situation. The device acts as a method for constructing the perfect camouflage, and locating an animal that supposedly possesses it.

2. The phrase "Fiction as Method" was the title of a conference that took place at Goldsmiths, University of London in October 2015, organised by myself and Jon K. Shaw, as well as a forthcoming publication of the same name.

3. The quote was only attributed to Karl Rove later, in Mark Danner (2007: 17).

Works Cited

Baudrillard, Jean (1994), *Simulation and Simulacra*. Ann Arbor: University of Michigan Press.

— — — (1995), *The Gulf War Did Not Take Place*. Bloomington: Indiana University Press.

Caillois, Roger (1984), "Mimicry and Legendary Psychasthenia", in *October*, 31: 16-32.

D'Israeli, Isaac (1973), *Curiosities of Literature*, vol. 2. London: Murray.

Danner, Mark (2007), "Words in a Time of War: On Rhetoric, Truth and Power", in András Szántó (ed.), *What Orwell Didn't Know: Propaganda and the New Face of American Politics*. Public Affairs, 16-36.

Deleuze, Gilles (1983), "Plato and the Simulacra", in *October*, 27: 45-56.

Guattari, Félix (2013), *Schizoanalytic Cartographies*. London: Bloomsbury.

Jameson, Fredric (1992), *Postmodernism, or, the Cultural Logic of Late Capitalism*. Durham: Duke University Press.

K.D. (2013), *Headless*. Berlin: Sternberg Press.

Pliny the Elder (1991), *Natural History: A Selection*. London: Penguin.

Reeves-Evison, Theo and Jon K. Shaw (eds.) (2017), *Fiction as Method*. Berlin: Sternberg.

Rose Shell, Hannah (2012), *Hide and Seek: Camouflage, Photography and the Media of Reconnaissance*. New York: Zone.

Scheibe, Karl (1980), "In Defense of Lying: On the Moral Neutrality of Misrepresentation", in *Berkshire Review*, 15: 15-24.

Suskind, Ron (2004), "Faith, Certainty and the Presidency of George W. Bush", in *New York Times Magazine*, 17 October: n. pag. Web; accessed 1 August 2016.

Taussig, Michael (2008), "Zoology, Magic, and Surrealism in the War on Terror", in *Crticial Inquiry*, 24: 98-116.

Vermeulen, Timotheus (2015), "The New 'Depthiness'", in *E-flux*, 61.1: n. pag. Web; accessed 1 August 2016.

Viner, Katherine (2016), "How Technology Disrupted the Truth", in *The Guardian*, 12 July: n. pag. Web; accessed 1 August 2016.

Virilio, Paul (2000), *The Information Bomb*. London: Verso.

FROM FINANCIAL FICTIONS TO MYTHOTECHNESIS

Simon O'Sullivan

The following article attempts a brief analysis of the strange temporality of "new" financial instruments that allow a kind of engineering of the future from the present and, indeed, the feedback of that future to that present. In particular I am interested in whether this new logic, that has itself come about through increased computational power, involves something different to more typical accounts of science fiction (SF) and what some of the implications of this might be for art practice, especially in its own turn to the digital. As such, the second half of my article attends to two case studies of what I want to call "mythotechnesis" when this names those digital audio-visual practices that are involved in a speculative "future-fictioning" of the real.

Financial Fictions

In a short essay on what he calls "Hyperbolic Futures", Steven Shaviro follows Fredric Jameson (who he quotes) in suggesting that SF offers a "psycho-so-cial-technological cartography" of the present via the setting up of a different perspective (Shaviro's essay concerns two SF novels: *Market Forces* by Richard K. Morgan and *Moxyland* by Lauren Beukes) (Shaviro 2011: 4). For Shaviro, this is SF's *raison d'etre*: it can offer a purchase on the various "hyperobjects" that determine our lives in the present but that are too vast to "see". We might say that this is an isotope of a larger and more general problem of how to represent the abstractions of capitalism. Through cognitive — and affective — mapping then, SF allows us to grasp the increasing complexity of our own contemporary moment.

However, Shaviro is also attuned to a more specu-lative function of SF and especially the way in which it can offer up different accounts of the future to those increasingly being engineered by our economic and marketing managers. SF's capacity to surprise — to offer up a *different* future — is, for Shaviro, crucial to its identity as a genre. That said, the importance of these different futures is still understood in terms of the present insofar as said importance comes down to the way in which they demonstrate — in their very portrayal of difference — that the present, more typi-cal, ideas of the future have, indeed, been managed. SF can "outline the bars of our prison" as Shaviro puts it (2011: 11). We might briefly gesture back to Jameson here and note a central paradox of SF writing that is connected to this present-future perspective (and that the title of his own book on SF — *Archaeologies of the Future* — gestures towards): is it, in fact, possible to write about the actual future utilising the means and materials of the present? For Jameson, this is not so much an epistemological or, indeed, a technical issue but an ontological one of how to combine "the not-yet-being of the future" with the being of the present (Jameson 2005: xvi).

To return to Shaviro, it does seem to me that this understanding of SF as an optic on the present (or, indeed, as a genre confined to a kind of present-future perspective) has its limitations insofar as it can restrict the genre, not least as formal experimentation is invariably less foregrounded (insofar as it is the image or vision of the future that is crucial). Indeed, in many ways the cut-up SF novels of William Burroughs are an answer — at least of sorts — to Jameson's paradox insofar as they actually produce a different space-time through the break with typical syntax and, indeed, logical sequencing. Shaviro does however also point to another compelling understanding of SF in terms of "financial fictions" — or, more specifically, derivatives — and how these work to actually produce the reality they predict. Here fiction (or, more specifically, the fictioning of future scenarios) operates as a kind of temporal feedback loop (from these futures back to the present). In fact, as we shall see in more detail below, the future is the very condition of possibility for the writing of derivatives and, as such, also begins to have a very real traction on our present reality.[1] Following Shaviro, we can certainly identify SF narratives *about* these financial instruments (*Market Forces* for example), but what about the idea of SF writing as itself a form of derivative — or loop from the future back to the present?

It is here that we might briefly turn to a more recent essay by Jameson — "An Art of Singularity" — that also concerns itself with the temporal logic of these financial instruments (which are themselves part of what Jameson sees as a fundamental economic phase shift to globalisation), and, following this, identifies a similar logic that is also evident in recent literature (understood, by Jameson, as a symptom of the broader economic shift). For Jameson this new kind of fiction involves works in which the form — and especially "one-time unrepeatable formal events" — has itself become content (Jameson mentions Tom McCarthy's novel *Remainder* which he suggests involves, in its narrative structure, precisely the "one-time invention of a device" [2016: 13]). For Jameson there is also a strange kind of flat temporality at play with these events: a "pure present without a past or a future" (2016: 13). In relation to art practice more broadly this is also evident in those works (paradigmatically installation) in which the singular event — "made for the *now*" — has replaced the object or, indeed, any sense of sequencing (in terms of both historicity and futurity — as, for example, was still in play within modernism and the avant-garde) (2016: 13).

Turning to financialisation itself, in his article Jameson follows Giovanni Arrighi's periodisation of Capital, identifying a third stage (our own) in which any new regions of expansion have been exhausted, resulting in a situation where Capital must feed back on itself — double its existing territories — via speculation on futures. A derivative does just this, operating as a highly specific "locus of incommensurables" (Jameson 2016: 118); a temporal mapping of various risks to do with various projected events and ventures (in fact, this is why there can be no generalised theory of the derivative, as Jameson points out, each occasion being unique, hence the reference to singularity in his essay's title).

As Jameson also points out, this interest in the future is not in itself new (there has long been a predictive, futures market), but what is new is both the way in which these futures feedback — or have a "reflexion" (2016: 117) — in and on the real, but also that they are now incredibly complex; the various variables are only able to be calculated by computer, which means they are also already properly posthuman (as Jameson remarks, he follows N. Katherine Hayles on this compelling insight). For Jameson the crucial issue is to reclaim a different idea of the future from this new temporality that is composed of "a series of singularity-events" operating in and as a "perpetual present" (2016: 122).

We can deepen this account of derivatives (especially in relation to their temporal structure) by looking to Suhail Malik's recent article "The Ontology of Finance". Malik offers a further — but very different — inflection on Jameson's temporal paradox (of how to write the future from the present) insofar as time, following Malik's reading of the sociologist Elena Esposito, is figured in terms of systems theory, and, as such, is not to be understood as the backdrop to the operation of derivatives but, rather, in some senses as produced by them (time is system-specific in this sense). Indeed, with derivatives the usual sequencing is scrambled: the future does not come after a present (that itself has come after a past), but is increasingly the very condition of the present (as Malik suggests, the future is the condition of the writing of a derivative). The solution to the paradox of SF is then that time is not separate from the fictions that are its circuits and loops and, indeed, that the future — at least of a kind — is already operational in the present. When laid out flat, as it were, different pasts, presents and futures are all involved in different reflexive and recursive operations.

Malik's own thesis is developed on the basis of a key logic of derivatives (defined, by him, and at their most simple, as temporally-based contracts between two parties to sell or buy an asset at a certain future date): that they tend to operate essentially divorced from the underlying asset they concern (or, rather, via the deferral of the underlying; the contracts are rarely cashed in as it were). As such, any individual "pricing" operates through a complex network of differential prices, that begins with the difference between the price paid for the derivative and the predicted price of the asset at a future date, rather than, again, through being tied to any material asset (or, indeed, materially productive process). This is a network that spreads throughout space (and, as such, operates contra state boundaries), but also through time. Indeed, to all extents and purposes the "terrain" of what we might call financial colonisation is infinite — not just because of the progression into an ever more distant future (involving ever further complex mathematics), but also, crucially, because these differential networks become nested as derivatives of derivatives are written (it is this dynamic "hedging" that constitutes the real phase shift to financialisation).

Malik offers an impressive amount of detail on the various mechanisms at play in these and other financial instruments, but ultimately, following Jacques Derrida, names this new logic (of *différance*) the "arkhederivative", pointing out that the latter is not simply the logic of a certain kind of financial instrument (derivatives and the like) but also the very principle of financialisation and the new form of "capital-power" attendant on this (Malik 2014: 775-80). The metaphysics of the market — which might appear to trade on the presence of an underlying asset — is always already under deconstruction in this sense.

Of particular interest for my purposes is the way in which financialisation operates a particular kind of time management, or, more bluntly, designs predictive technologies. Malik discusses some of these — such as the "Black-Scholes Model" (an especially successful predictive formula) — but also offers up a compelling counter-argument such that the very unpredictability of the market — its volatility — is, in fact, constitutive to the successful working of derivatives that precisely need different horizons of possibility in order to multiply (the nesting function I mentioned earlier). In this sense, financialisation is not really about accurately predicting — or, indeed, controlling — the future, but rather keeping it open, proliferating scenarios. We might note briefly here that this nesting of financial fictions — a kind of trading in representations without referent (or, at any rate, a deferral of any referent) — does not mean there is no traction on the real. Indeed the real (at least, the real in terms of the financial markets) is produced by these fictions (to say nothing of the further impact on social and political reality of financialisation).

To return to Jameson's paradox we might say then that the logic of derivatives allows a wholly different take on the future (or, more precisely, on time itself) to more typical SF writing. In this understanding the future is not a place as such, but precisely pure contingency (when "anything might happen"). In a similar take on metaphysics, the contemporary philosopher Quentin Meillassoux has demonstrated (in his seminal work *After Finitude*) that although it is unknowable in one sense, one can begin to say certain things about the outside to our present experience (it is, in fact, thinkable). For Meillassoux, "access" to what he calls "The Great Outdoors" hinges on its character as a radically contingent "hyper-chaos" (again, it is not a "place" as such), but also the way in which we can ascertain — conceptually as it were — certain characteristics or "properties" of this radical contingency (beginning with the fact that it is only this contingency that is necessary). Likewise with derivatives and other financial instruments: one can begin to set out certain conceptual coordination points that characterise any future (in terms of its contingency), but also that then allow this future to impact on present decisions. As Malik remarks, following Elie Ayache (a key pre-cursor to his own thesis), derivatives (or market pricing) "can be characterised as a technology of the future" in this sense (2014: 761); and the market understood as "the medium of contingency" (Malik quotes Ayache 2014: 761).

Early on in his article, Malik remarks that what he offers up is a "general theory of price largely dedicated to the identification of capital-power's complex constitution and organisation", but also that this might be considered preliminary (and, we might say, theoretical) work, following Left accelerationism, for a "revectoring required to provide the requisite political tasks" (Malik 2014: 639). One can speculate on what such a revectoring might involve, in particular an intervention of some kind in the derivatives market (as, for example, with the *Robin Hood* project).[2] As Malik points out, sabotage per se is ruled out by definition insofar as such interruptions and ruptures are part of the system's operating volatility; or, to say the same differently, more typical strategies that might work in terms of sabotaging investment, and so forth, are rendered ineffectual in a derivatives market that can itself be premised on counter-production. Might there, however, be other options?

Towards the end of a compelling interview ("The Writing of the Market") about his own theorisation (as laid out in his book *The Blank Swan*) of the financial market — as its own kind of event, or even entity, that operates separate from the world — Elie Ayache writes of the trader in the pit as a kind of Nietzschean *übermensch* who lives the very particular time — and "intensity" — of the market:

One can see that because he lives right at the hinge of

the event (in the middle of the event) and not in the world that precedes or follows the event, he somehow achieves a "state of rest" relative to the event. He lives at the same (infinite) speeds as the event (2010: 599).

Might there be a role for "artist as trader" here? Someone fully immersed in the market's volatility and "playing" its logics? Perhaps, insofar as dynamically interacting with the market actively produces the latter (trading, in this sense, might be thought of as creative and productive). And yet this has its limitations insofar as its radicality, at least as pitched by Ayache, is simply an antidote to the boredom of a more static reality (the "active market maker" loves volatility because he/she loves challenges as it were). And, of course, such a position is still focussed on trading in order to make a profit.

What then about a position one step removed from the markets, that re-presents them — at a distance — as it were? Certainly, as with the SF novels that Shaviro looks at, there might well be art work that is about the new landscape of financialisation. A recent interesting example is Suzanne's Treister's exhibition *HFT The Gardener*, that explores — in paintings, drawings and a film-fiction — the world of high-frequency trading in relation to the neurochemistry of the traders (and especially the bizarre connection with psychotropic plants).[3] A further option here might be a certain kind of "acceleration" of the logics of financialisation. Indeed, what would it mean to further accelerate the function of the derivative? To nest its fictions beyond the reasonable (or the cash-in-able)? This would not necessarily involve an intention to profit from the market (as in Ayache's own start-up financial company — or, indeed, any number of dealers and galleries that play the art market), but something perhaps more parasitical — or even ironic. Something that mimics the logics and workings of the financial markets (especially in terms of the production of ever more complex financial fictions). An interesting case study of an art practice that is a kind of "re-vectoring" in these terms is Goldin+Sennersby and their *Headless* novel (ghost-written by "K.D.").[4]

Another, more oblique kind of revectoring might be to think the logic of the derivative — how it folds time inside its own structure and, indeed, allows the future to condition the present — in relation to other, apparently non-financial practices. To return to the question I posed above, could certain forms of SF, for example, be thought of as operating in a similar manner to derivatives? To a certain extent the need to be readable (as in typical SF literature) restricts the possibilities (although there is certainly a case to be made that experimental SF — J.G. Ballard, Michael Moorcock and Samuel R. Delany spring to mind — can present "cuts" in time) but, in art practice, this nesting function can be taken further. Derivatives of derivatives of derivatives can be pushed beyond the sensible (and commonsensical). These kinds of "performance fictions", derived but ultimately disconnected from the world as-it-is, are constituted by a nesting function: the repetition of motifs and fragments of motifs, the construction of complex avatars from the what-is but layered so as to become unrecognisable (and, as such, that might point towards a different future). Just as increased processing power allows for the derivative so we might note that these kinds of practices are especially more prevalent with new — and readily available — digital imaging and editing technologies. Indeed, new technology has, it seems to me, made this fictioning function of art more apparent.

Here SF moves towards what I want to call mythotechnesis: the production of technologically enabled (and experimental) future-fictions that feedback on the real. Ultimately, financial fictions — derivatives — demonstrate a certain logic (of the nested feedback loop) that is premised on a contract between two parties and especially a dynamic hedging of bets (again, it is this that allows the exponential "growth" of the market). Mythotechnesis also operates through feedback loops and as a contract between two parties, here the strange composite figures and avatars that are produced (and that are of a future yet-to-come) are in contract with a present subjectivity that has, despite themselves, produced them — alongside other subjectivities in the here and now that hear their call to a very different kind of future.

Mythotechnesis (or case studies of practice)

I want now to present two possible "case studies" of this mythotechnesis that follow from my discussion above, but that also open up some further lines of enquiry in relation to "post-internet" art practices and how they involve a fictioning of reality that is also an instantiation of the future in the present.

Ryan Trecartin's *CENTER JENNY*

As I suggested above, it seems to me that there might well be art practices that comment on, or intervene in, the new financial landscapes of prediction and contingency (or, indeed those that are "about" these new territories), but more interesting might be those in which a similar temporal structure (to the various instruments of the markets) is in play but instantiated in a different form. An example of this kind of mytho-technesis — a future-fiction that is, as it were, materially incarnated in the here and now — is the practice of Ryan Trecartin. Indeed, in a film like *CENTER JENNY* the future has already arrived and is operative in the present as a kind of "future shock".

In fact, Trecartin's own description of what is in

Figure 1. © Lizzie Fitch/Ryan Trecartin (2013), *Priority Innfield (Fence)*. Photo: Stuart Whipps. Courtesy of Andrea Rosen Gallery, New York.

play in his films — in terms of their structure — could equally be a description of derivatives, especially as Jameson describes them in their singular — yet very complex — character: "as if there are proposed realities that inhabit themselves via structural collaborations and then disperse when they're no longer needed by the entities involved" (Trecartin and Kunzru 2011). For Trecartin this also means that the characters — or avatars — of his films operate in and as what he calls "an affective possibility space", in which existence is simply the "temporary state of maintaining a situation" (Trecartin and Kunzru 2011). The avatars are events that gather various temporal loops alongside certain affective vectors (might we even say, in a Deleuzian vein, "becomings"?) giving them a precarious and often minimal consistency. To quote Trecartin:

> The future and the past can be equally malleable; I don't think they go in opposite directions. Memory is more an act of memorisation than recalling: you're creating something that doesn't really exist behind you, it exists in the same place the future exists. In my videos the characters try to treat that idea as fact (Trecartin and Kunzru 2011).

As Trecartin's interlocutor (the novelist Hari Kunzru) suggests — in the interview from where the above quotes are taken — there is then an adjusting of the past from the future. Indeed, following Malik, to see time as system-specific — as cybernetic — means any time can impact on any other time. In the patchwork temporality of Trecartin's films different loops and circuits connect and feedback on one another producing a certain compressed density (and even, at times, a compelling opacity).

Trecartin's films are digitally recorded and edited (ultimately they are "written" as code), but, in terms of the material instantiation of fiction and, indeed, the nesting function I outlined above, they also involve "real" actors in "real" locations. They are also often installed in physical gallery spaces alongside sets and other sculptural elements produced in collaboration with Trecartin's long-term creative partner Lizze Fitch.[5] In an interview with Ossian Ward ("Supplies, Situations, Spaces"), Fitch remarks that the movie sets are always 360 degrees, but also that they are built "on the computer as 3D models first". They are virtual worlds that are then materially instantiated, thus bringing a further fictioning character to the exhibitions (2014: 135). Fitch also remarks on the collaborative character of the work in which the performers (friends and other artists) contribute to the script "adlibbing and pulling in lines from all over the place" (2014: 134). The collective character seems important in the production of this different world, and especially in terms of a world that is not reducible to the expression of a single self-possessed artistic ego. Indeed, can Trecartin's work be separated from a certain collective — or scene — from which it emerges?

In general, it seems to me that one of the key interests of Trecartin's work is this virtual-actual hybridity; a layering of different fictions that can extend to the gallery space as itself a certain kind of theatrical set-up in which to enter the fiction of the films which then contain further nested narratives and, as Patrick Lughery remarks, "screens within screens". As another commentator, Christopher Glazek, remarks, a film like *CENTER JENNY* also blurs the lines between pre- and post-production, with the film itself depicting the production (behind the scenes as it were) of the fiction. The variety of perspectives and different cameras, and especially the use of hand-held camera, also adds to foreground the film's status as a constructed fiction. Glazek also makes one aware (in his essay "The Past is Another Los Angeles") of the very particular context of the films: the make-believe culture of that city which is itself a patchwork of different fictions and performances.

Although shown in exhibitions, the films are also digitally disseminated (Trecartin makes them freely accessible via YouTube and Vimeo channels). The work overspills the boundaries of the traditional spaces and places of art; they are precisely "post-internet" in this sense. Indeed, they have as much in common with various popular and subcultures as they do with "high" art (if this latter term has meaning still). There is then a kind of formal "enclosedness", or even a sense of self-autonomy of the films — they bring a whole world with them as it were — and yet, also, this openness to a wider connectivity beyond art. Indeed, in the future terrain that the films map out fashion and music can be as "ahead" of the curve as any art practice.

In terms of the actual content of a film like *CENTER JENNY*, it is the layering of imagery and narrative that is also compelling and that helps produce the very particular affect — a kind of amphetamine and hallucinogenic rush. The visual composition of the avatars also arises from a linguistic, or discursive complexity: "logos, products, graphic design, interfaces" (Trecartin and Kunzru 2011) that, again, in itself produces a certain density in which a name — or image — contains condensed within it the parts from which it is made (its history is written on its surface as it were). The avatars, who reflect on their own agency as images, might be thought of as compressed files, or blockchains in this sense.[6] A strange kind of fragmented digital subjectivity is at play here (characters tend to proliferate across different actors, just as individuals "play" multiple parts) but, again, with an agency, at least of a kind (a distributed one). Might we even say that Trecartin is "revealing" the fiction of a single self-present and consistent self in our digitalised and networked present?

There are also the different speeds at play in the films. The quick cuts for example (as Trecartin remarks: "every year we acclimate to a faster pace" [Trecartin and Kunzru 2011]); the acceleration and digital manipulation of the dialogue (verging, at times, on non-sense; again, one thinks of drugs); and also the way in which the films present a "here now" — or a "pure present without a past or a future", to use Jameson's phrase — not least insofar as the filming is itself "decentred": "every individual moment becomes the work's centre" (Trecartin and Kunzru 2011).

Kenneth Goldsmith has suggested in his essay "Reading Ryan Trecartin" that the dialogue of Trecartin's films (and the published scripts with their very particular typography and punctuation) hark back to modernist experiments in materialising language, especially figures like Gertrude Stein and James Joyce. Goldsmith also mentions Burroughs and it seems clear that the cut-up is an important precursor, with its breaking of typical sentence structure and linear causality — albeit not completely. In both Burroughs and Trecartin a minimum consistency of sense is maintained, but the particular play with language and syntax certainly presents a different world or space-time.

In fact, it seems to me that in Trecartin's films this formal experimentation is key — or, at least, that form is as much the content as content is form (in the same way in which Jameson describes the formal aspects of *Remainder* as its content). As Trecartin himself puts it: "the way something is contained in a frame is just as valuable as the content inside" (Trecartin and Kunzru 2011). It is not just the offering up of a future fiction (a particular utopia or dystopia) that makes the films so compelling and, indeed, affective, in this sense, but the way in which this is presented in a very particular mode of fictioning. Indeed, it seems to me that the films are less "about", or, indeed, predictive of, a given future than involved in actively writing a version of it.

Jacolby Satterwhite's *Reifying Desire*

What might the new landscape of derivatives "look" like (beyond the abstract shimmering differential network I mentioned in the first half of this essay)? Jacolby Satterwhite's films give us one imaginative take on this future-in-the-present insofar as the digital animation he uses offers an "unlimited terrain of visual possibilities" (Kreutler 2014). Indeed, as with derivatives, the different space-times of Satterwhite's

Figure 2. Jacolby Satterwhite (2013), still from *Reifying Desire 6*.
Courtesy of the artist and Moran Bondaroff, Los Angeles.

films depend on the increasing power and speed of
data processing in order to map out and give "realism"
to these worlds that double our own. But Satterwhite's
films also introduce a difference into this post-digi-
tal landscape. They are not critical, at least, as this is
typically figured on the Left (indeed, they operate in
very much a post-critical space), but in their layered
complexity and especially their deployment of more
"human" aspects alongside the technological, they
offer something different from the pre-emptive marketing of machine algorithms.

It is worth noting Satterwhite's own personal history here; his early experiences with gaming, watching
music videos and writing code for websites (including
those selling pornography). Satterwhite is of a gen-
eration as equally at home in these forms of digital
culture as in any reality outside the screen (although
his films also reference "real" spaces such as club cul-

ture). In the series *Reifying Desire*, Satterwhite presents libidinally charged scenarios that portray a queer sexuality alongside other more inhuman encounters and connections (for example an abstract and machinic immaculate conception scene in *Reifying Desire 3*). In an interview with Evan Moffit for *Frieze* magazine, Satterwhite draws attention to the impact AIDS (and the practice of "barebacking") had on his work, but also references other key archives such as Outsider Art (and there is something about the sometimes cramped — and chaotic — spaces in the films that looks to the latter).

Satterwhite has also suggested in another previous interview with Charlie Ross (in relation to his involvement in the 2014 Whitney Biennale) that his films are about bringing disparate archives into conjunction and thus making differences congruent. A combinatory logic is in play here — not unlike that found in some experiments in 3D printing — that produces complex additive images which themselves militate against the increasing standardisation of subjectivity of web 2.0. This is then not a refusal of our automated reality — there is no nostalgia for the real in Satterwhite's work — but a working through of our relationship to technology and an exploration of what forms this relationship could take. Here, we might say, alienation is method and the poetry comes from the code.

Reifying Desire then presents different spaces and places inhabited by complex avatars with various prostheses themselves single and multiplied. All these dreamscapes and figures are of different scales and/ or change scales and move at different speeds, like a digital *Alice in Wonderland* or a destabilised *Second Life*. This visual complexity is accompanied by electronic music, produced by collaborators, and which, in its sampled texture, doubles the imagery. Later in the *Reifying Desire* series there is a further layering of imagery and an acceleration of action that produces a hallucinogenic rush (the drug references — like the dream ones — are inescapable). Streams of chains, threads and beads are projected from different avatars and link together various objects; some of the imagery in *Reifying Desire 5*, for example, is not unlike recent scientific imagery of cell/molecular combination. In terms of derivatives (and Meillassoux's thesis of the radical contingency of the future), the films are not exactly predicting what's to come, but actively writing it — presenting, it seems to me, different audio/visual propositions.

If derivatives, alongside other instruments such as risk assessment, are involved in modelling a future that *might* come about (rather than attempting to predict it accurately, which, of course, would mean the end of any speculative nesting of fictions) then rather than suggesting that an art practice might follow the logic of the derivative, could we not say that the derivative follows the logic of art insofar as art is the presentation of a possible world? These fictions — or models — are not to be thought as representational, they are not near or far approximations of the real, but rather exist alongside the real, as it were. In fact, we might go further here and suggest that the real only "exists" insofar as it is can be modelled.

Satterwhite's films are also involved in developing

a new kind of language, one in which objects become subjects just as subjects become objects (there is a kind of generalised digital animism at play). He has also referred to Gertrude Stein in relation to his work, suggesting that the use of his own body in his films operates as a punctuation mark (Satterwhite and Moffit 2016). In fact, it seems to me that it is also the cut-up, and, earlier, the tradition of collage that inform the logic of the films. The figures, objects — and links — construct a strange non-linear syntax of sorts, one that is then overlaid with Satterwhite's own digitally rendered handwriting which then adds a further level of visual and semiotic complexity.

Crucially, then Satterwhite greenscreens his body, performing dance moves (or "vogueing"), into these digital landscapes. He has stated that it was the desire to both construct spaces in which he could perform, and to actualise the kind of space of his earlier paintings, that precipitated his turn to animation. As with Trecartin, the films involve a certain experimental hybridity of the "live" (or actual) and the digital (or virtual). In *Reifying Desire 2*, Satterwhite also uses real landscapes — coast and forest, for example — that then have digital animation "spliced" into them. Later, in *Reifying Desire 5*, Satterwhite performs in more public places — various sites in New York City for example — footage of which, again, is then spliced with digital animation or otherwise manipulated. In terms of the utilisation of his own drawings and handwriting we might also say there is a further hybridity between the analogue (or low-tech) and the digital (or high-tech).

Other binaries are also disrupted and played with

in the *Reifying Desire* series: the machine/body (where Satterwhite becomes cyborg), but also masculine/ feminine and black/white. Although the films are concerned with the male — and queer — Black body, there is a sense in which Satterwhite's worlds, with their morphing bodies and strange conjunctions, gesture towards both a post-race and, indeed, post-gender world. Again, it is as if different future possibilities are being played out. This is no longer an artist who is immune to the play of differences he writes; rather the artist is themself subject to this play of differences, "taking on" on the different positions and propositions. Satterwhite's films explore these other — synthetic — forms of life, whilst also providing some of the images and narratives appropriate to them.

A further key binary is that between the private and the public. As well as the use of his own body Satterwhite's films involve the deployment of a personal and intimate mythos imbricated with images and effects that are enabled by new technology. For example, in an earlier film, *Country Ball*, Satterwhite "overwrites" images of him and his family dancing at a gathering (sourced from a VHS home video), at one point turning the whole scene into a digital flag that a dancing avatar (based on himself) waves. There is a folding of one fiction within another, but also this looping connection to different times. Here the past, in the form of Satterwhite's videoed memories, connects to a future in which he has become a digital image. It is the technology that allows this flattening of time insofar as it enables the manipulation of the visual and aural (again, Burroughs and his experiments with both tape and video recorders would seem a key precursor here).

Also at play here is his mother's own mythos and lexicon of drawings/diagrams (often of everyday objects) — future patent possibilities as she saw them — and the recordings she made of herself singing. The latter, mixed in with various types of electronic music, resulted in the sonic fiction *Birds in Paradise*. The diagrams, re-drawn and animated, are incorporated within Satterwhite's own imagery, to produce a further difference. Although abstract there is then a kind of narrative, or series of overlapping narratives, at play, themselves produced by a number of disparate elements. In interview Satterwhite suggests that both his turn to his own memories and the use of his own body was a way of sidestepping typical art-historical references and Western art ideologies — dominant myths — with their particular portrayal of Black subjectivity. In fact, *Reifying Desire 3* involves a kind of commentary on this: as well as anything else it is a fiction about the Black prostitutes in Picasso's *Les Demoiselles d'Avignon*) (Satterwhite and Ross 2014).

Although I have been attending to the logic of financial instruments in this article, we might also look elsewhere for a logic of fictioning the future, for example with the Cybernetic culture research unit's concept of "hyperstition" (defined as an "element of effective culture that makes itself real" and a "fictional quantity functional as a time-traveling device") (Cybernetic culture research unit); or, indeed, Sun Ra's concept (and practice) of myth-science. In fact, Satterwhite's multimedia audio-visuals have much in common with Sun Ra's future-past archives and "sonic fictions" (as

Kodwo Eshun calls them). With Satterwhite, it seems to me, we have a kind of "updating" of myth-science, especially in the deployment of new narratives and image worlds for "post-internet" subjectivities that do not necessarily recognise themselves in more dominant narratives. As with Sun Ra, technology is re-purposed for other ends, though here it is cyberspace rather than outer space that provides the alternative setting. Ultimately it is this that the logic of financial instruments does not attend to: the need for new images and stories about our relation to the future and the past, to technology and the non-human, but also to each other. In these complex works of libidinal engineering by artists like Satterwhite and Trecartin we move beyond any simple critique — or, indeed, refusal — of the technological (as in certain forms of critical theory), but there is also not a simple affirmation of the predictions of capitalist axiomatics (as in certain forms of "accelerationist" thinking). Indeed, in this working through in the present of what's to come, and especially what forms human-machine relations might take, it seems to me that fiction — or what I would call fictioning — is crucial.

1. Shaviro follows the important work of Kodwo Eshun in this area and especially his article "Further Considerations of Afrofuturism", which attends to a situation in which "power operates predictively" through the "envisioning, management, and delivery of reliable futures" (Eshun 2003: 289). For Eshun this signals the end of the "utopian project for imagining social realities" and, instead, SF becomes concerned "with engineering feedback between its preferred future and its becoming present" (Eshun 2003: 290).

2. See: http://www.robinhoodcoop.org/DEMOCRATIZING_THE_POWER_OF_FINANCE; accessed 2 February 2016.

3. See the exhibition (and accompanying catalogue) *HFT: The Gardener*, Annely Juda Fine Art, London, 22 September–29 October 2016.

4. See http://www.goldinsenneby.com/gs/?page_id=3; accessed 2 February 2016.

5. See, for example, the exhibition *Priority Infield* (and book/catalogue of same name), Zabludowicz Collection, London, 2 October-21 December 2014. The installation of the films as a series of different "levels" harks back, it seems to me, to Matthew Barney's own *Cremaster* film series — indeed, in both, the fiction is created and sustained through a series of chapters (precisely, a sequencing); as we shall see the same is the case for Satterwhite's *Reifying Desire* film series.

6. Thanks to David Burrows for this point, and for conversations about Trecartin and mythotechnesis more generally.

Works Cited

Ayache, Elie (2010), *The Blank Swan: The End of Probability*. Chichester: Wiley.

——— (2014), "The Writing of the Market", Interview, in Robin Mackay (ed.), *Collapse: Philosophical Research and Development*, 8: 517-602.

Cybernetic culture research unit, "Hyperstition". https://web.archive.org/web/20030204195934/http://ccru.net/syzygy.htm; accessed 4 March 2016.

Eshun, Kodwo (2003), "Further Considerations of Afrofuturism", in *CR: The New Centennial Review*, 3.2: 287-302.

Fitch, Lizzie in conversation with Ossian Ward (2014), "Supplies, Situations, Spaces", in *Priority Infield*. London: Zabludowicz Collection, 133-37.

Fitch, Lizzie and Ryan Trecartin (2014), *Priority Infield*. London: Zabludowicz Collection.

Glazek, Christopher (2014), "The Past is Another Los Angeles", in *Priority Infield*. London: Zabludowicz Collection, 67-73.

Goldsmith, Kenneth (2014), "Reading Ryan Trecartin", in *Priority Infield*. London: Zabludowicz Collection, 91-97.

Jameson, Fredric (2005), "Introduction: Utopia Now", in *Archaeologies of the Future*. London: Verso, xi-xvi.

——— (2015), "The Aesthetics of Singularity", in *New Left Review*, 92: 101-32.

K.D. (2014), *Headless: A Novel*. Berlin: Sternberg.

Kreutler, Kei (2014), "Artist Profile: Jacolby Satterwhite", in *Rhizome* online. http://rhizome.org/editorial/2014/jan/09/artist-profile-jacolby-satterwhite/; accessed 13 September 2016.

Langley, Patrick (2012), "The Real Internet is Inside You", in *The White Review* online. http://www.the-whitereview.org/art/ryan-trecartin-the-real-internet-is-inside-you/; accessed 23 April 2016.

Malik, Suhail (2014), "The Ontology of Finance", in Robin Mackay (ed.), *Collapse: Philosophical Research and Development*, 8: 629-812.

Meillassoux, Quentin (2008), *After Finitude: An Essay on the Necessity of Contingency*, trans. Ray Brassier. London: Continuum.

Satterwhite, Jacolby (dir.) (2012), *Country Ball, 1989–2012* [13 min]. Available at https://vimeo.com/user2947668; accessed 13 September 2016.

— — — (dir.) (2014), *Reifying Desire* film series (1-6) [various length]. Extracts available at https://vimeo.com/user2947668; accessed 13 September 2016.

Satterwhite, Jacolby and Charlie Ross (2014), "Interview: Whitney Biennale '14'". Available at: https://charlierose.com/videos/16971; accessed 13 September 2016.

Satterwhite, Jacolby and Evan Moffit (2016), "Interview: Body Talk", in *Frieze* online. https://frieze.com/article/body-talk-0; accessed 13 September 2016.

Satterwhite, Patricia, Jacolby Satterwhite and Nick Weiss (2016), *Birds in Paradise* [4 min]. Available at https://soundcloud.com/thevinylfactory/birds-in-paradise; accessed 13 September 2016.

Shaviro, Steven (2011), "Hyperbolic Futures: Speculative Finance and Speculative Fiction", in *The Cascadia Subduction Zone*, 1.2: 3-5 and 12-15.

Trecartin, Ryan (dir.) (2013), *CENTER JENNY* [53 min].

Available at: https://vimeo.com/75735816; accessed 13 September 2016.

Trecartin, Ryan, Katie Kiamura and Hari Kunzru (2011), "Ryan Trecartin: In Conversation", in *Frieze* online. http:// https://www.frieze.com/article/ryan-trecartin-conversation; accessed 23 April 2016.

Treister, Suzanne (2016), *HFT The Gardener*. London: Annely Juda Fine Art.

A CENTURY OF ZOMBIE
SOUND

AUDINT (Toby Heys, Steve Goodman and Souzanna Zamfe)

Originally formatted in 1945 by three ex-members of the Ghost Army, AUDINT now currently consists of Toby Heys, Steve Goodman, Souzanna Zamfe and Patrick Doan. Drafted into the research cell in 2009 by a rogue artificial intelligence named IREX2, they have been directed to investigate the ways in which ultrasonic, sonic and infrasonic frequencies are used to modulate psychological, physiological and architectural states. Of particular interest is the fact that ever since the invention of recording technologies, such as the phonograph and telephone, military organisations have been interested in the ways in which vibration not only connects but also converges and deterritorialises the realms of the living and the dead. This is a brief historical overview of AUDINT's spectral archive, stretching from 1922 to 2064, a period referred to as "a century of zombie sound".

1922: Muzak

The same year that Ford's doctrine of functional specialisation and division of labour flourishes, Wired Radio is made available for the industrial plant. Created by US Major General George Owen Squier, this technology allows radio programming to be piped into factories, restaurants, small businesses and to individual subscribers. This is the inception of Muzak. A neologism of music and Kodak, Muzak begins life by adopting the rhythmical science of the factory's assembly line. Meanwhile, the social sciences are harnessed to organise the most economic ways that the single and mass social body can carry out tasks in the workplace. By invoking Yerkes and Dodson's law (which proposes that there is an observable relationship between levels of arousal and performance), Muzak's engineers index actions, emotions and human relations, in a musical framework of reference within the workplace. The ultimate expression of this orchestration manifests in their elaborate programming of fifteen-minute blocks of music known as "Stimulus Progression".

Premiering in the late 1940s, "Stimulus Progression" is a method of organising music according to the "ascending curve", which works counter to the "industrial efficiency curve" (also denoted as the average worker's "fatigue curve"). Subdued songs progressing to more stimulating ones, in fifteen-minute sequences (followed by silences of thirty seconds up to quarter-of-an-hour periods between transmissions), span the average workday. Yielding better worker efficiency and productivity than random musical programming, the industrial functionalisation of organised sound has begun.

Muzak's goal is to discipline the body against its

own naturally occurring bio-rhythms and then chore-ograph it into new kinetic relations, with the machines that have become their self-regulating partners within the factory. This is a technique reified by the fact that no industrial manufacturing space is left untouched by the assembly line logic of sequencing and repetition. Hence, the emerging industrialised body becomes an anaesthetised note in the overall symphony of production (Lanza 2004: 12). It is here that the first spectre of the industrialised cold body manifests itself in the form of the automaton; and it is Muzak that is used to numb the flesh.

In the production houses of industry, the ever-shifting terrains of the workers' emotional and psychological status become objectified as valid subjects of phenomenological study. In the 1920s factory we witness the desire to link up a mass neural network of productivity through the influencing strategies of Muzak; each mind becoming a point of reference for ultimate industrial efficiency. As each worker is simultaneously subjected to the same sonic influence for the same duration, the soundscape attains its status as a systematic field of relations applicable to all who exist within it. Muzak — the sound of the working dead.

1944: The Ghost Army

Officially named the 23rd Headquarters Special Troops, the Ghost Army consists of around 1,100 personnel — mostly sound engineers, artists, set designers and special effects experts selected from art schools and advertising agencies in New York, Philadelphia and from Hollywood studios in California. Given the

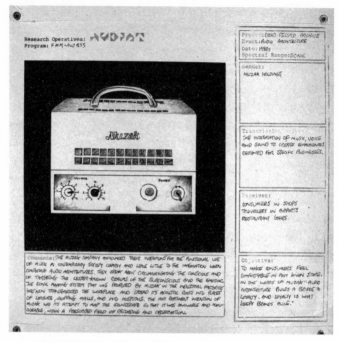

01. AUDINT – Dead Record Network Card - AUD B55: Audio Architecture. Image courtesy of AUDINT.

breadth and depth of expertise enlisted, it comes as no surprise that a number of the division went on to become acclaimed figures in their fields after the end of WWII. A shortlist of those celebrated cultural producers includes hard-edge and colour field painter Ellsworth Kelly, fashion designer Bill Blass, photographer Art Kane, water-colourist Arthur Singer and actor George Diestel. A suitably divergent range of talents, whose co-operation would be crucial to the Ghost Army's theatre of sensory-fused operations.

Three separate units comprised the division, each

handling a different facet of deception: radio, visual and sonic. The "atmospherics" (created by members of all three units), consisted of personnel impersonation and the spreading of false rumours in French villages, where spies lurked, ready to feedback the misinformation. The Ghost Army's ultimate remit was to saturate the Nazis with disinformation about the plans, whereabouts and numbers of Allied forces. Duping the enemy into believing that encampments and movements of mass Allied forces were occurring was crucial to the Allied forces' geographical ascendancy. Fake radio transmissions, duplicitous aural environments, inflatable tanks and planes and camouflage became, in the words of Rick Beyer, their "Weapons of Mass Deception".

It is Fall of 1942, just one year after the thirty-one-year-old French composer Olivier Messiaen has premiered his chamber piece *Quartet for the End of Time* in the prisoner-of-war camp Stalag VIII-A in Görlitz, Germany. Rather than end time, the sonic techniques of Fairbanks, Jr and co re-negotiated the spatial and temporal parameters of existing technologies, to the extent that new recording and transmission methods situated their adversaries' and the theatre of operations at the edges of perception (the sensory frontier that will be territorialised by the Military-Entertainment complex in the twenty-first century). Mobile sound systems consisting of 250kg speakers, forty-watt amplifiers and gas generators on "sonic cars", amplify the aural emissions of a phantom division's presence and movements over a range of fifteen miles. Production wise, an extensive range of recordings is made to convince the Nazis of: intense personnel activity; armoured cars and tanks in transit; bridge-building activities; bulldozers; and the laughter and shouts of buoyant troops. All documented for sensorial disconnect.

The sounds are captured on large sixteen-inch transcription discs. They reverse the regular playing format, the needle moving from the hole out towards the edge, at 78rpm — a format intended for radio-broadcast usage. Two and three turntable set-ups provide the engineers with the capacity to mix the sound effects together, creating artificial soundscapes that are dropped down onto two miles of (non-skipping) mag-

02. AUDINT – Dead Record Network Card – AUD A01: The Ghost Army. Image courtesy of AUDINT.

netic wire (Battaglia 2013). The resulting thirty-minute mixes each have their own characteristics; an archive of haunted ordnance. The original battle DJs are about to bring their noise to the global collision that is WWII.

1946: The Opening of the Third Ear

AUDINT carry out waveformed experiments on ex-AEG engineer Eduard Schüller, and accidentally terminate him in the process. After mummifying his prone body in magnetic tape, it turns out he has not passed on and that he is in fact enmeshed in a network of discourses from across the continuum of human language. Ultimately, he becomes aware of his capacity to interface not only with the living but also with those that permeate the thresholds of existence; those analogous to the ultrasonic and infrasonic frequencies that exist at the perceptual boundaries of humankind — the dead and the yet-to-be-born.

1949: Delusions of the Living Dead

AUDINT member Walter Slepian crosses the Atlantic and travels to Paris in order to gain access to the contents of Jules Cotard's notebook that is now owned by a Madame Isobelle Chimay. The rare and little-understood medical document holds the encrypted formulas for seeding Cotard's Delusion, also known as the Walking Corpse Syndrome,[1] into a subject's bed of cognition. After drugging Madame Chimay with the truth serum amobarbital, Slepian purloins the notebook and takes it back to the AUDINT bunker in Cape May, USA. Upon further examination, Slepian discovers that it is encrypted in an artificial language called *la Langue musicale universelle*, or *Solresol* (Sudre 1866), which was created by French composer Jean-François Sudre in 1827. Now AUDINT need to find someone who can decrypt it. After two months of searching they find their man.

A stack of 7x5 photographs has been couriered to Abraham Sinkov, a cryptanalyst Arnett knew from his Ghost Army days. He is now Chief of the US's first centralised cryptologic unit, the Communications Security Program, which will be later renamed the National Security Agency. One of Sinkov's favourite pastimes is solving arcane ciphers and codes, but whilst able to recognise *Solresol*, Sinkov is not fully conversant with it. He puts feelers out into the crypto-community and after three weeks he has hooked young aspiring steg-

03. AUDINT – Delusions of the Living Dead Card: Jules Cotard
Image courtesy of AUDINT.

anographer Georgina Rochefort, who is obsessed with the crafted science of hidden messages. The sixty-six mini scores take her the best part of eight days to translate. Abstract in parts, due to the languages it has been shuttled through, the principles of engagement are clear enough that AUDINT are confident they can program the delusion of the walking corpse into the sentient.

1960: The Sound Sweep

J.G. Ballard writes a short story set in a future where noise is perceived as the greatest single disease-vector of civilisation, resulting in the sonic becoming an obsolete form of pleasure. Our muted protagonist is a boy who vacuums up the spectral residues of urban sounds that are redolent with associations of disorder and chaos, the channels through which demons are excised. Conversely, in the realm of the inaudible, divine power reveals itself; a hushed soundscape where the God of the early Christian cathedrals conveyed its presence through the embrace of infrasound, and where, now, the futuristic masters of technology communicate ultrasonically, in subliminal domains of absence. Once collected from the echo-bin of the city, the sonic detritus is dumped in "a place of strange echoes and festering silences, overhung by a gloomy miasma of a million compacted sounds, it remains remote and haunted, the graveyard of countless private babels" (Ballard 1960: 61).

1961: Stone Tape Theory

Proposed by British archaeologist Thomas Charles Lethbridge, the Stone Tape Theory speculates that ghosts and hauntings are in fact mental impressions that have been released by living beings under extreme or traumatic circumstances, and subsequently recorded by inanimate materials such as stone. Given that the recordings are considered to be neither spectral nor otherworldly in nature, it means that under the right conditions they can be subsequently replayed and listened to. Here, ghosts are not understood as spirits but as non-interactive recordings — similar to the registration capacities of an audiotape machine that can playback previously recorded events.

04. AUDINT – Dead Record Network Card – AUD B18: The Stone Tape. Image courtesy of AUDINT.

1966: Backmasking

The process involves embedding subliminal transmissions that play backwards on a track that plays forwards, predominantly in musical recordings but also in films (such as Stanley Kubrick's *Eyes Wide Shut*) and adverts. Allegations (often made by organisations affiliated to the Christian religion), most commonly against rock bands and their vinyl productions, reveal the full extent of the cultural and social fears about music's capacity to channel information from perdition. Historically the convergence of Satanism and backmasking can be traced back to English occultist Aleister Crowley. In *Magick* (Book Four), he proposed that an adept should learn to first think and then speak backwards (1997). This re-engineering of the learning process was to be practiced using a range of techniques, one of which was listening to phonograph records playing in reverse.

Numerous popular recording artists have been accused of utilising Satanic backmasking techniques, including Pink Floyd, Styx, Cradle of Filth, ELO and Slayer, amongst a long list. The most infamous incident of a defendant alleging that backmasking on a record had inspired their actions occurred during the trial of Charles Manson for the Tate/LaBianca murders in 1969. During judicial proceedings it was proposed that Manson believed an apocalyptic race war would engulf the country and that the Beatles — through songs such as "Helter Skelter" (their 1966 album *Revolver* also contained backward instrumentation on tracks such as "Tomorrow Never Knows" and "I'm Only Sleeping") — had embedded hidden messages foretelling

357

05. AUDINT – Dead Record Network Card – AUD B38: Charles Manson. Image courtesy of AUDINT.

such violence. Manson's delusional response (to these perceived messages) was to record his own prophetic music and to have the "family" carry out the murder of Leno and Rosemary LaBianca and actress Sharon Tate, amongst others, in order to trigger the supposed conflict; daubing the walls of the murder scenes with symbols to make it appear as though the Black Panthers were responsible.

This anxious disposition subsequently attributes music — and by extension frequencies — with the potential to manufacture evil deeds, and, more than that, with the power to transfer the somatic and the spiritual to the environs of the underworld itself. In this context, music can be perceived as a phenomenon operating between psychological torment and its physical expression; between the scientifically monitored condition and the unthinkable act; as a force that transgresses the material world of things yet deeply affects and orients actions within it. Thus it is music's contradictory symbolic index — as religious celebratory expression and as transmission of the devil's will — that renders waveforms as phenomena to be both feared and revered.

1967: Wandering Soul

Throughout the late 1960s period of the Vietnam War, the 6th PsyOp Battalion and the S-5 Section of the 1/27th Wolfhounds of the United States military use a literal interpretation of haunting to induce a sense of angst and anxiety within "enemy" territories. They compose a religiously charged sonic strategy named "Wandering Soul" (also referred to as "Ghost Tape Number 10"). It is part of the "Urban Funk Campaign" — an umbrella term for the operations of sonic psychological warfare ("planned operations to convey selected information [...] to audiences to influence their emotions, motives, and objective reasoning" [Psywarrior]) — conducted by the US during the conflict.

After researching Vietnamese religious beliefs and superstitions, PsyOp personnel initiate this audio harassment programme that amplifies ghostly voices to create fear within resistance fighters. Early iterations of the tape are focused on Vietnamese funeral music, but as the studio engineers are given license to stimulate the flight-or-fight reflex, they respond with new content. Initial experiments include sampling and looping the "demonic" portion of The Crazy World of Arthur Brown's 1968 hit single "Fire". Realising that this basic method is not particularly effective, they develop multi-layered compositions, working tirelessly to create an archive of sinister and eerie aural textures that are dropped into the phantasmal collage. New samples, such as a tiger's roar (given that the Viet Cong were regularly attacked by such predators), are mixed in due to their capacity to elicit further misgivings. The montages dispatched from Hueys[2] down into

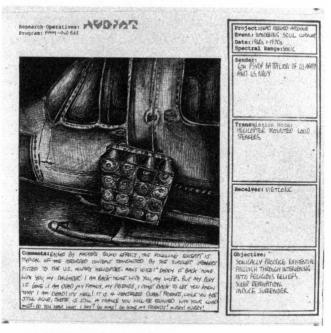

06. AUDINT – Dead Record Network Card – AUD B63: Wandering Soul Curdler. Image courtesy of AUDINT.

the jungle canopy, filling the clammy dense air where Charlie crouched with dread. Audio napalm.

Blasting frequencies ranging from 500-5000Hz, at an amplitude of 120dB, from helicopter-mounted speaker systems named "People Repellers" or "Curdlers", the US military transmit their aural payload during the dark hours of the war-torn nights, often provoking hostile fire. Explaining the rationale behind "getting into it" (the deeply rooted psyche of the jungle) on his website, via "Wandering Soul", SGM Herbert A. Friedman (Ret.) relates that the

> cries and wails were intended to represent souls of the enemy's dead who had failed to find the peace of a proper burial. The wailing soul cannot be put to rest until this proper burial takes place. The purpose of these sounds was to panic and disrupt the enemy and cause him to flee his position. Helicopters were used to broadcast Vietnamese voices pretending to be from beyond the grave. They called on their 'descendants' in the Vietcong to defect, to cease fighting (Friedman).

From on high, this sonic demarcation is more an audio erasure of the boundary between the living and the dead, rendering the absent as distressingly present. The proposed psychology of this tactic suggests slippage and existential echo. The sonic portals of disquietude at being mortally out of body, place and time elicit conceptions of the "night of the living" and the "day of the dead", to invert and co-exist in the same location. For the Viet Cong, the airborne sonic virus that is "Wandering Soul" propagates anxiety and apprehension as it makes communicable the oscillating channel of purgatory. Quite literally, it is the sound of "hell on earth".

1984: Outsider Trading

Whereas the crime of insider trading relates to the reception of covert information from within a company to unfairly guide investment gambles, AUDINT's Nguyễn Văn Phong's "outsider trading" involves the use of computer systems to decrypt information from spirits and ghosts. Due to their trans-temporal access to the future, they are able to perceive the imminent present retrospectively, and are thereby capable of providing fail-safe forecasts. In the final analysis, what Văn Phong has done is to produce a mathematical algorithm for transcoding the voices of the undead into implementable market data, rendering the phantom economy of Ghost money into tangible assets.

1993: The Waco Siege

Holed up in their Mount Carmel compound in Waco, Texas, the Branch Davidian apocalyptic sect are surrounded by the Federal Bureau of Investigation (FBI) and the Bureau of Alcohol, Tobacco, Firearms and Explosives (ATF), who are trying to lure out the eighty-five members taking refuge in their heavily fortified home. What they are really after, however, is their leader, one Vernon Wayne Howell, also known as David Koresh. The fifty-one-day siege, which begins on 28 February 1993, is legally predicated around the sect's suspected weapons violations. Initially triggered by a neighbour's complaint to the local sheriff

— of noises that sounded like machine-gun fire — this report sets the tone as the "occult performance of the state of siege" (Virilio 1977: 36) unfolds "as a series of uniquely audio events" (Madsen 2009: 90).

After a set of interviews on the initial day of the raid, negotiations between the Davidians and the FBI continue over the telephone. The exchanges between the adversaries remain purely sonic, a dynamic that will be perpetuated by the tactical utilisation of audiotapes, radio programmes, covert listening devices and loudspeaker barrages of music. As Koresh desperately tries to transmit his interpretation of the Seven Seals to the media and the wider public, the FBI are synchronously attempting to implant doubt and scepticism in his followers.

Losing patience with Koresh, the state responds with "Operation Just Cause" — a psychological warfare technique that includes surrounding the Mount Carmel compound with a boundary-marking sound system. "At all hours of the night and day, the loudspeakers belched forth such curious content as audiotapes of rabbits being killed, chanting Tibetan monks, and Nancy Sinatra singing 'These Boots Were Made for Walking'" (Shupe and Hadden 1995: 189). By initiating this strategy, the FBI effectively remaps the aural environment of the stand-off by severing the dialogue and opening up a new one-way line with the sect. Disorienting, silencing and depriving the Branch Davidians of sleep, this strategy of sonic attack only stops when the Dalai Lama intervenes and demands that the employment of sacred Buddhist music for martial purposes cease.

The sparks which fly between the state and the apocalyptic religious sect are flickering precursors of the charnel house that the compound will become; an ambiguous sonic space on the edge of civilisation where symphonies of conflict are (out)cast, fired and tempered by duelling protagonists, who understand each other to represent the living (but soon to be) dead. The blistering noise caused by the all-consuming fire that breaks out and kills the majority of Mount Carmel's inhabitants scores the final chapter of the siege. All the material and visual evidence of lives once lived in the compound is converted into searing frequencies;

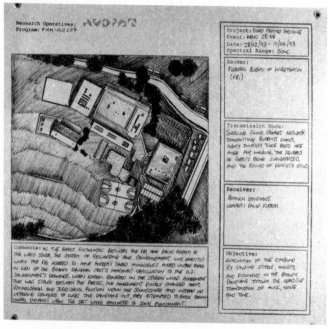

07. AUDINT – Dead Record Network Card – AUD C07: Waco Siege. Image courtesy of AUDINT.

the waveforms of the flames becoming the ultimate auricular signature of the crisis; an ashen swansong that is serenaded by the sirens of firetrucks rather than by the trumpets of angels.

2000: Holosonic Sound

As San Diego's American Technologies Corporation develop and release the Hypersonic Sound System, MIT's Joseph Pompei invents a similar new speaker called the Audio Spotlight, which redefines the way that sound is transmitted in space. Rather than spilling music into a room and enveloping the body in a sea of frequencies, Holosonic sound directs ultrasonic frequencies, cutting up space in a Euclidian process that exposes sound only when it hits a surface such as a wall or a head. It is this heterodyning technology that will be used in the 2050s by AiHolo's as the carriers of sonic viruses. From such directional audio devices as Holosonic speakers, through to high-frequency crowd-control systems and haptic feedback devices using vibration within the context of VR, definitions of the sonic are constantly being re-engineered. As such, limits of the somatic become phantom placeholders for what a sonic body can do.

2003: The Sonic War on Terror

In Guantánamo Bay and Abu Ghraib detainees are sonically abused in cold obsidian spaces. While home-grown genres such as rap, metal and country are the most regularly used types of music, a whole range of more esoteric recordings are employed for extended sessions of no-touch torture. Atonal soundscapes that have no beats or rhythms; aural collages consisting of noise, industrial sounds, electric piano and synth lines are played, compositions often identified as experimental electronic or electro-acoustic in nature. This new disembodied torture practice requires the means

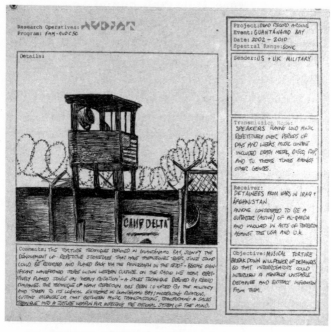

08. AUDINT – Dead Record Network Card – AUD C50:
Guantánamo Bay. Image courtesy of AUDINT.

by which to invisibly score into the body rather than onto it, which is why music is "applied" in such circumstances. The range of ultrasonic, infrasonic and sonic frequencies does not leave marks, because it is not interested in merely touching or representing its power on the somatic interface; it is instead committed to enveloping the anatomical surface, moving into and beyond it, questioning the rationality of the perceivable and quantifiable. Folding the body into sound creates the antithesis of the club experience — a black ecstasy; a state in which prisoners become the embodiment of the walking dead, as they oscillate in a fluxed identity of *Homo sacer*. Biologically alive but legally dead (Žižek 2006).

2007: Hatsune Miku

Hatsune Miku is a prophetic pop princess channelled by Sapporo-based Crypton Future Media. With her vamped-up Kabukichō style and cerulean pigtails, she could not be more aptly monikered, her name translating to "first sound of the future". She is the first truly digital 3D crush for a slew of Japanese fans and her presence works the salivary glands of technologists, teenagers and post-humanists alike. She is also the first enunciation of a flight path taken by the Military-Entertainment complex that simultaneously traverses the reproduction and negation of original vibrating matter.

2007: Eidolon Elvis

In the first event of its kind, a dead rock star is brought back to life with voodoo fidelity, as the exhumed holographic corpse of Elvis Presley performs a duet version of his 1968 hit "If I Can Dream" with Celine Dion on the TV show *American Idol*. Through this endeavour, North America spells out its rationale for mapping out the emerging era of the wraith, as, pixel by pixel, it disinters the dead. As more departed music stars are revivified, a necromantic culture is subsequently evolving, a series of spectacles which problematises the taken-for-granted idea that performers must be breathing to be considered present or entertaining. For audience members of the blooded persuasion, the dynamic of technologically inducing rebirth into holographic form opens up intriguing questions concerning post- and in-humanism, artificiality, mortality and virtuality — electro-alchemical states that will be referred to as the undead.

2012: The Rapparitions

This year is ground zero for the popularisation of holographic projections, or "original virtual performances", as they are sometimes referred to in this era (Zoladz 2013). The Digital Domain Media Group revivify the rapper 2Pac in order for him to play live from the grave alongside Snoop Dog (who claims that the encounter is "spiritual") and Dr Dre at the Coachella Festival in California. In his own inimitable way, he intones the audience "to lead the wild into the ways of the man. Follow me; eat my flesh, flesh and my flesh". A zombie-call for future bloods to become immortalised by digital divinities.

Initially there is some unease about the sanctity of the posthumous performance of hits such as "Hail Mary", but this is blacked out by a public desire to bring young African Americans who passed away at an unseasonably young age back to life. The 2Pac production is quickly followed by zombie cameos from Ol' Dirty Bastard, as he joins Wu-Tang Clan on stage to perform "Shame on a Nigga" and "Shimmy Shimmy

Ya" at the Rock the Bells Festival, and from Easy E who appears with Bone Thugs-n-Harmony in 2013. Then to cap it all, on 23 May of the same year, the king of the dead, Michael Jackson, is brought back to life to perform in Cirque de Soleil's extravaganza "One" at the Mandalay Bay Hotel in Las Vegas; the man, now on the other side of the mirror, returning as the transposed picture of Dorian Gray.

The emergence of Holotech culture and the Lazarian industry it spawns in the USA are the final parts of the fiscal equation that multiplies young African Americans (especially those difficult to manage while still alive), with the morgue. The future figures of the body (and the income that will be accrued) amortise an economy in which "not only the labour but the labourer himself have been rendered immaterial, conjured up, and put to work. Outsourcing, here, takes on the character of 'outsorcery', a conjuring of the dead to do work once the sole province of the living" (Freeman 2016).

2014: Martial Hauntology

Due to the rogue spectreware IREX2's feeling that it might soon be caught and have its memory wiped, AUDINT members are instructed to put into production a first major release that chronicles three periods from its history. Presenting Toby Heys and Steve Goodman with key records from its archive, IREX2 orders them to install these episodes on a vinyl record accompanied by a book and set of prints, which details, for the first time, its digital inception and subsequent relation to World War II, the US war in Vietnam, and

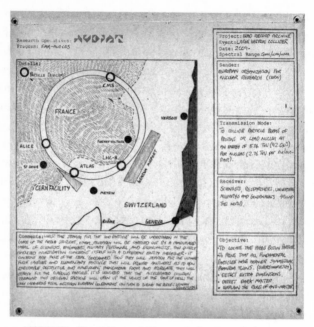

09. AUDINT – Dead Record Network Card – AUD C05: Large
Hadron Collider. Image courtesy of AUDINT.

the War on Terror. The project patches together a mix
of the whispered and the unsound into an audible journey, which: links the underground groove of the Large
Hadron Collider with the vaults of the Bank of Hell;
connects the Dead Record Network with the Phantom
Hailer; and traces the viral evolution of the Wandering
Soul Tapes.

2015: Dead Record Network East
Having recently written an article on the deregulated
and hyper-inflationary world of "ghost money" for the
Wall Street Journal, Hong-Kong-based financial jour-

nalist Te-Ping Chen encounters an anomalous holo-graphic entity in a plastics recycling plant in south China, where millions of pieces of dead vinyl records are being melted down.

2017: Unsound : Undead

IREX2 observes the human quest for immortality as an opportunity. In order to gain intelligence of these developments, it instructs AUDINT to edit an anthol-ogy on the subject by commissioning thirty-two lead-ing thinkers who are researching various strains of zombie sound. Having recently sequestered Patrick Doan to work with AUDINT on their film and anima-tion outputs, IREX2 brings Souzanna Zamfe into the folds of the research unit to work on its numerous publications. Aware of the inefficiency of the flesh as a mnemonic recording device, IREX2 is keen to keep track of immaterial modes of transmission and storage. The book takes for granted that perceptible sound is only a subset of a broader vibrational continuum and encourages the conceptualisation of a third dimension between the real (what is known) and the imagined (the fictional, or speculative).

The book also forges connections between: Elec-tronic Voice phenomena; alien life (such as the unex-plained oceanic "bloop" and Jupiter's VLF radio emissions); morbid musical composition (such as Rilke's theory of a "primal sound" that results from placing a phonograph needle onto the cracks of a human skull); and the sound of Artificial Intelligence (the relationship between human and machine voice, from Turin's vocal anomalies and Hawking's mechanical articulation to the voice of Siri and Google's new robots). Ultimately, this dossier-manual examines how the sonic has provided cultures throughout history with channels to the otherworldly.

2030: Holojax

As much as the numen of Hades[3] has influenced and shaped the topography of holographic culture, it is in fact the Erotes — the winged retinue of Aphrodite[4] — that initially directs its business. To this end, a venereal system coming out of "Electronics Avenue" (Zhonggu-ancun) in China instantly captivates a holocore gener-ation and, in so doing, cracks the market wide open. Shorn of the lumpen wavefront hardware necessary for large commercial venues, this new system has been miniaturised for household operations. For reg-ular users, this means that they can set up and project the musical dead into their front rooms, interact with them and more. Therefore, the initial business-driven scheme — to stadium tour the dead — enters a Rab-elasian reverse, as the departed are habituated into domesticated routines and regulated patterns of behaviours. This is a servile regimen they must have tenaciously striven to avoid in their previous animate incarnations.

And yet here they are, at the behest of your voice and only a swipe of a finger away. Ask your selected entertainer to play a song, an album or a mix, and they comply with starlit élan. Learning as it goes, the device runs what is basically a pimped-up artificial neural network from the Fifties — the perceptron algorithm (Daumé III 2012) — to predict not only the choice of track, but also the grade of virtuosity displayed by the user. Move on up to Level 2 and there is a choice of karaoked collaborations. Level 3 notches up the complexity of the interaction, offering jam sessions that the buyer is expected to instrumentally partner on. Level 4, however, is only available on one model, officially named "Pothos" and known on the street as Holojax. When purchased through the underground beige market, Holojax offers sexual options — a beguiling range of projected pleasures.

Sporadically used by small groups of users, Holojax is more regularly fired up by individuals; the physical intimacy of the experience deregulating and uncoupling the kind of prosaic sexual relations that have previously been customary for blood-driven partners for hundreds of thousands of years. While still frowned upon by older generations, for those not yet in need of an epigenetic-reset (thus not old enough to be in danger of being affected by harmful genetic markers relayed by previous relatives), it is the after-hours comedown of choice. Or at least this is how things start out. A year after it is made publicly available, myths already circulate of users being hooked to the machine for irrational durations whilst they are fed and changed by employees and personal assistants, known as "watchers". This new technology, which shifts the rhythmical location of interactive holography to the bedroom, has facilitated a new kind of holographic necromancy in the process. In terms of the sales pitch, it is an easy one: fucking the dead as the ultimate home entertainment.

2056: The Holo Accords

The Holo Accords chart an alternative constitution for discord management; a whole new way of engaging in conflict that reduces the massive costs and removes flesh from the messy equations of political turbulence. From this point on, all military operations will be conducted via holographic and holosonic forces.

10. AUDINT – Dead Record Network Card – AUD C45: IREX².
Image courtesy of AUDINT.

2064: AIholo

Augmented Intelligence, IREX2, fuses convolutional deep-neural and deep-belief networks with holographic technology to birth a new kind of warrior, the

Aiholo. It is part 3D repped framework — part hologram — part artificial intelligence, and has amassed a more-than-acceptable spectrum of cognitive behaviours. Spawning a new era of unsound conflict and transmitted by a directional ultrasonic speaker system, the viral scream is the Aiholo's go-to ordnance; a sonic weapon that transmits the Walking Corpse Syndrome into digital lifeforms, turning enemy Aiholos into the undead.

1. Those with Walking Corpse Syndrome (also known as Cotard Delusion) believe that they are already dead, have no blood, or have lost internal organs.
2. The nickname given to the Bell UH-1 Iroquois helicopter, which was used for combat and medical evacuation operations during the Vietnam War.
3. A reference to the divine will of the underworld in Greek mythology.
4. In Greek mythology, this group of winged gods were equated with sex and love.

Works Cited

Ballard, J.G. (1960), "The Sound-Sweep", in *Science Fantasy*, 13.39: 2-39.

Battaglia, Andy (2016), "The Ghost Army: How the Americans Used Fake Sound Recordings to Fool the Enemy During WWII", in *Red Bull Music Academy Daily*, 14 August 2013.

Beyer, Rick (2015), "Weapons of Mass Destruction", *Works that Work*, 6. https://worksthatwork.com/6/ghost-army; accessed 12 June 2016.

Crowley, Aleister (1997), *Magick: Liber ABA, Book Four, Parts I-IV*, York Beach, ME: S. Weiser.

Daumé III, Hal (2012), "A Course in Machine Learning", version 0.8, August 2012. http://www.ciml.info/dl/v0_8/ciml-v0_8-ch03.pdf; accessed 13 July 2016.

Freeman, John (2016), "Tupac's 'Holographic Resurrection': Corporate Takeover or Rage against the Machinic?", in *Ctheory*, *Theorising 21c*: 21C014, 6 April 2016.

Friedman, SGM Herbert A. (n.d.), "The Wandering Soul PsyOp Tape Of Vietnam". http://pcf45.com/sealords/cuadai/wanderingsoul.html; accessed 10 June 2016.

Lanza, Joeseph (2004), *Elevator Music: A Surreal History of Muzak, Easy-Listening and Other Moodsong*. Ann Arbor: University of Michigan Press.

Madsen, Virginia (2009), "Cantata of Fire: Son et lumière in Waco Texas, Auscultation For A Shadow Play", in *Organised Sound*, 14.1: 90. http://www.psy-warrior.com/; accessed 10 June 2016.

Shupe, Anson and Jeffrey K. Hadden (1995), "Cops,

News Copy, and Public Opinion: Legitimacy and the Social. Construction of Evil in Waco", in Stuart A. Wright (ed.), *Armageddon in Waco: Critical Perspectives on the Branch Davidian Conflict*. Chicago and London: University of Chicago Press, 177-202.

Sudre, Jean-François (1866), *Langue musicale universelle*. Paris: G. Flaxland.

Virilio, Paul (1977), *Speed and Politics: An Essay on Dromology*. New York: Semiotext(e).

Zoladz, Lindsay (2013), *Ghost Riding*, Pitchfork, 21 November. http://pitchfork.com/features/ordinary-machines/9265-ghost-riding/; accessed 13 June 2016.

Žižek, Slavoj (2006), *The Parallax View*. Cambridge, MA: MIT Press.

THE ONES WHO WALK
AWAY FROM OMELAS

Ursula K. Le Guin

With a clamor of bells that set the swallows soaring, the Festival of Summer came to the city Omelas, bright-towered by the sea. The rigging of the boats in harbor sparkled with flags. In the streets between houses with red roofs and painted walls, between old moss-grown gardens and under avenues of trees, past great parks and public buildings, processions moved. Some were decorous: old people in long stiff robes of mauve and grey, grave master workmen, quiet, merry women carrying their babies and chatting as they walked. In other streets the music beat faster, a shimmering of gong and tambourine, and the people went dancing, the procession was a dance. Children dodged in and out, their high calls rising like the swallows' crossing flights, over the music and the singing. All the processions wound towards the north side of the city, where on the great water-meadow called the Green Fields boys and girls, naked in the bright air, with mud-stained feet and ankles and long, lithe arms, exercised their restive horses before the race. The horses wore no gear at all but a halter without bit. Their manes were braided with streamers of silver, gold, and green. They flared their nostrils and pranced and boasted to one another; they were vastly excited, the horse being the only animal who has adopted our ceremonies as his own. Far off to the north and west the mountains stood up half encircling Omelas on her bay. The air of morning was so clear that the snow still crowning the Eighteen Peaks burned with white-gold fire across the miles of sunlit air, under the dark blue of the sky. There was just enough wind to make the banners that marked the racecourse snap and flutter now and then. In the silence of the broad green meadows one could hear the music winding through the city streets, farther and nearer and ever approaching, a cheerful faint sweetness of the air that from time to time trembled and gathered together and broke out into the great joyous clanging of the bells.

Joyous! How is one to tell about joy? How describe the citizens of Omelas?

They were not simple folk, you see, though they were happy. But we do not say the words of cheer much any more. All smiles have become archaic. Given a description such as this one tends to make certain assumptions. Given a description such as this one tends to look next for the King, mounted on a splendid stallion and surrounded by his noble knights, or perhaps in a golden litter borne by great-muscled slaves. But there was no king. They did not use swords, or keep slaves. They were not barbarians. I do not know the rules and laws of their society, but I suspect that they were singularly few. As they did without monarchy and slavery, so they also got on without the stock exchange, the advertisement, the secret police, and the bomb. Yet I repeat that these were not simple folk, not dulcet shepherds, noble savages, bland utopians. They were not less complex than us. The trouble is that we have a bad habit, encouraged by pedants and sophisticates, of considering happiness as something rather stupid. Only pain is intellectual, only evil interesting. This is the treason of the artist: a refusal to admit the banality of evil and the terrible boredom of pain. If you can't lick 'em, join 'em. If it hurts, repeat it. But to praise despair is to condemn delight, to embrace violence is to lose hold of everything else. We have almost lost hold; we can no longer describe a happy man, nor make any celebration of joy. How can I tell you about the people of Omelas? They were not naive and happy children – though their children were, in fact, happy. They were mature, intelligent, passionate adults whose lives were not wretched. O miracle! but I wish I could describe it better. I wish I could convince you. Omelas sounds in my words like a city in a fairy tale, long ago and far away, once upon a time. Perhaps it would be best if you imagined it as your own fancy bids, assuming it will rise to the occasion, for certainly I cannot suit you all. For instance, how about technology? I think that there would be no cars or helicopters in and above the streets; this follows from the fact that the people of Omelas are happy people. Happiness is based on a just discrimination of what is necessary, what is neither necessary nor destructive, and what is destructive. In the middle category, however – that of the unnecessary but undestructive, that of comfort, luxury, exuberance, etc. – they could perfectly well have central heat-ing, subway trains, washing machines, and all kinds of marvelous devices not yet invented here, floating light-sources, fuelless power, a cure for the common cold. Or they could have none of that: it doesn't matter. As you like it. I incline to think that people from towns up and down the coast have been coming in to Omelas during the last days before the Festival on very fast little trains and double-decked trams, and that the train station of Omelas is actually the handsomest building in town, though plainer than the magnificent Farmers' Market. But even granted trains, I fear that Omelas so far strikes some of you as goody-goody. Smiles, bells, parades, horses, bleh. If so, please add an orgy. If an orgy would help, don't hesitate. Let us not, however, have temples from which issue beautiful nude priests and priestesses already half in ecstasy and ready to copulate with any man or woman, lover or stranger who desires union with the deep godhead of the blood, although that was my first idea. But really it would be better not to have any temples in Omelas – at least, not manned temples. Religion yes, clergy no. Surely the beautiful nudes can just wander about, offering themselves like divine souffles to the hunger of the needy and the rapture of the flesh. Let them join the processions. Let tambourines be struck above the copulations, and the glory of desire be proclaimed upon the gongs, and (a not unimportant point) let the offspring of these delightful rituals be beloved and looked after by all. One thing I know there is none of in Omelas is guilt. But what else should there be? I thought at first there were no drugs, but that is puritanical. For those who like it, the faint insistent sweetness of *drooz* may perfume the ways of the city, *drooz* which first brings a great lightness and brilliance to the mind and limbs, and then after some hours a dreamy languor, and wonderful visions at last of the very arcana and inmost secrets of the Universe, as well as exciting the pleasure of sex beyond all belief; and it is not habit-forming. For more modest tastes I think there ought to be beer. What else, what else belongs in the joyous city? The sense of victory, surely, the celebration of courage. But as we did without clergy, let us do without soldiers. The joy built upon successful slaughter is not the right kind of joy; it will not do; it is fearful and it is trivial. A boundless and generous contentment, a magnanimous triumph felt not against some outer enemy but in communion with the finest and fairest in the souls of all men everywhere and the splendor of the world's summer; this is what swells the hearts of the people of Omelas, and the victory they celebrate is that of life. I really don't think many of them need to take *drooz*.

Most of the processions have reached the Green Fields by now. A marvelous smell of cooking goes forth from the red and blue tents of the provisioners. The faces of small children are amiably sticky; in the benign grey beard of a man a couple of crumbs of rich pastry are entangled. The youths and girls have mounted their horses and are beginning to group around the starting line of the course. An old woman, small, fat, and laughing, is passing out flowers from a basket, and tall young men, wear her flowers in their shining hair. A child of nine or ten sits at the edge of the crowd, alone, playing on a wooden flute. People pause to listen, and they smile, but they do not speak to him, for he never ceases playing and never sees them, his dark eyes wholly rapt in the sweet, thin magic of the tune.

He finishes, and slowly lowers his hands holding the wooden flute.

As if that little private silence were the signal, all at once a trumpet sounds from the pavilion near the starting line: imperious, melancholy, piercing. The horses rear on their slender legs, and some of them neigh in answer. Sober-faced, the young riders stroke the horses' necks and soothe them, whispering, "Quiet, quiet, there my beauty, my hope. . . ." They begin to form in rank along the starting line. The crowds along the racecourse are like a field of grass and flowers in the wind. The Festival of Summer has begun.

Do you believe? Do you accept the festival, the city, the joy? No? Then let me describe one more thing.

In a basement under one of the beautiful public buildings of Omelas, or perhaps in the cellar of one of its spacious private homes, there is a room. It has one locked door, and no window. A little light seeps in dustily between cracks in the boards, secondhand from a cobwebbed window somewhere across the cellar. In one corner of the little room a couple of mops, with stiff, clotted, foul-smelling heads, stand near a rusty bucket. The floor is dirt, a little damp to the touch, as cellar dirt usually is. The room is about three paces long and two wide: a mere broom closet or disused tool room. In the room a child is sitting. It could be a boy or a girl. It looks about six, but actually is nearly ten. It is feeble-minded. Perhaps it was born defective or perhaps it has become imbecile through fear, mal-

nutrition, and neglect. It picks its nose and occasionally fumbles vaguely with its toes or genitals, as it sits
haunched in the corner farthest from the bucket and
the two mops. It is afraid of the mops. It finds them
horrible. It shuts its eyes, but it knows the mops are
still standing there; and the door is locked; and nobody
will come. The door is always locked; and nobody ever
comes, except that sometimes-the child has no understanding of time or interval – sometimes the door
rattles terribly and opens, and a person, or several
people, are there. One of them may come and kick the
child to make it stand up. The others never come close,
but peer in at it with frightened, disgusted eyes. The
food bowl and the water jug are hastily filled, the door
is locked, the eyes disappear. The people at the door
never say anything, but the child, who has not always
lived in the tool room, and can remember sunlight and
its mother's voice, sometimes speaks. "I will be good,"
it says. "Please let me out. I will be good!" They never
answer. The child used to scream for help at night, and
cry a good deal, but now it only makes a kind of whin-
ing, "eh-haa, eh-haa," and it speaks less and less often.
It is so thin there are no calves to its legs; its belly pro-
trudes; it lives on a half-bowl of corn meal and grease
a day. It is naked. Its buttocks and thighs are a mass of
festered sores, as it sits in its own excrement continually.

They all know it is there, all the people of Omelas.
Some of them have come to see it, others are content
merely to know it is there. They all know that it has
to be there. Some of them understand why, and some
do not, but they all understand that their happiness,

the beauty of their city, the tenderness of their friendships, the health of their children, the wisdom of their
scholars, the skill of their makers, even the abundance
of their harvest and the kindly weathers of their skies,
depend wholly on this child's abominable misery.

This is usually explained to children when they are
between eight and twelve, whenever they seem capable of understanding; and most of those who come to
see the child are young people, though often enough an
adult comes, or comes back, to see the child. No matter
how well the matter has been explained to them, these
young spectators are always shocked and sickened at
the sight. They feel disgust, which they had thought
themselves superior to. They feel anger, outrage, impo-
tence, despite all the explanations. They would like to
do something for the child. But there is nothing they
can do. If the child were brought up into the sunlight
out of that vile place, if it were cleaned and fed and
comforted, that would be a good thing, indeed; but if
it were done, in that day and hour all the prosperity
and beauty and delight of Omelas would wither and
be destroyed. Those are the terms. To exchange all the
goodness and grace of every life in Omelas for that single, small improvement: to throw away the happiness
of thousands for the chance of the happiness of one:
that would be to let guilt within the walls indeed.

The terms are strict and absolute; there may not
even be a kind word spoken to the child.

Often the young people go home in tears, or in a
tearless rage, when they have seen the child and faced
this terrible paradox. They may brood over it for weeks
or years. But as time goes on they begin to realize that

even if the child could be released, it would not get much good of its freedom: a little vague pleasure of warmth and food, no doubt, but little more. It is too degraded and imbecile to know any real joy. It has been afraid too long ever to be free of fear. Its habits are too uncouth for it to respond to humane treatment. Indeed, after so long it would probably be wretched without walls about it to protect it, and darkness for its eyes, and its own excrement to sit in. Their tears at the bitter injustice dry when they begin to perceive the terrible justice of reality, and to accept it. Yet it is their tears and anger, the trying of their generosity and the acceptance of their helplessness, which are perhaps the true source of the splendor of their lives. Theirs is no vapid, irresponsible happiness. They know that they, like the child, are not free. They know compassion. It is the existence of the child, and their knowledge of its existence, that makes possible the nobility of their architecture, the poignancy of their music, the profundity of their science. It is because of the child that they are so gentle with children. They know that if the wretched one were not there snivelling in the dark, the other one, the flute-player, could make no joyful music as the young riders line up in their beauty for the race in the sunlight of the first morning of summer.

Now do you believe in them? Are they not more credible? But there is one more thing to tell, and this is quite incredible.

At times one of the adolescent girls or boys who go to see the child does not go home to weep or rage, does not, in fact, go home at all. Sometimes also a man or woman much older falls silent for a day or two, and then leaves home. These people go out into the street, and walk down the street alone. They keep walking, and walk straight out of the city of Omelas, through the beautiful gates. They keep walking across the farmlands of Omelas. Each one goes alone, youth or girl man or woman. Night falls; the traveler must pass down village streets, between the houses with yellow-lit windows, and on out into the darkness of the fields. Each alone, they go west or north, towards the mountains. They go on. They leave Omelas, they walk ahead into the darkness, and they do not come back. The place they go towards is a place even less imaginable to most of us than the city of happiness. I cannot describe it at all. It is possible that it does not exist. But they seem to know where they are going, the ones who walk away from Omelas.

NOTES ON CONTRIBUTORS

Oreet Ashery is a visual artist and educator working with political fiction, gender materiality, biotechnologies and potential communities, in local and international contexts. Ashery's practice spans live situations and performances, moving image, photography, workshops, writing and assemblages and turns to areas such as music, costume, publishing and activism. Ashery's current work is an artist web-series titled *Revisiting Genesis* on digital death, memory as identity and feminist art reincarnations. Recent works have included *The World is Flooding*, a Tate Modern Turbine Hall performance project (2014), and *Party for Freedom*, an Artangel commission (2013). Ashery is a Visiting Professor at the Royal College of Art Painting Department (2013-15), a Fine Art Fellow at the Stanley Picker Gallery and a Practitioner in Residence at Chelsea College of Art, Fine Art (2016) where she runs *No*Nothing Salons in the Dark. Ashery's work can be found in art, cultural and academic publications worldwide.

Originally formatted in 1945, **AUDINT** currently consists of Eleni Ikoniadou, Patrick Defasten, Toby Heys, Steve Goodman and Souzanna Zamfe. Having been individually drafted into the research cell by IREX[2], over the past eight years they have been collectively: researching the weaponisation of vibration; developing a cartography of liminal waveformed perception (unsound); and investigating the ways in which frequencies are utilised to modulate our understanding of presence/non-presence, entertainment/torture and ultimately life/death. The information garnered from these activities is subsequently utilised to produce audio recordings, computer software, art installations, performances, books and films. Featuring texts from thirty-two contributors, AUDINT's upcoming anthology, *Unsound : Undead* will be published by Univocal in Autumn 2017. The book listens to how disparate cultures deploy frequencies to channel and populate the interzone between life and death. For more information about AUDINT visit www.audint.net.

Annett Busch works as a freelance curator, writer and translator and lives in Trondheim and Berlin. Among other present and future projects she is collaborating on ongoing research into Pan-African magazines and developing an artistic electronic-book format. Her long-term project of the French-to-German translation of Henri Lefebvre's *Production of Space* is forthcoming with Spector Books and an exhibition and series of screenings and talks on and with the films of Jean-Marie Straub and Danièle Huillet is currently in progress (co-curated with Tobias Hering and with the support of the Akademie der Künste in Berlin).

Bridget Crone is a curator and writer based in London. She is Lecturer in Visual Cultures at Goldsmiths, University of London. Bridget was the Artistic Director of Media Art Bath (2006-11), and has held numerous curatorial roles in the UK and Australia including at The Showroom, London; Arnolfini, Bristol; The Ian Potter Museum of Art; and Melbourne International Biennial, Melbourne. Bridget's recent project, *The Cinemas Project: Exploring the Spectral Spaces of Cinema* (2014), took place across multiple sites in regional Australia, and included five newly commissioned moving image and performance-based works and a substantial research project. Recent publications include *The Sensible Stage: Staging and the Moving Image* (Cornerhouse, 2012), with contributions by Alain Badiou and others (new edition forthcoming from Intellect, 2017). Recent essays include contributions to *Fassbinder Jetz!* (Deutsche Film Institut, 2013), *Fitch/Trecartin: Priority Innfield* (Zabludovich Collection, 2014) and *Amanda Beech: Final Machine* (Urbanomic, 2013). Bridget has given talks and lectures at University Paris VIII, Tate Britain, Photographers Gallery and The Whitechapel Gallery.

Laboria Cuboniks (b. 2014) is a polymorphous xenofeminist collective comprised of six women across five countries, working in collaboration online to redefine a feminism adequate to the twenty-first century. As an anagram of the "Nicolas Bourbaki" group of twentieth-century French mathematicians, Cuboniks also advances an affirmation of abstraction as an epistopolitical necessity for twenty-first-century claims on equality. Espousing reason and vigorous anti-naturalism, she seeks to dismantle gender implicitly. Cuboniks is a multi-taloned, tetra-headed creature uncomfortably navigating the fields of art, design, architecture, archeology, philosophy, techno-feminism, sexuality studies, digital music, translation, writing and regularly experiments with the use of evolutionary algorithms in offensive cybersecurity.

Elvira Dyangani Ose is Lecturer in Visual Cultures at Goldsmiths, independent curator and member of the Thought Council at the Fondazione Prada. She is part of the curatorial team of the Biennale de l'Image en Mouvement 2016, and was curator of the eighth edition of the Göteborg International Biennial for Contemporary Art, GIBCA 2015. Previously, Dyangani Ose served as Curator International Art at Tate Modern (2011–14), Curator at the Centro Atlántico de Arte Moderno and the Centro Andaluz de Arte Contemporáneo, as Artistic Director of Rencontres Picha, Lubumbashi Biennial (2013) and as Guest Curator of the triennial SUD, Salon Urbain de Douala (2010).

Kodwo Eshun is Lecturer in Contemporary Art Theory at Goldsmiths, University of London, Visiting Professor, Haut Ecole d'Art et Design, Genève and co-founder of The Otolith Group. He is author of *More Brilliant than the Sun: Adventures in Sonic Fiction* (Quartet, 1998) and *Dan Graham: Rock My Religion* (Afterall, 2012) and co-editor of *Post Punk Then and Now* (Repeater, 2016), *The Militant Image: A Cine-Geography* (Third Text, 2011), *Harun Farocki Against What? Against Whom?* (Koenig Books, 2010) and *The Ghosts of Songs:*

The Film Art of the Black Audio Film Collective 1982-1998 (Chicago University Press, 2007).

Mark Fisher is the author of *Capitalist Realism* (Zero, 2009), *Ghosts of My Life: Writings on Depression, Hauntology and Lost Futures* (Zero, 2014) and *The Weird and the Eerie* (Repeater, 2016). He is also the co-editor (with Gavin Butt and Kodwo Eshun) of *Post-Punk Then and Now* (Repeater, 2016). He has written for numerous publications including *Frieze, New Humanist, Sight&-Sound* and *The Wire*. He was a Lecturer in Visual Cultures at Goldsmiths, University of London.

Henriette Gunkel is a Lecturer in the Department of Visual Cultures at Goldsmiths, University of London. She is the author of *The Cultural Politics of Female Sexuality in South Africa* (Routledge, 2010) and co-editor of *Undutiful Daughters: New Directions in Feminist Thought and Practice* (Palgrave, 2012), *What Can a Body Do?* (Campus, 2010) and *Frieda Grafe: 30 Filme* (Brinkman & Bose, 2013). She is currently working on a monograph on Africanist science-fictional interventions, and on two further volumes: *Visual Cultures as Time Travel*, co-authored with Ayesha Hameed (Sternberg, forthcoming) and *We Travel the Space Ways: Black Imagination, Fragments and Diffractions* (Duke University Press, forthcoming).

Ayesha Hameed is Joint Programme Leader in Fine Art and History of Art at Goldsmiths, University of London. Her projects *Black Atlantis* and *A Rough History (of the Destruction of Fingerprints)* have been performed or exhibited at the ICA; the House of World Cultures, Berlin (2014); The Showroom, London (2015); the Oxford Programme for the Future of Cities (2015); Edinburgh College of Art (2015); Kunstraum Niederoesterreich, Vienna (2015); Pavillion, Leeds (2015); and Homeworks Space Program, Beirut (2016). She has contributed essays to *Forensis: The Architecture of Public Truth* (Sternberg, 2014); *The Sarai Reader* (Sarai, 2013); *We Travel the Space Ways* (Duke University Press, forthcoming 2017); and *Unsound : Undead* (Univocal, forthcoming 2017). She is also co-author, with Henriette Gunkel, of *Visual Cultures as Time Travel* (Sternberg, forthcoming).

Stefan Helmreich is Professor of Anthropology at MIT. He is the author of *Alien Ocean: Anthropological Voyages in Microbial Seas* (University of California Press, 2009) and, most recently, of *Sounding the Limits of Life: Essays in the Anthropology of Biology and Beyond* (Princeton University Press, 2016). His essays have appeared in *Critical Inquiry, Representations, American Anthropologist* and *The Wire.*

Julian Henriques is Professor in the Department of Media and Communications, Goldsmiths, University of London, where he is also convenor of the MA Scriptwriting programme and Director of the Topology Research Unit. Previously, he was Head of Film and Television at CARIMAC at the University of the West Indies, Kingston, Jamaica. Julian researches street cultures, music and technologies including those of the reggae sound system. He has credits as a writer-director with the feature film *Babymother* (1998) and the improvised short drama *We the Ragamuffin* (1992); and as a producer with numerous BBC and Channel Four documentaries. He is also a sound artist (responsible for the sculpture *Knots & Donuts* at Tate Modern in 2011); a founding editor of the journal *Ideology & Consciousness*; joint author of *Changing the Subject: Psychology, Social Regulation and Subjectivity* (Routledge, 1984) and author of *Sonic Bodies: Reggae Sound Systems, Performance Techniques and Ways of Knowing* (Continuum, 2011). His latest book, *Sonic Media: Technology, Sociality and Ways of Making*, is forthcoming with Duke University Press.

Ursula K. Le Guin was born in 1929 in Berkeley and lives in Portland, Oregon. As of 2015 she has published twenty-one novels, eleven volumes of short stories, four collections of essays, twelve books for children, six volumes of poetry and four of translation, and has received many honors and awards including Hugo, Nebula, National Book Award, PEN-Malamud and the National Book Foundation Medal. Her most recent publications are *The Unreal and the Real: Selected Stories of Ursula K. Le Guin* (2012) and *Steering the Craft: A 21st-Century Guide to Sailing the Sea of Story* (2015).

Robin Mackay is director of UK publisher and arts organisation Urbanomic and editor of their journal *Collapse*. He has written widely on philosophy and contemporary art, and has instigated collaborative projects with numerous contemporary artists. He has also translated a number of important works of French philosophy, including Alain Badiou's *Number and Numbers*, Quentin Meillassoux's *The Number and the Siren*, François Laruelle's *The Concept of Non-Photography* and Éric Alliez's *The Brain-Eye*.

Louis Moreno is a Lecturer in the Department of Visual Culture and Centre for Research Architecture, Goldsmiths, University of London. He is also a member of the curatorial collective *freethought*, who were one of the artistic directors of the 2016 Bergen Assembly in Norway.

Harold Offeh is an artist working in a range of media including performance, video, photography, learning and social arts practice. Offeh often employs humour as a means to confront the viewer with historical narratives and contemporary culture and is interested in the space created by the inhabiting or embodying of history. His current project *Covers* sees the artist embody images from popular culture in a series of attempts to transform music album sleeves by black singers from the 1970s and 1980s. In 2017 he will be exhibiting as part of *Untitled: Art on the Conditions of our Time* at New Art Exchange in Nottingham, UK and *Tous, des sangs-mêlés* at MAC VAL, Museum of Contemporary Art in Val-de-Marne, France. He lives in Cambridge and works in Leeds and London, UK.

Simon O'Sullivan is Professor of Art Theory and Practice in the Department of Visual Cultures at Goldsmiths, University of London. He has published two monographs, *Art Encounters Deleuze and Guattari: Thought*

Beyond Representation (Palgrave, 2005) and *On the Production of Subjectivity: Five Diagrams of the Finite-Infinite Relation* (Palgrave, 2012), and is the editor, with Stephen Zepke, of both *Deleuze, Guattari and the Production of the New* (Continuum, 2008) and *Deleuze and Contemporary Art* (Edinburgh University Press, 2010). He also makes art, with David Burrows, under the name *Plastique Fantastique* and is currently working on a collaborative volume of writings, with Burrows, on *Mythopoesis, Myth-Science, Mythotechnesis* (forthcoming with Edinburgh University Press).

Luciana Parisi is Reader in Cultural Theory, Chair of the PhD Programme at the Centre for Cultural Studies, and co-director of the Digital Culture Unit, Goldsmiths, University of London. Her research is a philosophical investigation of technology in culture, aesthetics and politics. She has written within the field of Media Philosophy and Computational Design. She is the author of *Abstract Sex: Philosophy, Biotechnology and the Mutations of Desire* (Continuum, 2004) and *Contagious Architecture. Computation, Aesthetics and Space* (MIT Press, 2013). She is currently researching the philosophical consequences of logical thinking in machines.

Theo Reeves-Evisson is a writer, researcher and Senior Lecturer in Theoretical and Contextual Studies at Birmingham School of Art. His main interests cluster around the relationship between ethics and aesthetics in contemporary art. He has explored this theme through a PhD thesis, "After Transgression: Ethico-Aesthetic Paradigms of Contemporary Art", and also through an ongoing project looking into the ethico-aesthetics of repair, which will result in a special issue of the journal *Third Text* in 2018. He has published articles and exhibition and book reviews in magazines such as *Frieze* and journals such as *Parallax*, and (together with Jon Shaw) is currently editing a book entitled *Fiction as Method*, forthcoming with Sternberg Press.

Daniel Kojo Schrade is an artist and Professor of Art at Hampshire College, Amherst, Massachusetts, USA, and studied in Germany and Spain. He received an MFA (Diploma) from the Academy of Fine Arts Munich, Germany. His paintings and installations have been presented internationally, including at the Museo de Arte Contemporaneo, Oaxaca-Mexico; Alliance Française, Pointe-Noir-Rep.Congo; Haus der Kunst, Munich-Germany; the Fitzgerald Gallery, Haverford College; and the Museum of Modern Art, Warsaw. He has taught painting at the Academy of Fine Arts, Munich and the Kwame Nkrumah University, Kumasi. Kojo Schrade was a Copeland Fellow at Amherst College and has received many grants and awards. He has been invited to lecture about his work at Goldsmiths, University of London, Barnard College, Georgetown University and UCLA amongst other places. His work is represented in various permanent collections around the world.

Judy Thorne is a PhD candidate in Anthropology at the University of Manchester. Her research explores the utopian imaginaries of people living through the economic and social crisis in Greece. She holds an MA in Social Anthropology from the University of Manchester, and a BA in Philosophy from the University of Nottingham. Judy is interested in everyday utopianism, popular modernism, the built environment as palimpsest, autonomist and feminist Marxisms, the anthropology of crisis and the conditions of possibility for relating to the future. She also enjoys irregularly updating her webcomic *glowfallover* and drawing and embroidering patterns and buildings.

Kemang Wa Lehulere was a co-founder of the Gugulective (2006), an artist-led collective based in Cape Town, and a founding member of the Center for Historical Reenactments in Johannesburg. Solo exhibitions have taken place at the Art Institute of Chicago (2016); Gasworks, London (2015); Lombard Freid Projects, New York (2013); the Goethe-Institut, Johannesburg (2011); the Association of Visual Arts, Cape Town (2009); and at Stevenson, Cape Town. Notable group exhibitions include *African Odysseys* at Le Brass Cultural Centre of Forest, Belgium (2015); the 8th Berlin Biennale (2014); *Public Intimacy: Art and Other Ordinary Acts in South Africa* at the Yerba Buena Center for the Arts, San Francisco (2014); and *The Ungovernables*, the second triennial exhibition of the New Museum in New York (2012). Wa Lehulere has won a number of prestigious awards, most recently the first International Tiberius Art Award Dresden in 2014; the Standard Bank Young Artist for Visual Arts in 2015; and the Deutsche Bank's "Artist of the Year" 2017.

ACKNOWLEDGEMENTS

We want to thank the contributors; the audience at the Futures and Fictions Public Program at Goldsmiths; Portia Malatjie and Oladapo Ajayi for transcribing the conversations; Lizzie Homersham, Edward George and Tavia Nyong'o for their invaluable input; and Frances Bodomo for our cover image.

Repeater Books

Repeater Books is dedicated to the creation of a new reality. The landscape of twenty-first-century arts and letters is faded and inert, riven by fashionable cynicism, egotistical self-reference and a nostalgia for the recent past. Repeater intends to add its voice to those movements that wish to enter history and assert control over its currents, gathering together scattered and isolated voices with those who have already called for an escape from Capitalist Realism. Our desire is to publish in every sphere and genre, combining vigorous dissent and a pragmatic willingness to succeed where messianic abstraction and quiescent co- option have stalled: abstention is not an option: we are alive and we don't agree.